The Daily Telegraph

CASH
CLINIC

also by Niki Chesworth

The Sunday Telegraph
A–Z Guide to Family Finance

The Daily Telegraph
Guide to Paying Less Tax

The Daily Telegraph

CASH CLINIC

How to tackle common financial problems

NIKI CHESWORTH & NINA MONTAGU-SMITH

MACMILLAN

First published 2002 by Macmillan
an imprint of Pan Macmillan Ltd
Pan Macmillan, 20 New Wharf Road, London N1 9RR
Basingstoke and Oxford
Associated companies throughout the world
www.panmacmillan.com

ISBN 0 333 90876 7

1 3 5 7 9 8 6 4 2

A CIP catalogue record for this book is available from
the British Library.

Typeset by SetSystems Ltd, SaffronWalden, Essex
Printed and bound in Great Britain by
Mackays of Chatham plc, Chatham, Kent

Contents

Introduction

What makes the Cash Clinic, published every Saturday on the back page of the Your Money Section of the *Daily Telegraph*, so popular?

Just as with those must-watch property makeover programmes, it is a chance to see how other people live, an opportunity to compare yourself with them, and a very practical way to get some tips without having to go to the expense of paying an expert.

While many of us would like to have a money makeover, we are worried that if we go to a financial adviser we will be pressured into buying life insurance, taking out a pension or committing ourselves to long-term investments (even if these are the best financial decisions we could ever make). Some of us are also embarrassed to admit that our finances are in disarray or that we just do not understand how different financial products work.

Cash Clinic enables you to learn from others' mistakes, gives you a helping hand in finding out which areas of your finances may need to be reassessed, and enables you to benefit from financial advice without having to see an adviser.

After all, most financial problems – whether it be saving too little, failing to have adequate life cover, putting off planning for retirement or simply paying too much for financial products such as mortgages and loans – are shared by millions of others.

Cash Clinic deals with real people in real situations, making it much easier for readers to identify with their problems and to see how the financial advice could relate to their own circumstances.

As in many of the case studies featured in this book, you may not even realize you could improve your financial situation in such a variety of ways.

This approachable and easy-to-read guide to resolving common financial problems is based on Nina Montagu-Smith's real-life Cash Clinic cases published over the past two years. Even though interest rates have changed, the stock-market has fallen, tax thresholds have risen and new financial products such as stakeholder pensions have been introduced since some of the case studies were printed, the advice given by a wide panel of respected financial experts is still as valid today as when it was when first published. However, where relevant, tax rates and thresholds have been updated.

Although most of the Cash Clinic cases cover a wide range of financial issues – from saving and investing to pension planning – each one presents a particular problem that needs to be addressed. So the cases have been split into different chapters, which give advice to suit particular sets of needs. To introduce each chapter there is a guide to the salient issues and after each case study a summary of the lessons that can be learned.

GETTING FINANCIAL ADVICE

While the general advice given in this book will relate to many readers, it cannot replace specific advice given to suit an individual's needs and objectives. For that, readers will need to seek financial advice.

As there are around 1,000 savings accounts, almost 2,000 unit trust funds, some 3,000 shares quoted on the London Stock Exchange and around 4,000 different mortgages, it is almost imposs-ible for individuals to keep track of their finances themselves and ensure they are getting the best deal all of the time – they need to talk to someone who does this for a living.

So where do you go for help? There is no shortage of companies offering financial advice but many do not give impartial advice – they can only tell you about (i.e. sell you) the products of one company. For a more balanced view, you will need independent financial advice (although for less complicated financial products such as savings accounts, a visit to a comparative website that checks out the best rates may be the easiest option).

Financial advice will not usually cost you anything extra as advisers are usually paid a commission on products they sell, with this coming out of the charges deducted from the unit trust/ pension/life policy. However, for larger investments it can make financial sense to pay a fee instead and have the commission rebated. Most independent financial advisers allow you to do this.

Before talking to an adviser check:

- Who do they work for? Are they selling the product of a particular life company or bank or are they independent?

- What are their areas of expertise? Some are specialists in investments or pensions while others offer all-round advice.

In addition, check that you are comfortable talking to the adviser. Before recommending any financial products an adviser should conduct a thorough fact-find to find out as much as possible about your current financial situation, your attitudes to risk and your goals and plans for the future. Some of these questions may seem quite intrusive, so you need to feel happy talking to the adviser.

However, it will still be a case of 'buyer beware'. It is up to you to give the final say about any financial product, and even if you do seek financial advice you will still have to look after some areas of your finances yourself.

Financial advisers tend to concentrate on investments, life and pension products, so they may not advise you on ways to cut your household bills, the best type of bank account to suit your needs or where to put your short-term savings.

For some financial products, free impartial advice is harder to find. Mortgage brokers, for example, will often charge a fee, while banks and building societies will usually only advise on their own product range.

In addition, the cheapest investment products are often only available to those prepared to make their own decisions. Discount brokers, fund supermarkets and execution-only stockbrokers can pass on cost savings because they do not give advice. So if you want to invest for less, you will have to learn to be your own financial adviser.

HOW FINANCIAL ADVICE IS REGULATED

Financial advisers are regulated by the Financial Services Authority, which vets advisers and ensures they are adequately trained.

All advisers must be registered (to check go to www.fsa.gov.uk/register or call 0845 606 1234).

Although advisers have been 'polarized' into independent and tied (those who work for or sell only the products of one company) there are proposals to relax these rules. So it is even more vital to check how independent any adviser is and how they are remunerated. New 'multi-tied' advisers will recommend only a limited number of companies' products.

THANKS TO OUR FINANCIAL ADVISERS

Cash Clinic would not be possible without the help of numerous financial advisers who each week share their years of experience with readers and help our case studies.

The authors would like to thank all those who have provided advice. Readers who want to contact any of the experts in person will find their details listed in the Useful Addresses section at the end of this book.

1 Financial Planning

Financial planning involves more than just saving for the future, deciding to take out life insurance or investing for retirement. Individuals need to take a more holistic approach to their finances looking at everything from where their money goes to ways to pay less tax.

Subsequent chapters in this book look at the important areas of finance – including savings, investments, insurance and pensions. However, before buying any financial product it is important to know two things: first, what is the state of your finances today; and second, what you want to achieve financially in the future.

Too many of us have an *ad hoc* range of financial products: some life insurance, but not enough; a pension left with a former employer, but no long-term retirement strategy; a few shares, but not a balanced portfolio; an investment plan, but no savings.

This is because we buy – or rather, often are sold – financial products, instead of looking for financial solutions. Combined with a failure to look at our long-term goals, it means that these financial products often do not achieve what we want them to achieve.

This is one of the most common problems faced by Cash Clinic case studies. Some, like Case Study 3 in this chapter, that of Malcolm Shaughnessy, feature numerous savings accounts earning lower rates of interest than could be earned if the money was pooled into one account. However, it is important to look at finances as a whole – not just one area, such as your savings.

Review all of Malcolm's finances and it is obvious that he would be even better off using savings to repay his mortgage – upon which he pays a higher rate of interest than could ever be earned in any savings account. This will also fit into his plans to retire early. Before the experts reviewed Malcolm's finances he appeared to be in a strong position financially, with plenty of savings and investments and schemes in place to boost his pension on retirement. Yet all these products may not have achieved his long-term goals.

THE FINANCIAL REVIEW

How can anyone plan for the future if they do not know where their finances stand today?

Most of us have a good idea of what we are worth. Walk past an estate agent's window and it is tempting to compare the values of similar properties to your own. Reading through a paper, it is inevitable that an investor will take a quick glance at the value of his or her shares or unit trusts. And, of course, bank statements regularly remind us how much money we have to spend or how much money we have spent to put us in the red.

Yet it is only when we take the time to write down exactly what we owe and own that we get a true picture of our finances. To do this, write down your assets on one side of your balance sheet and your debts on the other.

Assets
These include:

• Property

• Pension

• Savings

• Investments

• Valuables such as antiques, jewellery, etc.

• Cars

• Household items

It is important to include all assets as these will be needed when calculating how much insurance – motor, buildings and contents –

you need to purchase and also when calculating the value of your estate for inheritance tax purposes.

When you are writing down what savings and investments you own, this is an ideal time to check that they are earning the best return in the most tax-efficient manner.

Time and time again, people in Cash Clinic case studies are found to own investments that are taxed when they could be tax-free if held in an individual savings account (ISA), savings that are earning pitiful rates of interest when they could be earning a decent return, and thousands of pounds in a few individual shares, when buying pooled investments such as unit trusts would spread the risks of investing. See Chapter 2: Savings and Chapter 6: Investments for tips and advice.

Now is also the ideal time to track down lost assets. Although most of us feel we have a good grip on our finances, the following should make you think:

- There are £19 million of unclaimed Premium Bond prizes.

- Some £5 billion is 'lost' in company pension funds by former employees who have left a pension fund behind but cannot be traced.

- Millions of windfall shares given away by building societies that converted to banks have never been claimed, including 40 million shares in the Halifax.

- There are millions of unclaimed life insurance pay-outs, including almost £40 million with the Prudential.

Debts
These include:

- Mortgage

- Overdraft

- Loans

- Credit cards

- Store credit and hire purchase

- Tax

Knowing what you owe is a vital part of the financial planning process. Borrowing costs money and can often mean the difference between a comfortable life and a hand-to-mouth existence.

As Case Studies 1 and 2 show, shopping around for the best rates can dramatically cut the cost of borrowing and help balance a budget. Credit cards and loans are covered in greater detail in Chapter 3 and mortgages in Chapter 4.

Now that you know what you are worth today, it is time to look at where your money goes.

Expenditure

As the Cash Clinic case studies show, it is only when all of an individual's outgoings are written down and added up that any waste can be identified – including money that is poured down the drain (or rather into the already fat coffers of financial institutions) in the form of unauthorized overdraft charges, excessive interest on loans or premiums on policies that are not needed or cannot be afforded.

Write down all items of expenditure and then make sure that you are getting value for money in each area by shopping around:

- The average family could save up to a third off insurance premiums, including £120 a year on home insurance and £150 on car cover, according to the AA.

- Mortgage apathy costs millions each year. A few minutes spent checking whether or not a £100,000 mortgage is the best deal could save £20,000 over the term of a twenty-five-year mortgage.

- The difference between a low rate and an average rate on a £5,000 loan borrowed over five years can be as much as £1,000 in extra interest over the term of the loan.

As our first case study, Carolyn Djanogly's, shows, even those struggling to make ends meet having already trimmed their expenditure to the bone can usually find savings – in this case by switching to a credit card with a lower rate of interest. The areas of finance where waste is most likely to occur are: household insurance, car insurance, life insurance, credit cards, current accounts, mortgages and household bills. Most of us could easily save more than £1,000 a year by ensuring we have the best deals on all financial products, according to a recent survey by an Internet money shop.

Income

The other side of the budget balance sheet is income. While expenses need to be minimized, income needs to be maximized. Although it may not be possible for everyone to earn more money from employment, it should be possible to earn more from assets and investments.

The average high-street current account pays a pitiful rate of interest of less than 0.1 per cent after tax. Yet it is possible to earn forty times as much by shopping around.

Budgeting

Once you have shopped round for the best deals, draw up a budget by writing down what you have coming in each month and what you spend.

If expenses exceed income, drastic action needs to be taken or else ever-mounting debts are inevitable. As our second case study, that of Jim and Miriam Cox, shows, circumstances – in this case the foot-and-mouth outbreak – are often outside an individual's control. However, that does not mean an individual cannot control the solution. This couple were forced to sell investments to make ends meet.

If income exceeds expenses, the remaining disposable income can be put to good use saving for a rainy day, protecting the family against disaster and investing for the future.

It is important to review your budget regularly as circumstances change. Budgeting is a discipline that can benefit everyone, not just those on low incomes.

A budget identifies:

- Areas of waste

- Areas where expenditure can be cut

- How much income is available to achieve financial goals

THE FINANCIAL PLAN

The next step is to decide what you want to achieve. It is important that any goals are realistic and prioritized.

Dreaming of retiring on a fat pension at age fifty when that is only ten years away and the individual has no pension plan in place may be totally unrealistic. Few could afford to build up a pension fund of £100,000-plus in such a short space of time.

Aiming to pay off a mortgage ten years early by switching to an affordable, flexible home loan and overpaying by £100 a month, on the other hand, is more likely to be an attainable goal.

Goals should be split into the shorter-term, medium-term and long-term.

For example:

- Short-term: three to six months to one year – reduce/repay overdraft, switch to a cheaper mortgage, start to save £30 a month, repay £100 a month off credit card debt.

- Medium-term: one to two years – clear all debts, free up enough income to use £7,000 annual individual savings account (ISA) allowance, maximize pension contributions.

- Long-term: two-plus years – retire early, pay off mortgage by the age of fifty.

Goals need to be prioritized. After all, there is no point investing all spare savings for retirement, if an individual has no rainy-day savings and as a result ends up in serious debt because of an unforeseen financial disaster. (Money invested in a pension fund is tied up until retirement, so individuals need to have savings they can access as well as those they cannot.)

The priorities should be:

- Making today's budget balance – that means trimming expenses and maximizing income by shopping around for the best rates.

- Freeing up enough extra cash to set aside as rainy-day savings – ideally at least three months (preferably six) of living expenses.

- Ensuring your family, income and home are adequately protected – few can afford all the different insurance policies on offer but a minimum of life cover and home and contents insurance is a must, and for the self-employed some form of income protection policy such as permanent health insurance.

- Then setting aside something for the longer-term future – a spread of investments in a tax-free ISA and some form of pension provision.

Achieving goals will usually mean making sacrifices, as Case Study 4 in this chapter, that of Brian and Ursula Parr, shows. The Parrs want to generate an extra £5,000 a year from their substantial capital but this would mean generating an income of 9 per cent a year from their investments. Such a high return would inevitably lead to an erosion of capital, the advisers warn. So they will have to sacrifice capital to get the income they require.

Remember, financial planning has to be an ongoing process. Ted Bloomfield, in Case Study 6 in this chapter, had £76,000 invested in individual shares but, as our financial advisers pointed out, these were in 'old economy' stocks and, as he did not manage his own portfolio, he was not maximizing his returns on this substantial investment.

Of course, any financial decision has consequences and Ted was warned to liquidate his portfolio gradually to minimize capital gains tax liabilities. The amount that can be realized as a gain (remember that is the profit, *not* the sale proceeds) each year tax free is currently £7,700 (the 2002/2003 tax threshold). That is roughly the same as the tax-free ISA allowance, so he could make a gain up to the capital gains tax threshold free of tax and then invest most of the proceeds free of tax. So tax planning is a vital part of financial planning.

TAX PLANNING

Tax is one of the biggest bills we pay each year, although we may not realize this as tax is usually deducted at source from pay, savings and investments.

While we may spend time shopping around for the best deals on our mortgages, cars, groceries and household goods, very few of us spend enough time trying to save on our tax bills.

As a result, nine in ten adults in the UK pay more tax than they have to, and some 41 million of us could be better off if we made the most of easy ways to save tax, according to IFA Promotion, the organization that promotes independent financial advice. This waste totals almost £6 billion a year, with the average person paying £140 in unnecessary tax.

It is not just waste that is an issue. There are valuable tax breaks that need to be maximized.

Income tax

Everyone has a personal allowance (the amount that can be earned before paying tax) which rises for the over-sixty-fives. These allowances rise at the start of each tax year (6 April).

Tax Year	2002/2003
Basic personal allowance	£4,615
Age sixty-five to seventy-four	£6,100
Age seventy-five and over	£6,370

The age-related allowances are reduced by £1 for every £2 earned in excess of an income threshold (for the 2002/2003 tax year) £17,900 earned until the basic personal allowance is reached. In addition, married couples where one of the partners was born before 6 April 1935 qualify for a married couple's allowance. It is important that these allowances are maximized – for tips, see below.

In addition, income tax is charged at different rates according to the level of an individual's income. The first £1,920 of income above an individual's personal allowance (the 2002/2003 band) is taxed at 10 per cent, then income from £1,921 to £29,900 is taxed at 22 per cent and anything above £29,900 at 40 per cent. Again these thresholds usually rise at the start of each new tax year.

Some of the easiest ways to save on income tax include:

- Invest in a tax-exempt ISA (the maximum investment allowed is £7,000 in each tax year – £14,000 for a couple). That way savings and investments escape tax.

- Once they have used up their ISA allowance, couples should put income-generating assets and savings in the name of the spouse who pays tax at a lower rate – that way they will pay less or no tax (if that spouse is a non-taxpayer).

- If one partner does not use up his or her personal allowance it is wasted. So income should be put into the non-taxpayer's name to use up the allowance.

- Likewise, if one partner pays tax at a higher rate and the other at the starting or basic rate, more income should be in that person's name so less tax is paid. Generally assets must be given as an outright gift to the lower-earning spouse.

- Opt for investments that grow rather than those that produce an income if you do not need that income today. Most investors do not pay capital gains tax, in which case growth will be tax-free whereas income will be taxed. (Note: the 10 per cent tax deducted on dividends cannot be reclaimed by non-taxpayers.)

- Non-taxpayers should make sure they are not paying tax unnecessarily. They should register to receive all interest gross (ask the Inland Revenue for form R85).

- Note that savings interest and dividends are added to all other income when determining at what rate you are taxed. This extra income could push a basic-rate taxpayer into a higher-rate tax band.

- Make sure you are not missing out on any tax allowances or tax credits. Employees can do this by checking their PAYE (pay as you earn) tax code. The children's tax credit, working families' tax credit, and the pension tax credit, which will be introduced in April 2003, have to be claimed.

Capital gains tax

In each tax year an individual can make £7,700 of gains (the 2001/2003 threshold) free of tax. Selling assets each year to use up the allowance rather than selling them in one go and suffering capital gains tax (CGT) of up to 40 per cent on all gains above the threshold can result in large tax savings. So if an investor owns a large portfolio, he can sell up to the CGT threshold each year – and no more – keeping gains tax free. It means an investor who has made gains of £20,000 on shares could pay no tax on these by selling them over three years rather than all at once.

Capital gains are charged at an individual's top rate added to other income to determine which tax band they fall into. Starting-rate taxpayers only pay 10 per cent on gains above the CGT allowance of £7,700 (provided these gains do not push the taxpayer into a higher tax bracket), basic-rate taxpayers pay tax at 20 per cent (even though this is lower than the basic rate of 22 per cent) and higher-rate taxpayers 40 per cent. It therefore makes sense for couples to put assets which could be liable to CGT in the name of the lower-rate taxpayer. Some £400 million could be saved in CGT if couples simply transferred assets between spouses to maximize their tax allowances.

Other ways to minimize CGT include:

- Shelter investments in an ISA as these escape CGT. The annual investment limit is £7,000.

- Own assets for longer. CGT is tapered with the amount of gain reduced by a set percentage the longer it is held. Non-business assets reduce from 100 per cent to 95 per cent if the asset is owned for three complete years before being sold. If you owned the asset on or before 17 March 1998, you qualify for an additional year of tapering. This tapering gradually increases until only 60 per cent of the gains are chargeable to CGT after ten years. Tapering reduces the effective rate of CGT to 12 per cent for basic-rate taxpayers and 24 per cent for higher-rate taxpayers after ten years.

Although your main home usually escapes CGT, if you own two – as do Ted and June Bloomfield in the final case study in this chapter, one will be liable to CGT when it is sold.

Inheritance tax

Rising house prices and increasing wealth mean inheritance tax is a tax paid by increasing numbers of people – not just the seriously rich. Upon death £250,000 (the 2002/2003 allowance, which usually rises at the start of each new tax year) of an individual's estate escapes inheritance tax – anything above that is taxed at 40 per cent. Yet an extra £1,240 million could go to chosen heirs instead of the taxman in the form of inheritance tax if more people planned ahead.

Although inheritance tax is so easy to avoid that it is often referred to as a 'voluntary' tax, sometimes it is unavoidable. However, instead of leaving future generations with a large tax bill, it is possible to buy a life policy written in trust that will pay the tax bill – the advice given to Brian and Ursula Parr in our fourth case study.

Even if there is no inheritance tax problem today, rising house prices could mean there is one tomorrow. Follow these tips:

- Make a will. Even if there are no tax implications, a will sets out who gets what, saving rows at what is already a difficult time.

- Most couples leave everything to each other but this is not always wise. Anything left to the spouse is automatically exempt from inheritance tax, so each spouse's individual inheritance tax allowance will not be used. The other drawback of leaving everything to the spouse is that upon death of the second spouse the estate is even larger, leading to a potentially higher inheritance tax bill.

- Give away assets before death. Any asset given away seven years or more before death escapes inheritance tax. If the individual who makes the gift dies within the seven-year period, the asset is only partially exempt from inheritance tax, with inheritance tax paid at a reduced rate.

- Make use of the annual gift allowances. Up to £3,000 can be given away each year, with this amount falling outside the estate for inheritance tax. Couples can give away £6,000 between them and if the allowance is not used in one year it can be carried forward to the next.

- In addition, it is possible to make gifts of £250 to any number of people free of tax.

Tax and investing

Investing for the future makes common sense; investing in a scheme that is tax-free makes financial sense. Yet far too many savers and investors are paying tax on their nest eggs. Over £550 million in tax could easily be avoided if everyone sheltered their investments and savings in a tax-exempt ISA. See Chapter 2: Savings and Chapter 6: Investments for more advice.

Tax and pensions

Getting money back from the Inland Revenue – in the form of tax relief – is another area where savings can be made. Optimizing contributions to personal and company pension schemes could result in an additional £1,000 million of tax relief being paid. Contributions to pension plans attract tax relief at the individual's highest rate, so in order to invest £100 a higher-rate taxpayer need only part with £60 – the remaining £40 is invested by the Inland Revenue. See Chapter 5: Pensions, for more advice.

Case Study 1

PROBLEM: PLANNING FOR THE FUTURE WHILE MAKING ENDS MEET TODAY

Vital Statistics
Name: Carolyn Djanogly
Age: Thirty-two
Location: North London
Occupation: Photographer
Income: Very little from occasional commission
Savings: 2,000 which will soon run out
Pension: Scottish Equitable
Investments: Scottish Amicable endowment
Mortgage: None
Borrowings: £5,000 HSBC car loan; £1,000 on HSBC Visa card
Insurance: None

Carolyn Djanogly gave up her career as a television director to pursue her dream of becoming a professional photographer. She has published a book, *Centurions*, a photographic tribute to the 100 people who have helped to shape the twentieth century socially, politically or culturally, from which she receives a royalty on every copy sold.

Carolyn spent nine years in television until 1996, working full-time as a researcher and then as a director for both the BBC and Granada, before going freelance in 1993. She said: 'I was miserable as a television director, particularly when I was freelancing, so in October 1996 I took the radical decision to leave television for ever.

I had always been passionate about photography and I had the idea
for my book.'

After two years living off the money from her last job and
working three days a week as a secretary, she finally ran out of
money and was forced to borrow from her parents and two friends.
But in January 1999, she was rescued by sponsorship from fund
manager SG Asset Management.

Carolyn said: 'I realized that their advertising campaign was very
like the way I take photographs, so I approached them and they
said they would back my book.'

As a result of struggling to make ends meet at times she has
become acutely aware of the value of money. She said: 'I have
become very cautious with money. I only spend my money on
staying alive, I don't go shopping and I don't take holidays.'

Carolyn also does some photographic commissions to help with
expenses, with the aim of setting herself up as a professional photographer. To do this she will need £8,000, with £5,000 of this being
spent on photographic equipment and the rest on stationery and
computer equipment.

The last of her sponsorship money, and the money she borrowed,
is in her HSBC current account – about £2,000 in all – and must last
her until she gets her first payment from the proceeds of the book.
Depending on how successful the book is, she may need it to last
even longer.

Her current account has a £1,800 overdraft facility, which she
may need to tide her over. There are no other savings.

As far as investments are concerned, Carolyn had opted out of the
State Earnings-related Pension Scheme (SERPS) in 1989 and diverted
the payments to a Scottish Equitable fund until 1993, when she went
freelance. She said: 'If things go well, I will start this up again.'

Carolyn also continues to pay £52 a month into a Scottish
Amicable endowment fund that was tied to a mortgage she had
between 1989 and 1994.

Carolyn, who rents a flat in Highgate for £200 a week, said: 'I am
unsure what to do with this and I thought I might be able to attach
it to another mortgage. After all, I do need a roof over my head.'

On the borrowings front, Carolyn has a £5,000 HSBC car loan which she took out last year. She repays £120 a month. There is also £1,000 outstanding on her HSBC Visa card.

WHAT THE EXPERTS SAY

The advisers to Cash Clinic agreed that until Carolyn has more cash flow, there is no point in thinking about saving for the future.

'The income she has left is insufficient to invest, especially given the fact that she needs to maintain contingency reserves,' said Adrian Shandley, of independent financial advisers (IFAs) Balmoral Associates in Southport.

Mark Bolland, of IFAs Chamberlain de Broe in London, said: 'We know that Carolyn needs at least £1,000 a month for the rent, endowment and car loan alone. On top of this will be food, utilities, travel, council tax and so on. At this rate, the £2,000 she has remaining from her sponsorship money will be used up very quickly.'

He added, however, that she can start making plans for the money she will be paid by the publisher of her book.

The first thing to deal with, therefore, is debt, according to Mr Bolland. He said: 'On a personal basis, it would doubtless be preferable to clear the debts to her friends first. However, if they are able to wait a while longer, then she should tackle the Visa and car loan first – financially, these loans are priorities because they cost a lot more.'

Kim North, of IFAs Pretty Financial Partnership in London, agreed and added: 'She should consider transferring the debt to a card with a special offer such as RBS Advanta.'

Mr Shandley also felt that Carolyn could find a better deal for her current account in order to squeeze the most value possible out of the small amount of funds she has left. He said: 'The funds in the HSBC bank account may be better moved to Standard Life Bank.'

Ms North also liked Standard Life, pointing out that it pays four-and-a-half times more interest and that Carolyn's existing savings were earning less than inflation.

Ms North said that Carolyn could link her Standard Life account to the HSBC current account and use the HSBC account for day-to-day expenses only.

The advisers agreed that Carolyn's £200 a week rent is 'dead money', but recognized that she might find it tricky to obtain a mortgage in her present financial situation. By way of illustration, Ms North said a mortgage of £100,000 at a discount rate would have initial monthly repayments of half what she spends on rent now. This is something Carolyn should make a priority as soon as she has a more stable income stream.

The advisers agreed that she should keep her Scottish Amicable endowment going. Mr Bolland said: 'This was set up in 1989 and may actually be worth quite a bit now. Having borne the costs of the policy already, and given that Scottish Amicable is a sound with-profits office, there may be a good argument to maintain the policy.'

Ms North noted that the surrender value of the endowment at present would probably be nominal, but Mr Bolland suggested that Carolyn obtain a quote for the potential proceeds of the policy at auction. He said: 'This will enable her to consider whether the cash that she could generate by selling the policy now could be profitably used, as opposed to any longer-term investment benefit of keeping the investment going.'

LESSONS TO BE LEARNED

- Endowments are long-term investments and once they have been taken out the maximum returns are only earned if they are kept for the full term. However, it is possible to sell them (if they are with-profits policies) if you are desperate for money. You will usually receive more than if you surrender (cash in) the policy with the life company.

- Even if you only have modest savings or a small amount in your current account, it is possible to earn far more interest by switching to a better rate.

- Competition among credit card issuers means that switching to a cheap introductory rate from another provider can lead to instant interest savings.

- Rent money is dead money. Low mortgage rates mean that home loans are often cheaper than paying rent.

Case Study 2

PROBLEM: HOW TO REDUCE DEBTS AND BUILD UP SAVINGS WHEN INCOME FALLS

Vital Statistics
Names: Jim and Miriam Cox
Age: Forty-two and forty-one
Location: Wollaston, Northamptonshire
Occupations: Farrier and laughter therapist
Combined income: Variable
Savings: None
Pension: Standard Life personal pension supporting part of
    mortgage
Investments: Jupiter ISA supporting rest of mortgage
Mortgage: Abbey National £48,000 interest-only home loan
Borrowings: £2,600 overdraft on Nationwide current account
Insurance: Joint life cover from Standard Life

Miriam Cox suffered a big drop in income when she switched to a part-time job to focus on her true vocation: depression therapy – and this could not have happened at a worse time. Her husband Jim then saw his income from his business as a farrier – someone who shoes horses – plummet as a result of the foot-and-mouth outbreak.

Through her company, Harmony Unlimited, based in Wollaston,

Northamptonshire, Miriam runs study groups two evenings a week and offers one-day and all-weekend workshops for people trying to combat depression.

She earns £10,000 a year from her part-time clerical job. Miriam said: 'My husband's business dropped by 90 per cent because of foot-and-mouth. Last month I took only £112 through my business – that was it. Next month I am doing a couple of workshops, but the income from those will really depend on how many people are on them. Last year I made nothing at all from the business – I was more like £3,000 down.'

The couple share a Nationwide Flex current account, which is overdrawn by £2,600 – 'pretty well up to the limit'. However, they are about to receive £2,000 from cancelling their separate life insurance policies. They have recently taken out a £100,000 joint life insurance policy with Standard Life, costing £36 a month, instead.

Miriam has a personal pension fund but it is supporting her mortgage. She took it out with Standard Life in 1996 and pays in £110 a month; her husband pays in £83 a month.

The couple also have a Jupiter ISA supporting £10,000 of their £48,000 mortgage with Abbey National. They pay £50 a month into the ISA and £200 in interest to the bank between them. There are no other savings.

WHAT THE EXPERTS SAY

The advisers to Cash Clinic said that Miriam needs to reduce her outgoings as a matter of priority before she will be in a position to save.

Maxine Harvey, of independent financial advisers (IFAs) Torquil Clark in Wolverhampton, said: 'The emphasis in the short term must be on reducing outgoings until things pick up again and they can start to build an emergency fund.'

The first thing Miriam must do is to repay as much of the overdraft as she can. The advisers recommended using the £2,000 cashback from the insurance policies to do this. Kerry Nelson, of

IFAs Deep Blue Financial in Hampshire, said: 'This will reduce monthly interest charges which would be higher than any interest she would receive from a savings account, at the same time reducing the anxieties of continually using an overdraft and taking the strain off what monthly drawings she is able to take from the business.'

On the subject of pensions mortgages generally, Ms Harvey said: 'I always get nervous when people say they have a mortgage covered by a pension. This means you have to wait until you retire before you can repay your mortgage and, in the meantime, you keep paying interest. The longer term aim has to be for Miriam and her husband to cover the mortgage some other way.'

Next, Miriam should see if she can reduce her pension fund contributions until she can better afford to save. Ms Harvey said: 'In the short term, as cash flow is an issue, it is worth checking the pension projections to see if there is an opportunity to reduce contributions to have the chance to build an emergency savings fund.'

Miram could choose a mini-cash individual savings account (ISA), which provides tax-free interest, as long as the Jupiter ISA the couple are contributing to is not a maxi ISA. This is because it is not possible to contribute to both a mini and a maxi ISA in one tax year.

Colin Jackson, of IFAs Baronworth in Essex, said that Mr Cox should make use of his own ISA allowance to let the couple spread risk across fund managers when they are earning more money.

LESSONS TO BE LEARNED

- Use any surplus cash – in this case the proceeds of the sale of life insurance policies – to reduce debts rather than boost savings. Interest charged on borrowing usually far exceeds what can be earned on savings.

- Linking a pension to a mortgage has drawbacks – the pension must be used to repay the mortgage, so there is less upon which to retire, and it cannot be used to repay the mortgage until retirement so the mortgage cannot be repaid early.

- As in the previous case study, there are no short-term savings. Everyone needs an emergency fund for a rainy day.

- Where possible, reduce long-term investment commitments (in this case the pension contributions) to free up cash to pay off debts and build up savings.

Case Study 3

PROBLEM: PLANNING FOR EARLY RETIREMENT AND DAUGHTER'S INHERITANCE

Vital Statistics
Name: Malcolm Shaughnessy
Age: Fifty
Location: Teesside
Occupation: Engineer
Income: £35,000 p.a.
Savings: £5,200 in bank and building society accounts
Pension: Final salary scheme; Scottish Widows additional voluntary contributions scheme
Investments: £1,200 in shares; MGM and Scottish Amicable endowments; Liverpool Victoria, Equitable Life and Standard Life savings plans
Mortgage: Abbey National £36,000 interest-only home loan
Borrowings: None apart from mortgage
Insurance: None

A review of his retirement plans has been forced on Malcolm Shaughnessy after an expensive split from his long-term partner, whom he had planned to marry.

Malcolm, a planning engineer with Corus, formerly British Steel, in Teesside, who has two grown-up daughters, Kirsty, thirty-one, and Louise, twenty-six, from a previous marriage, and one grandson, would like to stop work at fifty-seven and arrange his affairs so his daughters and grandson do not have to pay more inheritance tax than necessary. He believes he can save an additional £400 a month from his salary.

'I am only fifty but I am concerned about inheritance tax and I want to work out the best way to leave things to my daughters,' he said. He is concerned about what he should do about his mortgage.

At the moment, Malcolm has a five-year fixed loan with an extended two-year tie-in that he took from Abbey National two years ago. It is fixed at 6.35 per cent but the redemption penalties will last until he is fifty-five (in 2005), and he wishes to retire at fifty-seven. Ideally he would like to pay off the £36,000 loan in full well before retirement.

He said: 'I pay £191 in interest to the bank each month and have an MGM endowment to support it, which costs £151 a month. The redemption penalty is 180 days' gross interest but really I would like to switch to a flexible mortgage, but I don't know if this is the right thing to do.' He will be able to kick-start the early repayment of his mortgage with a £3,300 windfall he received when Scottish Widows was taken over by Lloyds TSB.

He has been contributing £55 a month to a Scottish Widows free standing additional voluntary contribution (FSAVC) plan for twelve years and six months ago started to pay into his company final salary pension scheme AVC. Malcolm, who has been in his company scheme for twenty-four years and currently earns £35,000 a year, believes he will get a lump sum of around £45,000 plus two-thirds of his final salary when he retires at fifty-seven if he continues with the AVCs.

Malcolm holds around £1,400 of shares in all, including £1,000 in Corus, but has no personal equity plans (PEPs), individual savings accounts (ISAs) or pooled investments such as unit and investment trusts.

He has, however, favoured lower-risk investments in the form of insurance company savings plans and endowments, of which he has several, costing him almost £100 a month.

Malcolm also has £2,950 cash saved on deposit with a variety of building societies, £650 in a tax-exempt special savings account (TESSA), a surplus of around £400 in his current account and £1,200 in his Co-op savings account.

WHAT THE EXPERTS SAY

Malcolm will not have to worry too much about inheritance tax planning, the advisers to Cash Clinic said, as his estate is worth less than the inheritance tax nil-rate band. However, David Wright, of independent financial advisers (IFAs) Johnstone Douglas in Croydon, south London, said: 'If Malcolm thinks there may be a liability, he should start to consider possible transfer of assets, setting up trusts for his daughters and his grandson.'

Kevin Minter, of IFAs David Aaron Partnership in Milton Keynes, said: 'One course of action he may wish to take is to place his existing endowment policies in a trust, which will mean they are outside his estate if they pay out a death benefit prior to maturity. He will still be able to use the proceeds at the end of the term on the assumption that he survives.' Adjusting existing endowments for them to be held in trust is usually straightforward; simply request a standard form from the life company that issued the endowment.

As far as the mortgage is concerned, the advisers were divided. Mr Wright urged Malcolm to put his Scottish Widows windfall payment towards his mortgage and to switch his mortgage away from Abbey National to the Woolwich, which offers a flexible home loan.

Mr Wright said: 'If he switches to the Woolwich, he could overpay the mortgage every month and additionally switch his current and savings account to the Woolwich. These accounts can be combined to reduce the net borrowing.'

The Woolwich flexible mortgage rate is set at 0.75 points above the Bank of England base rate, well below the 6.35 per cent Malcolm is currently paying. However, he must also take into account the redemption penalty he will have to pay to Abbey National which will reduce the savings he will make.

Both Darius McDermott, an IFA from Chelsea Financial Services in London, and Mr Minter thought Malcolm should also consider saving up now to repay the loan after the redemption penalty period.

Mr McDermott said: 'I would consider saving part of the money from maturing investments to reduce the mortgage when the redemption penalties are no longer in force, not before.'

His next priority is to build up a lump sum over the next seven years to repay the loan and maximize capital to take into retirement. The advisers thought he should do this by way of regular savings into an ISA.

Mr McDermott said: 'I feel that a more flexible vehicle would be appropriate here, to run alongside his main pension and AVCs, which are relatively rigid.'

LESSONS TO BE LEARNED

- Write endowment policies in trust – that way they fall outside of an individual's estate for inheritance tax purposes. However, if the individual survives until the policy matures, he or she can still benefit from the proceeds.

- Transfer assets to future generations while still young. Any gift made more than seven years before death is exempt from inheritance tax provided it is a gift without reservation, which means it has to be an outright gift.

- What can appear to be a cheap-rate mortgage may work out more expensive in the long run. For the first two years of Malcolm's mortgage he was paying a competitive rate, but then interest rates fell and he was paying more than the going rate. However, his mortgage locks him in for the first seven years.

- Those who want to retire early need mortgages that enable them to do so. Flexible mortgages are ideal.

- Additional voluntary contributions (AVCs) are a good way to boost a pension as they attract tax relief. However, they are fairly restrictive and rigid. They must be used to buy an annuity (to give an income for life) and cannot be taken as a lump sum. In addition, AVCs linked to an employer's scheme must be taken at the same time as retirement – it is not possible to take them earlier or later. ISAs – although they do not attract tax relief – are more flexible and can complement AVC investments.

Case Study 4

PROBLEM: GENERATING ANOTHER £5,000 A YEAR AND PROTECTING AGAINST INHERITANCE TAX

Vital Statistics

Names: Brian and Ursula Parr

Ages: Sixty-four and fifty-six

Location: Blackpool

Occupations: Mr Parr is retired; Mrs Parr is a catering manager

Combined income: £23,000 p.a.

Savings: £138,400 in bank and building society accounts

Pension: Mrs Parr has company pension schemes; Mr Parr is drawing his pension

Investments: £73,500 in unit and investment trusts; £7,620 in shares

Mortgage: None

Borrowings: None

Insurance: None

A £57,000 bingo win in March this year boosted Brian and Ursula Parr's savings on deposit by more than 50 per cent. They are now concerned that they may have too much in cash and are worried about inheritance tax.

Although Brian has retired, his wife Ursula is still several years away from stopping work. Brian, who lives with his wife in Blackpool, said: 'I am not sure if I am sitting OK or if I should have more in equities. I have increased the amount we hold on deposit because of our age. However, although it seems sensible to reduce our risk profile, I am not totally averse to taking the odd chance with investments.

'I want to generate another £4,000 to £5,000 a year to supplement our income and I want to prepare against inheritance tax liabilities for our son and his family. We have quite a bit invested and we do not have any debts, so what we have would definitely be subject to inheritance tax.'

The couple have left everything to each other in their wills and then to their son in the event of both their deaths.

Brian put £40,000 of his wife's bingo winnings into a Northern Rock one-year fixed-rate bond in her name. The rest is distributed around other savings accounts, bringing the total on deposit to almost £1,400. They keep a surplus of £2,500 in their Lloyds TSB current account and live on Ursula's salary of £13,500 a year from her job as a catering manager at a local police station, and income totalling £9,500 a year from Brian's two pension funds from the Army and the Royal Mail. The bulk comes from the Army, which he left eighteen years ago.

Ursula plans to retire in March 2004. She already has one paid-up pension fund from a previous job with Lancashire County Council which is projected to pay her a lump sum of £8,000 plus an annual pension of £2,500 and she will also receive £1,600 a year from her current pension fund.

The Parrs have invested a large amount in pooled funds: a total of £73,500 invested in unit and investment trusts – some of it in personal equity plans (PEPs) – in a wide range of sectors, including international, European capital growth, North American, South East

Asian, UK growth, emerging markets and technology funds. The couple also have around £7,600 tied up in CGNU and BG Group shares.

WHAT THE EXPERTS SAY

The Parrs should address the problems of inheritance tax and capital gains tax before working out how to generate more income, the advisers to Cash Clinic said.

Kim North, of independent financial advisers (IFAs) Pretty Technical Partnership, said: 'The Parrs should rearrange their wills to pass more on to their son on the first death so that they can make good use of inheritance tax allowances.'

Adrian Shandley, of IFAs Balmoral Associates, said the Parrs could consider taking out a whole-of-life policy in trust for their son to help pay for the anticipated inheritance tax liability. These policies produce a lump-sum benefit whenever the policy-holder dies.

Mr Shandley said: 'Because the Parrs are both still relatively young for inheritance-tax planning purposes, the cost of such a policy should be relatively modest. However, this would involve paying a monthly premium to a life assurance company, which would represent another outgoing in retirement.' He recommended a whole-of-life policy from Allied Dunbar for this purpose. Alternatively, the couple could take some of their capital from their cash deposits and place it in an insurance company bond. This could be put in trust for their son, thereby removing the capital from their estate, providing they do not die in the next seven years. However, it is important to watch out for the initial charges levied on these bonds, which can be as high as 7 per cent. Many brokers will be happy to rebate most or all of the initial commission to substantial investors.

Mr Shandley said the couple should consider reducing the amount they keep on deposit. 'I would recommend phasing some of this capital into managed or unit-linked investments as they give better growth prospects for the longer term. If the Parrs are deter-mined to retain a substantial amount of capital on deposit for reasonable access, then I would recommend the use of a series of fixed-term building society bonds to give liquidity at any point in time, while also gaining a higher rate of interest, through rolling over a series of fixed-term bonds.'

The advisers said that if the Parrs wish to generate more income from their investments, they should consider switching from growth-based investments to income-bearing ones, as the need for income rises after Ursula's retirement.

Ms North said that if the Parrs wish to increase their income by £5,000 after tax a year, they will have to obtain a yield of more than 9 per cent a year from their current investments besides their pensions. She added: 'If they want £4,000, they will need more than 7 per cent a year from their investments. Their current portfolio is very growth-oriented and is medium to high risk. The couple will need to change to income funds and use individual savings accounts (ISAs) to hold them.'

Ms North added: 'A yield of 9 per cent in today's markets will mean a depreciation of their capital, so the Parrs need to set their income sights a little lower, or accept that their asset value will fall.'

Matthew Brown, of the IFAs Argent Consulting in London, said that although Mr and Mrs Parr have used up their ISA allowances for the year, they can start again with new allowances from April next year. He suggested they consider switching to corporate bond funds when their need for income rises.

LESSONS TO BE LEARNED

- Do not leave your heirs a large inheritance tax bill. Consider taking out a whole-of-life policy written in trust to pay the bill – this way, the lump sum escapes inheritance tax. However, this can be expensive. The earlier the policy is taken out, the lower the premiums. Both new and existing policies can be placed under a trust with forms available from life insurance companies Alternatively, invest in an insurance bond written in trust.

- Over the long term, savings accounts often fail to beat or even match inflation. If investing for five years or more, consider investing some of your savings in stock-market-based investments which can produce higher returns.

- Review investments to make sure they match goals. Mr and Mrs Parr need income but have invested in growth investments.

- Make the most of tax allowances. By using up their £7,000 annual ISA allowances (£14,000 a year between them), the Parrs can earn income free of tax.

Case Study 5

PROBLEM: WORRIED ABOUT CAPITAL GAINS TAX AFTER INHERITING CASH AND A HOUSE

Vital Statistics
Names: John and Jane Crawford-Baker
Ages: Fifty-two and forty-eight
Location: Crawley, West Sussex
Occupations: Ambulance officer and database administrator
Combined income: £39,000 p.a.
Savings: £5,650 in cash savings
Pension: Mr Crawford-Baker is in the NHS final salary scheme; Mrs Crawford-Baker is in her company final salary scheme and has a frozen local government final salary scheme
Investments: £52,000 in stock-market investments
Mortgage: £48,000 Woolwich repayment mortgage

Borrowing: £12,000 First Direct three-year car loan
Insurance: None

When Jane Crawford-Baker inherited a £120,000 house in Northern Ireland from her father, she and her husband, John, decided to leave Sussex and improve the property. Jane also inherited £70,000 in cash and her husband had recently had a £18,000 inheritance from his godmother. He now plans to retire when he turns fifty-three.

The couple, who are both are in their second marriage and have no children, are concerned about the implications for capital gains tax if they keep their current house, which is in both their names, in Crawley, West Sussex, and rent it out in the meantime. Jane said: 'We want to modernize my father's house and then sell it in about five years' time, so there could be capital gains tax if it is not our main home.'

Jane is a database administrator for building and civil engineering benefits schemes, looking after holiday pay and pension schemes for employees. She earns £15,000 a year plus a £1,000 mortgage subsidy, while her husband earns £23,000 as an ambulance officer.

The couple share a joint account with First Direct which they run down to zero every month, putting any surplus into a First Direct high-interest cheque account. 'It's for if we know something is going to crop up in a shortish amount of time, but there's only about £150 in it at the moment,' says Jane. Her husband also has £5,500 in a maturing Halifax tax-exempt special savings account (TESSA).

The couple have around £52,000 in total invested in the stock-market, with some of this in tax-exempt personal equity plans (PEPs) – £10,500 in Jane's plan and £14,000 in John's. Neither has an individual savings account (ISA) and the rest of their capital is in pooled investments, apart from a few individual shares.

Both are lucky enough to be members of final salary pension schemes.

They have around £39,000 of their £48,000 Woolwich repayment mortgage outstanding to consider before they can move to Northern

Ireland. Jane bought the Crawley house for £64,000 in 1995 on a sixteen-year loan and it is now worth £115,000.

The couple also have a £12,000 First Direct three-year car loan, costing £435 a month, to repay.

WHAT THE EXPERTS SAY

The advisers to Cash Clinic agreed that the couple are right to be concerned about capital gains tax (CGT) liability.

Tom McPhail, of independent financial advisers (IFAs) Torquil Clark, said: 'If they move to Ireland and rent out their property in West Sussex, then they may be liable to CGT on disposal of the property.'

However, he said the Crawford-Bakers' liability could be reduced, depending on the length of ownership against the length of time they let the house out as rented accommodation. He explained: 'Any gain relating to the period when it was their principal private residence will not be taxable. In addition, they can effectively let the property out for up to one year before it would start being treated as not being their principal private residence.'

Vivienne Starkey, of IFAS Equal Partners in London, said the Crawford-Bakers should check with their mortgage company that it is content for them to rent the property out. She recommended that the couple treat renting out their home as a business and prepare a proper plan, addressing issues such as how much the rent will be, who will manage the property, collect the rent, deal with problems and organize repairs.

She supported the couple's idea for paying off the car loan. 'A basic-rate taxpayer would have to earn 12.4 per cent gross interest on their savings to cover the 9.9 per cent annual percentage rate (APR) on the First Direct loan.'

She said that, before using inheritance money to repay the mortgage, they must decide how much they will need for the renovation of the house in Northern Ireland. The advisers said that in order to prepare for their move and retirement, the Crawford-

Bakers need to get their savings in order. Mr McPhail recommended that John consider moving the cash in his TESSA to get a better rate.

Mrs Starkey said they should also move money in their First Direct account as alternatives such as Egg pay more than twice as much. However, she warned: 'It is up to savers to monitor their accounts.'

On the investments side, the advisers urged the Crawford-Bakers to make use of their ISA allowance for the tax year. Mrs Starkey said: 'They should both consider using their full £7,000 allowance for this tax year if the capital is not needed elsewhere. They will have an allowance of £7,000 each for the following tax year.'

LESSONS TO BE LEARNED

- The longer an asset is held, the lower the CGT. This should be taken into account when making any investment and deciding how long to hold it.

- Second properties – particularly buy-to-let – are popular investments. However, it is vital to do your maths. Treat letting out a home as a business to maximize rental income, minimize tax liabilities and reduce the headaches involved in being a landlord.

- Everyone should make use of their annual £7,000 ISA allowance. If they do not use it, they lose it. Over five years a couple can invest £70,000 in these schemes free of tax. So the Crawford-Bakers could shelter all their stock-market investments from CGT – then they only need worry about their second home.

Case Study 6

PROBLEM: CAPITAL GAINS TAX ON SALE OF A SECOND HOME AND SHARES

Vital Statistics

Name: Ted and June Bloomfield
Ages: Sixty-two and fifty-eight
Location: Norfolk and Leytonstone, London
Occupation: Mr Bloomfield is a motorbike spares shop owner
Income: £7,800 p.a. from shop; £2,000 p.a. from annuity
Savings: £5,600 in building society and bank accounts
Pension: Drawing pension
Investments: Property worth £400,000 total, plus a large number of
    shares
Mortgage: None
Borrowings: None
Insurance: None

Much of Ted and June Bloomfield's capital is tied up in property and shares. When Ted, who runs three motorbike spares shops in East London, is working in London on Thursday, Friday and Saturday, he stays at their house in Leytonstone, which is worth about £150,000. The rest of the time he lives with his wife June in the couple's home near Kings Lynn in Norfolk, which is worth about £250,000.

The couple have no children or other dependants.

At the moment, the shops pay for most of the Bloomfields' living expenses plus a wage of £150 a week to Ted. He is also drawing a pension from his NPI personal pension plan. It has a £5,000-a-year annuity, but Ted is currently taking just £2,000 a year in the hope of receiving rising income in future. He also took £23,000 as a tax-free lump sum from his pension fund when he was sixty but had to use £18,000 of this to do up the shops and make them more profitable. The remaining £5,000 went to pay off his business over-draft.

Ted, who has been married to June for sixteen years, said: 'I did intend to retire when I was sixty, but I couldn't really have afforded it. The shops turn over some money and our expenses are paid, but that's about it.'

'We would like to class the Norfolk house as my wife's main residence and the London property as mine and then we want to close down the shops. The council is taking over one of them in a property development scheme. They will turn it into three flats, do them up and rent them out for us. We will be guaranteed £110 a week for each of the flats and after five years, the building reverts back to us.'

The couple also have a large number of shares, with more than £76,000 invested directly in companies including Avon Rubber, Rolls-Royce, Cable & Wireless, Abbey National, Alliance & Leicester, British Gas, Centrica, Anglian Water and BT.

They do not have any pooled funds, personal equity plans (PEPs) or individual savings accounts (ISAs). June has her own personal pension plan with Sun Life of Canada worth £20,000. She plans to begin drawing an income from that in two years' time when she is sixty. She also has £5,000 in a Nationwide TESSA 2 account, which is due to mature in two years. Ted has £600 in savings. The couple do not have a mortgage or any other borrowings.

WHAT THE EXPERTS SAY

The advisers to Cash Clinic said that the Bloomfields need to keep an eye on potential capital gains tax (CGT) liabilities because of their shareholdings and investment in property.

Laura Hammond, of independent financial advisers, (IFAs) Thomson's Wealth Management in London, said: 'The couple will benefit from the capital growth of the value of the new flats, although they will have to pay CGT on the full gain as the flats do not fall under the primary residence exemption.

'The Bloomfields cannot class different properties as their main residence as married couples who live together can only have one main residence for CGT. Anyone with more than one home can make an election as to which home should be treated as the main residence. The choice must be made within two years of buying the property. This can be changed if necessary – but the change cannot be backdated by more than two years.'

Tim Cockerill, of IFAs Chartwell Investment Management in Bath, said that the couple should start looking at generating more income from their investments: 'They will need their investments to provide an income. The present spread of equities is very exposed to market volatility, which has been increasing in recent years. Many of the stocks they hold are in the "old economy" and – although this isn't necessarily a negative – the long-term prospects of the portfolio are not, I feel, outstanding. I would consolidate this portfolio into unit trusts. This way their investment is managed on a full-time basis, there is a much better spread of assets and that will reduce the risk profile. However, they will have to watch the CGT position when selling.'

Adrian Shandley, of IFAs Balmoral Associates, said: 'I would advise them to consider disposing of the shareholdings gradually to be CGT-efficient.'

Ms Hammond suggested the couple consider a share exchange scheme with a fund manager so that they can reinvest straight into individual savings accounts (ISAs) that will provide a tax-free wrapper around their investments. Inland Revenue rules make it impossible to transfer existing shares directly into an ISA; investors have to sell and rebuy the shares first if they want to continue to hold them. She said: 'Most of the share exchange schemes sell the shares for the client and do not impose commission charges. Some will even pay the offer price for shares they transfer into their own portfolios.

'The Bloomfields should invest £7,000 each into a maxi equity ISA now because of the diversification and tax benefits. They can use share exchange again after the start of the new tax year in April to transfer a further £7,000 each into ISAs.'

Both these amounts are within the current CGT personal allowance of £7,700 a year (the 2002/2003 allowance), so the couple should avoid CGT provided they do not have CGT liabilities elsewhere.

Ms Hammond agreed that the Bloomfields should have some exposure to corporate bond and fixed-income funds when they exchange their shares because they are safer and provide income.

The advisers did not agree, however, on what June should do with her pension. Mr Shandley said: 'I would advise her to draw her Sun Life pension as soon as possible, taking the maximum tax-free cash as the couple have no children or dependants and therefore the flexibility of tax-free cash is paramount.'

Ms Hammond, however, said: 'If the income from the flats is sufficient for them, then she can defer her pension. It would then continue to accumulate in the pension fund and, when she draws down the pension, she may benefit from a higher annuity rate because she is older.'

Ms Hammond added that June should look to the open market for an annuity when she does come to take it, rather than just going with the one on offer from her pension company.

LESSONS TO BE LEARNED

- To maximize income in retirement, it is possible to take a reduced pension in the first few years so that income increases as you age – when you may need the money more or, as in the case of Ted Bloomfield, no longer earn a living.

- Do not put all financial eggs in one basket. The Bloomfields have far too much of their capital in 'old economy' stocks and have not spread the risks of investing.

- Maximize CGT allowances. Everyone can make tax-free gains of £7,700 a year (the 2002/2003 tax allowance). So those with substantial portfolios should consider realizing this amount of gains each year rather than selling shares in one block and incurring CGT.

- Like too many people, the Bloomfields have investments that are taxable when they could invest them in an ISA tax free. Using a share exchange scheme, as recommended, can cut the costs of switching shares into an ISA. However, before doing this investors should check their CGT position.

- Couples inherit from each other free of inheritance tax when the first spouse dies. However, they should consider the inheritance tax position upon death of the second spouse. If they have dependants or children (which the Bloomfields do not) they should leave assets to the next generation to use up as much of the £250,000 inheritance tax threshold as they can (the 2002/2003 allowance) and reduce the size of the estate upon death of the second spouse.

- Always shop around for the best rates on annuities, as Mrs Bloomfield has been advised to do. It is possible to boost retirement income by a third by taking the open market option instead of simply accepting the annuity offered by the company with which you have a pension.

2 Savings

Saving is out of fashion. Consumer borrowing is rising to record levels, while millions of us have less than £500 set aside to tide us over should financial disaster strike.

Part of the problem is low interest rates. With the cost of borrowing down to levels last seen in the 1960s, it is not surprising that consumers would rather borrow to buy goods than save up first.

In addition, low interest rates mean low savings rates – and these are often so poor they cannot even match the low rate of inflation. So in 'real' terms savers are seeing their capital fall – instead of rise – in value.

However, saving does still make financial sense. Consider this:

- Home buyers do not usually receive help in paying their mortgage for the first nine months after losing their job. Without savings or insurance, how would you keep a roof over your head?

- Living life up to the limit on an overdraft, credit card and with personal loans means that when disaster strikes it may not be possible to borrow any more to pay for essentials such as repairing the boiler/buying a new car engine, etc.

- Stock-market investments can fall – as well as rise – in value, as has been seen in recent times, whereas money on deposit is not at risk.

- Some items of expenditure are too much to bear out of disposable income. It costs as much as £43,000 to send a child to private day school for six years, with a further £12,000-plus to cover uniforms and extra activities. That would eat up over £90,000 of pre-tax income for a higher-rate taxpayer – roughly

£18,000 a year. Few could afford such costs out of disposable income and instead must save.

Many of us think 'it could not happen to me'. However, it could. In Cash Clinic Case Study 11 in this chapter, Sue Ledger's life changed dramatically following redundancy and the sudden death of her husband. In her early forties she was left with her son's school fees to pay and no job. Fortunately the couple had adequate life insurance, her husband had a good pension and they had also saved for the future.

Think about it – would you be in such a good position should disaster strike?

FINDING THE BEST RATE

Although interest rates are at an historical low and the majority of interest-bearing current accounts are paying less than 0.1 per cent interest after tax, it is still possible to earn a reasonable return from money on deposit.

The best buys in the savers selection produced by financial comparison guide MoneyFacts now show that the highest rates are paid by so-called direct accounts which are managed by:

• Telephone

• Post

• Internet

To set up an account – even on-line – savers, unless they are existing customers, need to supply identification and send a cheque by post. So an account will take several days to set up. In some cases cash cards are issued to give access to cash, but in others savers have to send written notification that they wish to access their money.

Savers can also boost their returns in the following ways:

Tiered rates

The more that is invested, the higher the rate of interest, so investors should pool smaller savings accounts into one larger one.

Notice periods

The longer investors are prepared to tie up their cash, the higher the rate of interest given. However, there may be penalties for early access to cash.

Bonuses

Several of the best-buy accounts only pay the best rates to those who save for a minimum period – six months or a year – when they are paid a bonus.

Fixed rates

These are only given on bonds savings accounts, which usually require a minimum deposit of £1,000 and last for a set period from six months to a year. However, if interest rates rise in the meantime, savers could find that they are locked into a rate that is no longer competitive.

How to shop around

Traipsing up and down the high street looking for the best rates from different banks and building societies will take time and may not even help savers to find the best rate as some of the more competitive savings institutions – including supermarkets and on-line banks – do not have bank branches.

Savers should read the financial pages of newspapers, including the *Daily Telegraph's* Your Money section on a Saturday, and regularly check out rates at on-line comparison websites such as www.moneysupermarket.com. Details of on-line savings providers can be found at www.find.co.uk.

TAX-FREE SAVING

Savings' interest is usually paid with tax deducted at 20 per cent. Higher-rate taxpayers must pay an additional 20 per cent tax to bring the rate up to 40 per cent. However, basic-rate taxpayers – even though they pay tax on income at 22 per cent – have no extra tax to pay. Lower-rate taxpayers can reclaim 10 per cent of the tax deducted and non-taxpayers should register to receive income gross (without tax deducted) by filling in form R85 available from the Inland Revenue. However, no tax at all need be paid if savers invest in a tax-free savings account.

ISAs

Tough competition among savings institutions for individual savings account (ISA) business means that these tax-free accounts also pay among the highest rates of interest – even if the tax breaks are taken out of the equation.

Designed to encourage people to save more, ISAs enable savers to put their money into cash (savings), share-based investments and life insurance company investments (not to be confused with life insurance policies).

In addition there are three types of ISA:

- **Maxi ISAs** have an overall investment limit of £7,000 and all the investments must be bought from one provider. Most maxi ISA investors invest the full amount in stocks and shares. However, some ISA providers also allow them to invest up to £3,000 in savings.

- **Mini ISAs** enable investors to buy all three types of investment (savings, stocks and shares and life insurance investments) from different providers. Most savers take out mini cash ISAs which have a maximum investment limit of £3,000. As with maxi ISAs, if investors buy all three types of investment the maximum investment limit is £7,000 (£3,000 in stocks and shares, £3,000 in savings, £1,000 in life insurance investments).

- TESSA-only ISAs allow investors in TESSAs that mature after their five-year term is up to reinvest up to £9,000 of the capital (not interest) in a tax-free ISA.

It is possible to open a cash ISA with as little as £1 and further investments can be made at any time – either lump sums or regular payments.

Banks, building societies and National Savings all offer ISAs and, as with savings accounts in general, they are not always easy to compare.

Some have notice periods while others allow instant access; some only pay the top rates of interest to those who invest the maximum allowed; others accept deposits of just £1; some guarantee a set rate or give bonuses to investors while others have variable rates.

To help savers to select the best-buy ISAs, the Government introduced what is known as the CAT standard. This stands for fair Charges, easy Access and decent Terms and conditions. There is one drawback – the standard is voluntary.

For the cash element of an ISA to be CAT-marked the ISA provider must:

- make no charges

- have a minimum transfer/investment of £10

- allow withdrawals within seven working days or less

- not pay interest that is more than 2 per cent less than the bank base rate

However, opting for a cash ISA that meets the CAT standard is no guarantee that it is the best deal for an individual saver. Some cash ISAs do not meet the CAT standard because they have notice periods and minimum investments of more than £1, yet they pay far higher rates than those paid by ISAs that meet the CAT standard.

Once an ISA investment is made, the allowance is used up. It is not possible to invest £3,000, then withdraw £1,000 of this and reinvest £1,000 in the same tax year. Once savers withdraw money from an ISA, the tax break is lost. So it pays to invest for the long term.

The ISA rules state that investors:

- must be aged eighteen or over

- must be resident in the UK for tax purposes

- cannot hold an ISA jointly with anyone else or on behalf of another person

The fact that joint accounts are not allowed should benefit couples who can shelter £6,000 of savings a year between them.

TESSAs

The Tax Exempt Special Savings Account (TESSA) may have been withdrawn from sale on 6 April 1999 and replaced by ISAs, but, that does not mean they have lost their tax breaks.

Any money invested in a TESSA can continue to grow tax-free and investors can continue to invest regular amounts (up to set limits) until their TESSA matures at the end of five years. Over this five-year term the maximum that can be invested is £9,000.

Although new TESSAs cannot be opened, existing investors can switch their account to another TESSA provider to earn a higher rate. However, some TESSA providers do not accept transfers and others charge exit penalties if savers wish to take their business elsewhere.

TESSA savers should think twice about closing their accounts as if they do so they will lose all the tax breaks (as with ISAs, all interest is paid free of tax).

Once the TESSA matures, investors have these options:

- to take all the proceeds

- to place the capital (not any interest earned) of the maturing TESSA into a TESSA-only ISA

- to transfer the capital proceeds into the cash component of a maxi or mini ISA

The most tax-efficient option is a TESSA-only ISA as savers can shelter up to £9,000 of capital in these schemes and retain the £3,000 cash ISA allowance.

Transfers into cash ISAs or TESSA-only ISAs must be done within six months of the TESSA maturing.

National Savings
In addition to offering a cash ISA, National Savings and Investments has several tax-free schemes. However, savers should not be seduced by the tax breaks. Some accounts pay very poor rates of interest.

National Savings Certificates
- Fixed-interest certificates pay a guaranteed income over five years – hence the term 'fixed'.

- Index-linked certificates, as the name implies, pay interest at a fixed percentage above the annual rate of inflation (the retail price index).

- The minimum investment in both is £100 and the maximum in any one issue is £10,000.

- Savers who withdraw their money before the term of the account is up (two years or five years depending on the certificate) will suffer as reduced interest is paid and no interest in some cases.

Children's Bonus Bonds
These are bought by adults for children and are not children's savings accounts (accounts for children to operate themselves are run by banks and building societies).

- Anyone over sixteen can invest in a bond for a child aged under sixteen.

- Bond are sold in units of £25 and the maximum that can be held in any one issue is £1,000 a child. However, this limit applies to each issue so children can hold up to £1,000 in earlier or future issues.

• Bonds pay a bonus if held for five years.

The Ordinary Account

The first £70 of interest (£140 with joint accounts) is tax-free. However, as the rate of interest paid on the ordinary account is so low (currently well below 2 per cent), investors are usually better off investing in an account that is taxable.

Premium Bonds

Although these are not technically a savings account, the prizes paid out are equivalent to a competitive rate of interest. Prize money is tax-free.

TAXABLE SAVINGS

Some types of savings earn interest that is paid gross – that is, without tax deducted – but this interest is still liable to tax and should be declared to the Inland Revenue. These include the following National Savings products: Capital Bonds, Income Bonds, the Investment Account and Pensioners' Bonds.

There are advantages in receiving interest gross. Non-taxpayers do not have to register to receive tax-free interest and starting-rate taxpayers do not have to reclaim part of the tax deducted. Also, there is a delay of up to twenty-one months between earning interest and having to include it on tax returns and pay tax on it.

Other savings pay interest with 20 per cent deducted at source.

CURRENT ACCOUNTS

Most interest-bearing current accounts pay an interest rate of less than 0.1 per cent after tax so it is not surprising that few people think of their bank account as a savings account.

However, while the average earner will pay in excess of £1 million into their current account over a thirty-year working life they will earn less than £40 in interest, according to Virgin One Account. Paying salaries into an account which combines a current account with a mortgage – so that all income automatically reduces debt – can improve this return to over £4,000.

Alternatively, sweep any credit balances into a savings account that pays a higher rate of interest.

SAVING VERSUS INVESTING

Saving is safe. Investing is riskier.

However, there is a price to pay for safety and certainty. Historically, stock-market-based investments have performed better than cash on deposit over most five-year periods, whereas savings rates often fail to beat inflation and as a result over the longer term the value of money on deposit falls in 'real' terms.

However, as the last year or two has proved, investors can be better off with savings accounts as at least their capital is protected when the stock-market tumbles, leaving investors nursing losses.

A compromise is a savings vehicle that is, in fact, a stock-market investment. These investment bonds are often sold to those who want the safety of a savings account but with a higher return.

Life insurance companies sell with-profits bonds (which allow 5 per cent withdrawal tax-free each year), school fees plans and endowment investments (usually ten-year-plus investments with the proceeds tax-free), while friendly societies have their own tax-exempt accounts into which £270 a year can be invested free of tax.

While these investment plans may be safer than riding the rollercoaster of the stock-market, they can however still leave investors out of pocket because they often have high charges and are inflexible. In Cash Clinic Case Study 12 in this chapter, Jeff Sugden and Anna Fronek paid £1,000 into an endowment but when they wanted to cash it in early they only received £500 back.

Before buying a long-term investment scheme (most have minimum investment periods of ten years), investors should ensure that they can continue to make the monthly investments for the full term. If they cannot make such a long-term commitment they should opt for more flexible investments such as stocks-and-shares ISAs. These are covered in greater depth in Chapter 6: Investments.

Corporate bonds funds are also often sold as alternatives to savings accounts. These unit trusts pay a higher rate of interest than most savings accounts, but there is an element of risk that the capital can be eroded. Invest via an ISA and the income is paid tax-free.

SAVING FOR SPECIFIC EVENTS

While it is advisable to have savings for a rainy day, most of us also save for specific events such as a deposit on our first home, driving lessons, holidays, school fees and weddings.

There are some specific savings vehicles for these purposes.

Saving for a child's future

Banks and building societies have accounts specifically designed for children. These often make saving fun and children may receive free perks such as a teddy bear, a £10 gift voucher or calculator. The rates vary from the very competitive to the very poor (rates of less than 0.1 per cent), so parents should shop around. As children have their own tax allowance (it is the same as for adults), they can usually earn interest free of tax. However, parents should note that if their child earns more than £100 in interest a year from money given by their parents, it is the parents who could pay tax on this interest. This rule is to stop parents putting savings into accounts in their children's names to escape tax.

When it comes to investing for children – rather than children saving their pocket money for themselves – National Savings has the Children's Bonus Bond, a five-year bond paying a fixed rate of interest that is reasonably competitive.

These accounts are controlled by parents or guardians until the child is sixteen, then he or she can either cash it in or wait to get the final bonus at the age of twenty-one.

Friendly societies, which are mutual organizations similar to life companies, offer ten-year children's savings plans which are tax-free. However, the maximum investment is only £25 a month or £270 a year and they are not flexible. To get the maximum returns investors have to invest for the full term.

School fees planning

It can cost over £90,000 to send a child to a private day school from the age of five onwards and a further £25,000 plus to help them through university. Families with more than one child are therefore looking at a bill of £200,000-plus.

Much depends on how long the parents – or grandparents – have to invest. With three young children, Ross and Jane Marshall, in Cash Clinic Case Study 10 in this chapter, are advised to opt for share-based investments as they have long enough to ride out the ups and downs of the stock-market. Martin and Janet Hardy, however, in Case Study 7 in this chapter, have older children. As the eldest is eighteen and starting university it is too late for the Hardys to invest to help pay for his education. Their only option is a savings account.

School fees plans are investment bonds packaged by several life insurance companies. The advantage is that these mature on a set date so a series of bonds or plans can be bought which mature in consecutive years. These policies also iron out the rises and falls in the stock-market, making them safer than many other share-based investments.

The life company pays tax on the underlying investments, so there is no further tax to pay for basic-rate taxpayers. Higher-rate taxpayers, however, must pay 18 per cent more tax – the difference between the basic and higher-rate tax – when they cash in the policy. Only if the policy has an element of life insurance (as is the case with endowments) are the proceeds tax-free.

ISAs are more flexible, have lower charges, are tax-free, can be sold at any time to fund school fees and the contributions can be varied. Pooled funds such as unit trusts are the favoured option as they spread the risks of investing across a wide number of shares.

Zeros are a type of investment trust share that pays no income. Their full name is zero dividend preference shares and, as their name suggests, investors are not entitled to any dividends. Instead, at the redemption (pay out) date investors receive a set price which is equivalent to earning a set percentage a year on their investment (usually more than they would earn in a savings account). Several zeros can be purchased with different redemption dates with these dates coinciding with the start of a new school year. As they have a set redemption price, investors know exactly what they will receive and when (although there are risks with these products and there are no guarantees). No income means there is no income tax to pay. However, the proceeds may be liable to capital gains tax if they exceed the individual's annual allowance (currently £7,700 for the 2002/2003 tax year).

Saving for a wedding

The average wedding now costs in excess of £11,000 and increasingly it is the young couple who pay for a proportion of the costs (although traditionally it is the bride's father who should find this large lump sum).

While a broad spread of investments can be used for school fees planning because of the long time-scale, when it comes to saving for a wedding the shorter time-scale (few couples are prepared to wait five years or more to get married) means that savings are often the only option.

Whether the saving is being done by a parent or by the young couple themselves, the priority should be safety combined with a high rate of interest and tax breaks. The only option, therefore, is a cash ISA into which each partner can pay up to £3,000 a year.

Case Study 7

PROBLEM: SAVING FOLLOWING A DROP IN INCOME

Vital Statistics

Names: Martin and Janet Hardy
Ages: Forty-six and forty-four
Location: Warrington, Cheshire
Occupations: Trainee Church minister and supply teacher
Combined income: £14,200 net p.a.
Savings: £3,000 in National Savings; £3,800 in Halifax savings account
Pension: £8,000 in Standard Life personal pension plan
Investments: None
Mortgage: £13,000 endowment mortgage from Birmingham Midshires
Borrowings: Student loan
Insurance: Standard Life endowment; £5,000 life cover from Canada Life

After a career as an accountant, Martin Hardy decided to become an ordained minister with the United Reformed Church five years ago.

'I saw redundancy destroy one or two people because they were over fifty and so had no chance of re-employment,' said Martin. 'Then I experienced redundancy myself and I received a lot of support from the Church. That is when I decided I had had enough of industry and wanted to do Church work.'

Currently in his final year of training at college in Manchester, Martin has a salary of only £11,800 – compared to £20,000 when he was an accountant – however, this is tax-free as it is made up of a £5,500 grant from Warrington Council topped up by the United Reformed Church. He has topped up income for the past three years by taking the full student loan each year of £1,700. When he is ordained, his salary from the Church will rise to £15,000.

Martin's wife Janet works part-time as a supply teacher and brings in around an extra £2,400 a year. This is also tax-free as it falls within her personal tax allowance.

The Hardys' eldest son, Timothy, eighteen, has just started at Sheffield University. Martin said: 'He is expected to take out a student loan of £3,500 a year. However, because our income is low we do not have to pay for him to go. He receives a grant of £1,200 or £1,300 and has to pay his fees out of that. We hope to give him an extra £2,000 a year as well. We are conscious that our second son, Andrew, who is sixteen, wants to go to university as well in a couple of years.'

The couple have a third son, Matthew, who is nine.

The Hardys have a joint current account in which they keep the bare minimum of funds and Martin also has a student account, currently holding about £6,000, which must last until the end of June.

The couple have no savings of their own but have saved £3,000 in National Savings bonds for their children. They put £1,000 into a five-year Capital Bond for Timothy in January 1998 and at the same time £1,000 each for the other two children in five-year Children's Bonds. The Hardys also have a Halifax savings account for the three boys and try to put in about £100 a month. At the moment there is around £4,000 in the account and that money is used for things the boys need, such as school trips.

Martin has a Standard Life personal pension, into which he transferred funds from his previous job a few years ago. There is about £8,000 in the fund. Janet does not have a pension but Martin will be able to expect support in his old age from the Church.

He said: 'My pension is one area of concern that we have.'

The Hardys have never invested money in the stock-market but have a £13,000 endowment mortgage from Birmingham Midshires, which they took out in 1981.

WHAT THE EXPERTS SAY

The first thing that the Hardys should do is make the money they have saved work harder, the advisers to Cash Clinic said.

Philippa Gee, of independent financial advisers (IFAs) Gee and Co. in Shrewsbury, said: 'The £6,000 held in the student account will be required during the next year. However, during its short life-span, it is still important to maximize its impact and therefore I would suggest transferring the funds to an account which will pay a higher rate of interest while offering easy access.

'A similar exercise should be undertaken with the savings account for the children, again to generate a higher level of interest.'

Ms Gee added that if the Hardys were prepared to tie the money up for a few years – particularly for their two younger sons – they could go for an account with a fixed return.

Stephanie Garner, of IFAs Millfield Partnership, recommended a savings account from Egg, the telephone and Internet banking arm of Prudential. She said: 'The couple should also make sure they have completed the appropriate R85 form to obtain gross interest as they are non-taxpayers.' They can get a copy of this from the Inland Revenue.

Janine Starks, of IFAs Chase de Vere in Bath, recommended Northern Rock's Base Rate Tracker Account for the savings. She said: 'Remember, though, that once Mr Hardy begins working for the Church and is a taxpayer, he will have to pay tax on his half of the interest. It would therefore be better to keep the savings in Mrs Hardy's name.'

She recommended that the Hardys consider investing the proceeds of their youngest son's National Savings Children's Bond in a pooled fund – a unit trust, investment trust or open-ended investment company – when it matures in 2003. She said: 'The key to stock-market investment is having time on your side, to ride out the ups and downs – and children have the time.'

Ms Starks also emphasized the importance of the Hardys saving for themselves as well as their children. She said: 'In order to have savings other than their pension at retirement, it is important to begin the savings routine as soon as possible. This should be possible once Mr Hardy begins his full-time job with the Church next year. Retirement is still twenty years away, and given this time-span, a stocks-and-shares individual savings account (ISA) could be used.'

She recommended that the Hardys start a regular savings plan and make monthly payments into the ISA of anything from £20 (the maximum annual investment limit is £7,000 if investing in stocks and shares using a maxi ISA, and £3,000 if investing in cash savings).

Ms Starks said: 'It will be possible for the couple to have an ISA each and to invest in different funds.'

The couple could also make a single-premium pension contribution at the end of the year if there is any surplus cash, said Ms Gee, but should concentrate on cash savings for the time being.

Ms Garner agreed, saying: 'Janet could contribute to a personal pension on a one-off basis, which would be a suitable method of funding due to her fluctuating earnings.

Even though she is a non-taxpayer, she would still be entitled to tax relief on her contributions using the new stakeholder pensions.'

LESSONS TO BE LEARNED

- However little there is to invest, it is still worth shopping around for a better rate – even if the money is only being saved for a year or less.

- Couples where one spouse is a non-taxpayer and the other a taxpayer (as will be the case when Martin starts work) should put savings into the name of the non-taxpayer so that they escape tax, and register to receive interest gross by filling in form R85 available from the Inland Revenue.

- Savings are safe but over the longer term stock-market-based investments tend to produce better returns. So when investing for retirement or on behalf of children when there may be ten, fifteen or twenty years to invest, consider stock-market investments. Pooled investments such as unit trusts spread the risks and by investing via an ISA all the proceeds are tax-free.

- Prioritize savings. The Hardys have been advised to build up some cash savings before investing in pensions and long-term schemes. Only when there are sufficient savings to pay for immediate needs and emergencies should investors consider tying up their money in stock-market investments. Remember, once money is invested in a pension that is it – it is locked up until retirement or until age fifty with a personal or stakeholder pension.

Case Study 8

PROBLEM: BUILDING UP SAVINGS AS WELL AS INVESTING FOR TWO DAUGHTERS' FUTURES

Vital Statistics
Names: David and Judith Plaistow
Ages: Thirty-five and twenty-nine
Location: Nottingham
Occupations: Company sales director and full-time mother
Income: £30,000 p.a.
Savings: £2,120 in bank accounts
Pension: Standard Life personal pension and Legal & General personal pension (Mr Plaistow); frozen NHS final salary scheme (Mrs Plaistow)

Investments: 16 per cent stake in the company Mr Plaistow works
    for; £37,000 Friends Provident endowment; home worth £85,000
Mortgage: £13,000 interest-only home loan from Cheltenham &
    Gloucester
Borrowings: None apart from mortgage
Insurance: £150,000 life cover with Standard Life

David and Judith Plaistow have just £1,300 in savings for themselves
– not a lot to protect their finances against disaster and provide for
their two children, Anna-Louise, two, and Elizabeth, five months.

David, who has a 16 per cent stake in the Nottingham franchise
of The Message Pad, a call centre business, used to be a trader in
the City of London until the stock-market crash in 1987 brought
that to a halt and he went to Nottingham University to study European business and French as a mature student.

Judith left work as a nurse to be a full-time mother and so the
couple live off David's salary, which was £30,000 last year and is
expected to rise by about £5,000 a year from now on. He gives his
wife a monthly allowance, paying it into her separate account from
his NatWest current account.

The couple do have a joint savings account at Alliance & Leicester
with about £1,000. 'It is easy access so we can get at it quickly if we
need it,' says David. He also has a Nationwide savings account with
£300 invested.

The couple have savings accounts with Tesco for their children
and put in about £10 a month each. Their elder daughter has about
£550 and their youngest, £270.

David said: 'As my salary goes up, I would like to save more for
them if I can. When they finish education, I want them to have a
sum they can use for, say, a deposit on a house. We will also use
money in these accounts to fund things like school trips.'

He has two personal pensions as he has also contracted out of
the state earnings-related pension scheme (SERPs). He pays £100 a
month to a scheme with Standard Life, which he has held for three
years, and his SERPs payments go into a Legal & General scheme

he has held since 1989, which is worth around £7,700. Judith has a frozen NHS pension scheme.

However, David said: 'I am a bit concerned about the way that pensions are run with annuities. I am not happy that the insurers who sell annuities get to keep all your capital. So, I am thinking about putting money into ISAs.' However, until now he has made no ISA or other stock-market investments.

His main investment is his 16 per cent stake in the Nottingham franchise of The Message Pad but this too is a concern. He said: 'When the company is floated my stake could potentially be close to a quarter of a million pounds. Then I will have all my eggs in one basket. I don't know if it is wise to have so much invested in one company.'

The couple have a £13,000 interest-only mortgage from Cheltenham & Gloucester backed up by a Friends Provident endowment. David has also taken out £150,000 life cover with critical illness from Standard Life, costing £22 a month.

WHAT THE EXPERTS SAY

The Plaistows' prime concern is to begin planning for the future. But first they must build up a cash fund for emergency expenses, the advisers to Cash Clinic said.

John Owen, of independent financial advisers (IFAs) Willis Owen in Nottingham, said: 'Mr Plaistow enjoys a reasonable salary by East Midlands standards but has very little in the way of immediate access savings for emergencies. He should focus on increasing this before worrying about increasing contributions to either his pension or an ISA.'

Kevin Minter, of David Aaron Partnership, another IFA, said: 'The emergency funds they have, currently standing at £1,300, are not enough for a couple with two young children.'

Mr Owen recommended an easy-access savings account with Northern Rock. He particularly liked the bank's base-rate tracker account, which was paying seven times as much interest as the couple were earning on their Alliance & Leicester account.

Mr Owen said: 'Alternatively, a simple transfer into the Alliance & Leicester mini cash ISA would shoot the rate up and still retain easy access.' He said the couple should aim to save around £5,000.

The advisers agreed that once the Plaistows have saved enough cash, they should turn their attention to providing for the future.

Adrian Shandley, of IFAs Balmoral Associates, said: 'David should be warned that he is not paying nearly enough into his pension. You should aim for a minimum of between 7 per cent and 10 per cent of your income.

'Many people are now turning away from pensions in favour of other investments such as ISAs as they are more flexible, don't die with you in retirement, and do not rely on annuities. However, you do not get tax relief as you invest.'

A lot therefore depends on David's tax status. Mr Minter said: 'He is creeping towards higher-rate tax. When he gets there, pensions will provide 40 per cent tax relief for him on the contributions.'

Mr Minter said that David should balance pensions with other forms of investment as well. 'He needs to strike a balance between his requirements for retirement income and savings for the medium term.'

He recommended that David open an ISA for regular savings. As it is not possible for anyone to buy both a mini and a maxi ISA in the same tax year, if the Plaistows want to start a maxi ISA for stock-market savings as well as a mini cash ISA, they should each hold one of them.

The couple should consider investing in the stock market for their children, the advisers said. Mr Minter recommended the Witan Investment Trust as it has consistent returns and low charges. He said: 'Bearing in mind that these savings could be held for nearly twenty years, placing them in a deposit account is likely to provide poor returns over that period.'

David will also benefit from new capital gains tax tapering rules. Mr Minter said: 'His 16 per cent stake in the franchise company certainly appears to be one of his biggest assets. He will now be able to receive taper relief, effectively reducing capital gains tax down to 10 per cent, despite him being a higher-rate taxpayer, as long as the shares are held for two years.'

LESSONS TO BE LEARNED

- Sort out savings before investing in the stock-market. The Plaistows have just £1,300 saved – not enough for a family with two young children.

- Taxpayers should consider cash ISAs as the rates paid are higher than for many savings accounts and interest is earned tax-free.

- Long-term savings – like the money the Plaistows wish to set aside for their daughters – should be in tax-free stocks and shares ISA accounts rather than in deposit accounts as over the longer term these are likely to produce higher returns.

- Couples should each make the most of their tax allowances – both can invest in ISAs.

- Even if tax has to be paid, minimize the amount. David can cut the rate of capital gains tax on his shares – a business asset – to just 10 per cent if he holds on to the shares for two years.

- The recommended minimum investment in a pension is 10 per cent of income. Pensions are discussed in greater detail in Chapter 5.

Case Study 9

PROBLEM: HOW TO SAVE UP TO LEAVE JOBS AND TRAVEL THE WORLD

Vital Statistics
Names: Richard Ardron and Mariella Wilson
Ages: Twenty-seven and twenty-five
Location: West London
Occupations: Teachers
Combined income: £42,000 p.a.
Pensions: Occupational
Borrowings: Student loan; personal loan
Insurance: Life cover

Richard Ardron and Mariella Wilson have thrown caution to the winds, resigned from their jobs, and are going travelling around the world. But they have just four months to save for the trip, something Richard is less worried about than Mariella. When it comes to managing money, she and Richard are like chalk and cheese.

Mariella said: 'When we started saving, Richard had a budget plan which I just couldn't stick to, so now I am paying him £100 a month and he is saving it.'

While they work out their periods of notice, Richard and Mariella, who are teachers at the same comprehensive school in Hounslow where they met, live separately in West London.

Richard is department head for business studies and economics, while Mariella is acting head of department for history. Both earn £21,000 a year and have been teaching at the school for three-and-a-half years. Richard's rent in Ealing is £317 a month and Mariella 's in Putney is £400 a month.

The two plan to leave the country in July, flying first to India and Nepal for four weeks and spending a further six weeks elsewhere in South-East Asia. After that, they will go on to Australia. 'We may teach to raise further money while we are abroad,' Richard said. 'But, really, that is what we are trying to get away from so we won't unless we have to.'

When the couple first decided on the trip six months ago, Richard opened a joint Standard Life savings account into which he pays £350 a month, including the £100 Mariella pays to him. He said: 'I chose that account because at the time it had the best rate and no penalties for making withdrawals.'

Richard also has a current account and savings account with First Direct, the telephone banking arm of Midland Bank, and Mariella has a current account with Lloyds. Richard said: 'I have a £250 overdraft facility, but I never use it. Mariella is about £400 overdrawn.'

They have no building society accounts, tax-free savings or investment schemes such as individual savings accounts (ISAs).

Both are contributing £100 a month to the Teachers' Superannuation pension scheme and have been doing so for three-and-a-half years.

The pair have already saved £1,600 in their Standard Life account. Richard also plans to sell his car and Mariella has cashed in £2,000 of National Savings Income Bonds given to her by her grandfather when she was a child.

Mariella said: 'I cashed them in in order to have the correct amount in my bank account to get my visa for Australia, but I will use that money to buy tickets and then replace it before we go.' She also holds a small number of TSB shares her father bought her fifteen years ago.

The couple would like to go away with around £5,000 each after raising the money to pay for their round-trip airline tickets – £1,200 each. They plan to open an account in Australia and transfer money from England.

On the borrowings side, Mariella pays £22 a month to pay back her student loan but she will qualify for deferment while out of the country. Richard borrowed money from his parents instead and is paying them back at the rate of £50 a month. This will come to an end just before he goes abroad.

Neither has any other major borrowings. Mariella does not hold a credit card, but Richard has a First Direct Visa card and a Goldfish Mastercard.

WHAT THE EXPERTS SAY

The advisers to Cash Clinic agreed that Mariella and Richard still have some way to go before they will have saved their target of £12,400.

Charles Dickson, of Charles Dickson Financial Planning in Surrey, said: 'So far they have saved £1,600, have a further £2,000 from the National Savings Income Bond and are saving £350 a month. At this level, they will have saved £5,350 by the end of July so they are going to be short of their target.'

Mr Dickson said that the sale of Richard's car may not be enough to make up the shortfall. Additionally, Mariella could sell her TSB shares to go towards the savings. He said the couple should consider ways to decrease their outgoings or increase their income in order to save a greater amount before they leave the country in the summer.

He said: 'Out of their combined net income of about £2,400 per month, £717 is spent on rent. As teachers, it may be possible for them to earn extra income by doing outside tutoring.'

All the advisers agreed that Mariella and Richard had made an excellent choice of savings account.

Mr Dickson suggested that Mariella and Richard opt out of the teachers' pension scheme in the run-up to their departure. He said: 'This would save their 6 per cent contribution. They can make up what they lose by making additional voluntary contributions (AVCs) to their scheme when they return. This could add up to an additional £800 to go towards the trip.'

If they do work while they are away, Mr Dickson pointed out, they need to check their tax status before they go. He said: 'As they are leaving four months into the tax year, and will not return to work until we are into the next tax year, they will be entitled to a tax rebate. They will only have earned £7,000 each and will be entitled to their full tax allowance, which will be £4,615 each.'

This means the couple will only have to pay tax on the remainder of £2,385 each, so they should get a rebate of over £500 each when they get back. Mr Dickson said: 'When they leave their jobs, they should send their P45s to their tax office with a letter confirming that they will not be working for the remainder of the year. A point to remember, however, is that if they do work while abroad, those earnings may be liable to UK tax.'

LESSONS TO BE LEARNED

- Saving up a specific sum in a specific time means sacrifices. Mariella and Richard may have to sell shares and a car as well as working as tutors and stopping pension contributions in order to raise enough to go travelling.

- Interest charged on borrowing can easily wipe out money earned on savings. Richard has the right idea – he clears credit card balances in full so no interest is charged.

- Before taking risks, have a fall-back position. For most people, it is emergency savings. For Mariella and Richard it is the ability to work when they travel, should they run short of funds.

Case Study 10

PROBLEM: SAVING TO FUND THE PRIVATE SCHOOL FEES OF THREE CHILDREN

Vital Statistics
Names: Ross and Jane Marshall
Ages: Both thirty-six

Location: Edinburgh

Occupations: Mr Marshall works for Scottish Power; Mrs Marshall is a part-time GP

Combined income: £65,000 p.a.

Pensions: Scottish Power money purchase scheme (Mr Marshall) and NHS scheme (Mrs Marshall)

Investments: Savings schemes with Sun Life, Scottish Widows and Friends Provident; Edinburgh Fund Managers Investment Trust Individual savings account (ISA); Mercury Emerging Markets Unit Trust ISA; Foreign & Colonial EuroTrust and Foreign & Colonial Investment Trust; Scottish Power share–save schemes; 500 Halifax shares

Mortgage: £71,000 endowment loan from Northern Rock

Borrowings: None apart from mortgage

Insurance: Scottish Widows and Axa Equity & Law endowments supporting mortgage

Choosing the right school for their three young daughters has proved to be a learning experience for Ross and Jane Marshall.

'We are very much in favour of sending our children to the local school,' said Ross. 'But we both value education and after it received a bad report we may be forced to take the step of sending them to private schools.'

The Marshalls must now plan how they will pay the day-school fees for their daughters, Bridie, six, Robyn, five, and Philippa, two.

The couple have a combined gross income of £65,000 a year and have always shared a joint account, which is usually in credit.

Each month they pay £400 by direct debit into an easy-access Halifax savings account which now has around £3,000 in it. They also have 500 Halifax windfall shares. Ross said: 'We use the Halifax account for emergencies and things like holidays. It is a stop-gap account.'

The couple pay £120 a month into a Sun Life Multivestor savings scheme for the girls and have been doing that for one-and-a-half years. Ross said: 'We want to set up a small nest egg for them to put towards something important.'

The Marshalls also have a ten-year savings plan with Scottish Widows to which they have been contributing £50 a month for the past eight years. Similarly, they pay £40 a month into a ten-year Select Savings Plus plan with Friends Provident, which has been going for seven years. 'I think that if you drip-feed money out of your account into savings then you can't spend it,' said Ross.

Ross has an individual savings account with Edinburgh Fund Managers through which he invests £75 a month. This was originally a personal equity plan (PEP). Jane also took out a PEP (these are tax-free schemes that were withdrawn in 1999 when ISAs were introduced) at the same time which has been converted to an ISA and invests £50 a month in emerging markets.

Ross also invested £2,000 with Foreign & Colonial after he inherited a small amount of money and invests £250 a month into three separate share-save schemes with Scottish Power. Of his £250 of premium bonds, Ross said: 'They have never yielded a sausage in ten years.'

On the pensions front, Jane is lucky enough to be a member of the National Health Service final salary scheme, while Ross contributes to the company scheme with Scottish Power. He pays £350 a month into this, including £195 in additional voluntary contributions. He has been part of the scheme for four years. He is also a member of two company pension schemes to which he contributed before joining Scottish Power.

The Marshalls' £71,000 mortgage is a five-year fixed rate with Northern Rock taken out a year ago. 'It knocked £110 off our monthly repayments,' says Ross.

The couple pay £55 a month to a Scottish Widows endowment and £70 a month to an Axa Equity & Law endowment to support the mortgage. They pay £355 interest a month. The mortgage is due to run to 2013.

WHAT THE EXPERTS SAY

Private schooling for three children is an enormous financial commitment and the Marshalls need to start getting organized immediately, the advisers to Cash Clinic said.

Kim North, of independent financial advisers (IFAs) Pretty Technical Partnership, said: 'They will probably be aware that this will be a huge commitment as day schools can charge up to £39,000 between the ages of thirteen and eighteen and boarding schools up to £67,500 for one child. Multiplied by three, this necessitates serious financial planning.'

Rebekah Kearey, of IFAs Roundhill Financial Management in Brighton, said the Marshalls' investment portfolio is fairly risky as a large proportion is invested directly in the stock-market in investment trusts.

She said: 'These tend to be more volatile than their unit trust and open-ended investment company [OIEC] sisters. Volatility is fine, so long as there is no need to draw capital at a fixed time, so the Marshalls should be careful their investments are supported by some other more steady ones, especially if the portfolio is to be used to fund school fees in the next few years.'

School fees have traditionally increased at a rate faster than inflation and earnings and so they normally need to be funded well in advance. As the Marshalls have only recently considered private education, they have few reserves and will probably have to fund the bulk of the fees out of income for the first few years.

Ms Kearey estimated that it will cost the Marshalls in the region of £460,000 to educate their daughters privately, taking into consideration future inflation. However, she said: 'This could be reduced by about £20,000 if they fund a series of investments now, which can meet the fees in increasing proportion from 2005.'

She said the investments to fund the fees could be made up of a portfolio of ISAs, unit and investment trusts, open-ended investment companies and insurance bonds.

Graham Bates, of Bates Investment Services in Leeds, suggested that the Marshalls use the proceeds of their Scottish Widows and Friends Provident savings schemes to help with school fees in the early years. He also suggested they consider an advance on their mortgage to help pay the fees.

Ms North said the Marshalls' Halifax shares, currently worth around £3,900, could also go towards school fees. Mr Bates said: 'Regular savings in ISAs should be maintained as these can be realized for fees later on.'

Mr Bates did not approve of Jane's choice of emerging markets. He said: 'They should select a UK or European fund.'

LESSONS TO BE LEARNED

- Do not take risks with money that is needed for a specific purpose at a set time. If the stock-market falls just before the money is needed, the investments will have to be sold at a loss and the investor cannot hold on for markets to recover. The Marshalls have too much of their money in high-risk funds such as the emerging markets instead of safer UK and European funds.

- There is more than one way to save. Do not forget to look at ways to trim outgoings to free up money to save. The Marshalls switched their mortgage to a better deal and saved £110 a month.

- Make the most of tax breaks. The Marshalls are using their ISA allowances which enable them to invest tax-free and yet are also very flexible, allowing them to cash in their investments when they need them to pay school fees without any penalties.

- Ten-year life insurance savings plans such as the ones the Marshalls have bought from Scottish Widows and Friends Provident require a long-term commitment. There can be penalties for those who stop contributions or cash in their policies early.

Case Study 11

PROBLEM: FUNDING PRIVATE EDUCATION FOLLOWING BEREAVEMENT AND REDUNDANCY

Vital Statistics
Name: Sue Ledger
Age: Forty-two
Location: Nottingham
Occupation: Housewife
Income: £9,600 net p.a.
Savings: £46,500 in bank and building society accounts
Pension: None
Investments: £23,500 invested in pooled funds; home worth
    £125,000
Mortgage: None
Borrowings: None
Insurance: £25,000 term assurance

Sue Ledger's life has changed greatly in the past year following the sudden death of her husband, John, and redundancy. She is now a full-time mother to her seven-year-old son, Nathan, whom she is determined to keep in private education.

She said: 'I was finally made redundant at the end of last year, so I am a full-time housewife now. If I get another job, it will only be part-time.'

She received £15,000 in redundancy pay – the equivalent of one year's salary. This has been added to the £23,000 proceeds of two endowments which matured on her husband's death last year.

Around £5,000 has already been used to pay school fees, the purpose Mrs Ledger would rather keep these savings for. The rest – around £33,000 – is in an Egg Internet account.

Sue, who receives £800 a month after tax from her husband's

pension, said: 'My husband's death was unexpected and I was not prepared for the future financially. I am concerned about having a pension and longer-term savings.'

She has only a small pension of her own from a previous employer. She said: 'I contributed to a pension when I was working but I didn't put much into it.'

At the moment, a lot of her savings are in cash form. There is £10,500 in a follow-on tax-exempt special savings account (TESSA) with Leeds & Holbeck. This matures in two years' time. Sue also has £3,000 saved in a Bradford & Bingley mini cash individual savings account (ISA), which she took out in August 1999.

She also has a total of £23,500 invested in unit trusts, mainly in PEPs and ISAs in general growth funds. However, the Jupiter European PEP inherited from her husband, worth £8,500, had the tax wrapper removed.

Sue said: 'I would like to take out a new ISA, but now that I no longer have a salary, I am not certain I will have the money to do it. I think the money is there for my son's school fees, but I wonder if I should be doing more.'

The mortgage on Sue's home, worth around £125,000, was repaid when her husband died and she has no other borrowings.

Sue is also concerned about provision for her son if anything should happen to her. She has £25,000 term assurance from Cornhill, costing £6 a month. She said: 'That is all I have, so I do need to set up something proper for my son.'

WHAT THE EXPERTS SAY

The priority for Sue is to protect her son in the event of anything happening to her, the advisers to Cash Clinic said.

Philip Pearson, an independent financial adviser (IFA) with WMC Investment Managers in Dorset, said: 'To provide the necessary funds to maintain her son's education to age eighteen and to provide the guardians with an income of around £500 a month indexed against inflation, assets in the region of £250,000 will be required. There is, therefore, a shortfall in the region of £31,000 between Sue's present savings, life assurance and the value of her home.

'I therefore recommend life assurance of a period of eleven years using a low-cost term assurance policy from Standard Life which will provide a sum assured of £31,000 for a fixed monthly premium of £5.91.'

Mr Pearson also suggested that Sue have both term assurance policies written in trust to ensure that the trust fund is used for her son's benefit in a tax-efficient way.

Harris Frazer, of IFAs Assured Benefit Consultants in Manchester, explained: 'The benefit of writing the policy in trust in this way is that the money would be outside of her estate for inheritance tax purposes.'

He said Sue should take out life assurance worth around £400,000 to provide her son with an income of £20,000 a year. He said: 'Scottish Equitable would provide her with this level of cover for £42.10 a month.'

David Wright, an IFA with Alexander Forbes, based in Croydon, south London, recommended a family income benefit policy, rather than term assurance, to provide income of £20,000 a year over fourteen years to coincide with her son's twenty-first birthday.

He said: 'This type of insurance is a cheap but effective way of providing protection for dependants. The cost would be £20.32 a month.'

The second thing for Sue to consider is how to cover her son Nathan's school fees. Mr Wright said: 'Her present savings and investments will not be enough to pay for school fees.'

To cover school fees in the future, Sue should invest in ISAs the advisers recommended.

Mr Wright said: 'At the moment, Sue's portfolio is heavily weighted in the UK. An international fund will provide some diversification as it invests globally.'

Mr Frazer recommended that Sue use a with-profits bond to pay for school fees. He said: 'Because of her need for a secure return, it is important that the money is invested in a product with minimal risk to the capital. With-profits policies grow by adding bonuses, both annual and terminal. With-profits policies tend to experience a smoother growth rate than equity-backed investments as some profits are held back in good years to supplement poorer years. The Inland Revenue will allow Sue to make a partial encashment of the bond each year of up to 5 per cent of its initial value with no immediate tax to pay.' With-profits policies are complicated products, so Sue must be clear about the charges and the cost of cashing in the bond early if she needs to later.

For her own financial future, Sue needs her own pension. Following the introduction of stakeholder pensions in April 2001, she can now contribute to a pension – and receive tax relief – even though she has no earnings from employment.

LESSONS TO BE LEARNED

- Saving for a rainy day is not enough. Insurance is also vital. Thankfully Sue's husband had taken out life insurance before he died. Now, however, it is up to her to ensure that she too has adequate life insurance to protect her son's financial future.

- Do not put all your nest eggs into one basket. Sue's portfolio is heavily weighted in the UK and she was advised to diversify overseas. Likewise, many of her investments were direct equity investments such as unit trusts. With-profits bonds iron out rises and falls in the stock-markets and are less risky.

- Always consider the tax implications of any financial decision. Sue has been advised to use up her £7,000 a year ISA allowance to shelter investments from tax and to write life insurance policies in trust so that the proceeds escape inheritance tax.

- Women need pensions too. It is still far too common for men to have adequate pensions and life insurance and for their wives to have little or none.

Case Study 12

PROBLEM: SAVING FOR A WEDDING WITH TWO YOUNG CHILDREN, DEBTS AND A MORTGAGE

Vital Statistics
Names: Jeff Sugden and Anna Fronek
Ages: Thirty-two and twenty-five
Location: Consett, Co Durham
Occupations: Fireman and customer services assistant
Combined income: £32,000 p.a.
Savings: £1,600 in Universal Building Society savings account
Pensions: Fire Service occupational pension (Mr Sugden); Norwich
    Union personal pension (Miss Fronek)
Investments: Scottish Widows mini equity ISA; two Scottish
    Widows twenty-five-year savings plans; two Homeowners
    Friendly savings plans; two children's Tunbridge Wells
    Equitable savings plans
Mortgage: £28,000 Halifax repayment mortgage
Borrowings: £1,200 student loan; £7,000 Lloyds Direct personal loan
Insurance: None

Jeff Sugden and his partner, Anna Fronke, have their hands so full
with their two young children that they have little time to concentrate on finance.

The couple, who plan to marry in July, are trying to save for their
wedding but find they have little left at the end of the month.
Balanced against this, they have the task of repaying £8,200 in
student and personal loans.

The couple, whose two children, Anya and Tommy, are aged two
years and nine months, have a joint income of £32,000. Jeff, a
fireman, earns the bulk of this – £21,750 – as Anna works part-time

in the customer services department of manufacturing group Eurosil.

Anna, whose parents moved to Glasgow from the Czech Republic when she was ten, said the couple spend £30–£50 a week on childcare. She said: 'We usually have between £100 and £200 left over at the end of the month which we could save, but invariably end up spending.'

They have around £1,600 in the Universal Building Society in Newcastle, earmarked for their wedding, and both have made a start with long-term savings. Both of them contribute to pension schemes – Jeff to his Fire Service occupational pension and Anna to a Norwich Union personal pension, into which she pays £31 net a month.

She also has a mini equity individual savings account (ISA) from Scottish Widows, with a UK Equity Index unit trust which tracks the FTSE 100. She invested £1,000 in January last year, but has not added to it since.

The couple took out a Scottish Widows twenty-five-year Premier Savings Plan in March 1998, each investing £50 a month. Anna added: 'We also have two tax-free savings plans with Homeowners Friendly, started last October, into which we save £25 a month each. I am not sure if these are performing well or not.'

The couple are keen to save for their children as well. So far, each of the children has an eighteen-year Tunbridge Wells Equitable savings scheme into which their parents pay £10 a month.

On the borrowings side, they have a £28,000 Halifax repayment mortgage, which they switched to from an endowment mortgage. Anna said: 'We did have a twenty-five-year Axa Sun Life endowment, which we took out in October 1997, but we cashed it in last year. We had paid in about £1,000 and only got £500 back, but we really wanted a repayment mortgage.'

The couple have managed to reduce the term of their loan to twelve years, but Anna is concerned that they could be repaying less. She said: 'We are paying interest at Halifax's standard variable rate. We would like to pay down the mortgage as quickly as possible and wonder if we should remortgage, but we are tied into it until 2002.'

The couple also have a total of £1,200 to repay in student loans – they are repaying £58 a month – and a £7,000 Lloyds Direct personal loan. Anna said: 'We are shifting this to an Egg credit card and are repaying £300 a month.'

Anna has £20,000 term assurance with Axa Sun Life costing £8 a month over its ten-year term. Jeff has a special Fire Brigade insurance package with Royal & Sun Alliance also costing £8 a month.

WHAT THE EXPERTS SAY

The couple are right to focus on the short term for now, the advisers to Cash Clinic said.

Mark Bolland, an independent financial adviser (IFA) with Chamberlain de Broe, said: 'They should make the cost of the wedding the priority and ignore everything else for a while. The £200-odd that is left over at the end of each month should be put away towards the cost of the wedding as well. This would come to about £1,200 which can be added to the £1,600 already saved. They have the £1,000 in the ISA which could be sold to provide extra cash.'

He suggested they borrow more on their Egg card if they need extra funds for the wedding but added: 'They should watch the interest rate as the cheap rate only applies to transferred balances and the introductory rate only lasts for six months.'

Anna Bowes, of IFAs Chase de Vere, suggested the couple look for a savings account paying a higher rate of interest to help with their wedding fund. She said: 'The account they currently have is paying only 1.5 per cent gross. After tax, this is 1.2 per cent, which is well below inflation.'

As the couple have not used their ISA allowance for this tax year, they could consider a mini cash ISA. Ms Bowes said: 'If they have access to the Internet, then smile.co.uk is offering a good rate.'

Once they have saved enough for the wedding, the couple can turn their attention to investments. Mr Bolland was unhappy with their current range. He said: 'They are investing £145 a month into endowment-type vehicles. While these policies should be main-tained, because there is little point in paying the charges to get out, they are paying too much into expensive and inflexible vehicles.

'As they have discovered to their cost with the Axa Sun Life endowment, getting out of these things can be expensive. They would be better off using ISAs for investments.'

James Dalby, of IFAs Bates Investment Services said: 'Anna has already taken some steps with equity investment. I would suggest she maintains her Scottish Widows ISA but makes new regular contributions to another provider when the time comes.'

He said she should also pay attention to her pension, increasing contributions as the couple's budget allows.

On the mortgage side, the advisers recommended that the couple wait until the end of their tie-in period before remortgaging. How-ever, Ms Bowes said: 'In the meantime, they could approach Halifax and investigate switching to a more favourable rate without paying the redemption penalty.'

LESSONS TO BE LEARNED

- Cash ISAs do not have to be long-term investments. Although the tax breaks offered by ISAs are lost if the initial investment is withdrawn (so it is best to keep savings in these schemes for as long as possible), savers who would otherwise not use their ISA allowance should consider a cash ISA for short-term savings. The rates are often far better than for other savings accounts and interest is earned tax-free.

- Keep track of savings and investments. It is not unknown for savings rates to fall to uncompetitive levels once banks and building societies launch newer accounts. The same applies to investments. Anna admitted that she did not know how well their Homeowners Friendly Society investment plans were performing.

- Some investments require a long-term commitment and early
  encashment means that investors do not always get their money
  back. As our case study shows, cashing in an endowment early
  meant that Jeff and Anna received back only £500, even though
  they had paid £1,000 in premiums.

3 Credit Cards and Loans

Consumer credit has risen to record levels in recent years, topping £700 billion, thanks to low borrowing costs and the ease with which even those with poor credit ratings can borrow money.

On average each of us has in excess of £10,000 of borrowings. However, many of us are paying over the odds for this credit, despite the fact there are so many cheap deals on offer.

Competition from new providers, particularly in the credit card market, has led to a cut in rates – some companies even charge nought per cent interest for limited periods. Even so, millions are paying three or four times more interest than they need to because they have failed to take advantage of these better rates.

Part of the problem is apathy. And part of the problem is confusion.

What were once simple products are now increasingly complicated. Credit cards have introductory rates, rates for balance transfers (debit balances transferred from another credit card) and different rates for cash withdrawals and purchases, making them increasingly hard to compare. Personal loans are no longer simple: they come under a range of names from home improvement loans to consolidation loans.

In addition, different types of borrowing are better for different purposes. So it is not just a case of choosing the best credit card but also of comparing cards with overdrafts and loans.

OVERDRAFTS

Overdrafts are better for very short-term borrowing and to cope with fluctuations in cash flow rather than as a long-term facility.

- A permanent overdraft can work out far more expensive than a personal loan. With a loan, borrowers reduce the amount they owe each month, whereas with an overdraft there is a temptation to keep borrowing up to the limit. This means borrowers never get out of debt.

- Make the most of free borrowing. Many current accounts now have buffer zones, with all borrowing up to this amount (ranging from £50 to £500) either fee-free, interest-free or both.

- Shop around for the best rate. Overdraft interest rates can be almost twice as high with some banks as with others.

- Unauthorized overdrafts should be avoided as they have penal rates of interest and exceedingly high charges. Whenever possible, agree all borrowing in advance.

- Remember that overdrafts are a facility which can be withdrawn at any time. Relying on an overdraft for long-term borrowing is risky. If the bank feels that borrowing is out of control or that the customer can no longer afford such a high overdraft, it can ask for immediate repayment.

- Watch out for arrangement fees. Agreeing an authorized overdraft can cost 1 per cent of the amount borrowed. This fee may be charged again and again each time the overdraft arrangement is renewed.

- Many accounts still charge a monthly or quarterly fee – as well as interest – to those who are overdrawn. Check when charges are levied. Those who are overdrawn for just one day a month throughout the year could pay a total of £60 in annual charges. Those who dip into the red just once a quarter will pay just four lots of monthly charges with an account that charges if it dips into the red during the month, whereas they will be charged for an entire year's borrowing if they select an account that charges quarterly.

Switching to get a better deal

It is a sad fact that more people will change their spouse than their bank account. However, times are changing. In the past, few customers bothered to switch banks because of the hassle involved – and many banks did not make it easy.

Today many banks will do the hard work for customers, transferring all direct debits and standing orders.

There are several steps that can be taken to make life easier:

1. Customers should first choose an account to suit their needs rather than trying to fit their financial needs round what is on offer.
   - Choose the right buffer zone. Those with small overdrafts may find that they do not have to pay any charges at all if they pick an account with a large buffer zone.
   - Go for low interest and no charges. Those who are regularly overdrawn should avoid charges – these are often higher than interest costs. Only those with very large overdrafts should opt for charges in return for a very low rate of interest.
   - Check the charging period. Dipping into the red as one charging period ends and another begins means two lots of overdraft charges instead of one.
   - Consider gold or premier accounts if borrowing large sums. These accounts have higher charges than standard current accounts, but often come with a £10,000 borrowing facility at a very low rate.
   - Avoid packaged accounts that charge whether the customer is in the red or not. They are only worthwhile if the customer uses all the extra services that they are paying for in the monthly fee. Many customers do not.

2. When you open a new account, wait for it to be up and running before using it.

3. Keep adequate funds in the existing and new accounts (or have sufficient borrowing facilities for each). That way, you will not end up paying for bounced cheques.

4. Decide on a transfer date and ask for pay or pensions to be paid into the new account from that date.

5. Ask for a new mandate form from any companies paid by direct debit and send these forms to the new bank.

6. Tell the existing bank to stop all direct debit payments – and standing order payments – from the transfer date.

7. Send a list to the new bank asking for standing orders to be paid from the transfer date.

8. Only close the old bank account once arrangements are running smoothly with the new one.

CREDIT CARDS

Credit cards are now a viable alternative to overdrafts, with many issuers charging less for credit than a bank charges for current account borrowing.

Competition among issuers has led to the scrapping of annual fees on almost every card, whereas many banks still charge customers for overdrafts.

Add to this the convenience of credit cards (no need to carry cash and no problems about exceeding the cheque guarantee limit) and the extra consumer protection and it is no wonder that more of us have credit and store cards than overdrafts.

More than a fifth of money borrowed is now on credit cards. However, it is estimated that some £3 billion is wasted each year by cardholders who fail to switch to one of the low-rate cards and instead pay interest of four times the bank base rate.

Half of all credit cardholders repay their balance in full each month so the rate of interest is immaterial. Those who clear their balances (rather than repaying just some of what they owe) escape interest provided they pay within the interest-free period. This varies from fifty-two to fifty-nine days – however, some card issuers give less than this (in a few cases there is no interest-free period) so cardholders need to beware.

Even those who do not need to borrow money can benefit from using a credit card. In addition to having up to fifty-nine days' free credit (so their money can be earning interest elsewhere before it is used to pay off the balance), they receive more consumer protection. If goods purchased using a credit card are faulty or are bought from a supplier who then goes bust before delivering the goods or services, and these cost more than £100, the card issuer is jointly liable with the retailer under the Consumer Credit Act. So if the retailer refuses a refund, the cardholder can demand compensation from the card issuer. Another reason to use a credit card is that some card companies offer free purchase protection. This is insurance against theft or accidental damage – sixty to one hundred and twenty days after purchase.

For those who borrow, no fees and low interest rates are vital. However, comparing deals is not always easy.

- **Standard interest rate**: this is the rate charged once any special introductory rate ends. Often the cards with what appear to be the lowest introductory rates have very high standard rates, so after the introductory rate ends after six months, borrowing costs are no longer competitive.

- **Introductory rates**: these usually last for just six months and many only apply to any transferred balances, not balance transfers. Every time money is paid off the outstanding balance, it is usually used to reduce the balance transfer on the cheaper rate rather than the new spending debt which is charged at a higher rate. It may therefore be better to switch debts to a card with a cheap rate for balance transfers and then use another card which has a competitive standard rate for new spending.

- **Fines**: cardholders who exceed the borrowing limit or miss a payment (a minimum of 3 per cent of the outstanding balance or

£5 must be repaid each month) can be fined. This is one way that the new low-cost card issuers recoup some of their costs. Read the small print carefully.

Some four in ten cardholders do not know what rate of interest they are paying on their credit card. So that is the first thing to check.

Those who do not repay their balance every month or are paying interest at the standard rate will generally be better off switching to a card with an introductory deal.

Gold and platinum cards are increasingly less elite (the minimum salary requirement may be as low as £10,000 or £20,000), but annual fees charged by many companies can make them less competitive. Once again, competition has led to more issuers removing annual fees and cutting interest rates.

To switch cards, all cardholders have to do is fill in the details of their current card on the application form for the new one. The new card issuer should then arrange for the transfer of the balance.

When using a card there are several pitfalls to watch out for:

- Avoid using a credit card to withdraw cash from a cash machine. With a credit card it usually costs a minimum of £1.50 or £2 per withdrawal, so it can cost £2 to take out just £10.

- Using a card abroad saves exchanging cash, carrying cash (which has risks) or buying travellers' cheques. However, card issuers add on foreign exchange loading of usually 2.75 per cent and may not always give the most competitive rate of exchange.

- Keeping hold of an uncompetitive credit card because of a loyalty scheme does not always pay (unless it is a cashback scheme) as most cardholders fail to make adequate use of these schemes and if they do, have to spend so much that it does not always make the offers worthwhile. As a result, many card issuers have scrapped these schemes.

PERSONAL LOANS

Borrowing a set amount at a set rate for a set term (usually six months to ten years) gives borrowers certainty – certainty about monthly payments (so no nasty surprises if interest rates rise) and that the debt will be repaid in full at the end of the term. One of the drawbacks of overdrafts or loans is that debts are often never repaid – all borrowers do is pay interest and some of their outstanding debts before incurring even more.

Personal loans are better for those borrowing for a year or more for a specific purpose. Those needing a facility (the ability to borrow rather than a set amount of money) can opt for credit cards or overdrafts.

There are, however, drawbacks to loans. They are not usually flexible. So there is no facility to increase what is owed or to change monthly payments if circumstances change. Repaying the loan early usually leads to penalties.

For those who need flexibility rather than certainty, newer forms of borrowing such as all-in-one accounts or offset mortgages which combine mortgages, loans, credit cards, savings and current accounts may be cheaper (mortgage rates are lower than personal loan rates so the interest will be less). These enable the borrower to increase the amount owed up to an agreed limit and to repay any amount at any time. As interest is charged on the daily outstanding balance, interest is saved the day money is paid into the account. These types of loan are covered in greater detail in Chapter 4: Property.

A few personal loans do offer flexibility. Borrowers are given a pre-agreed credit limit and must make a minimum payment each month. However, there is often a price to pay – variable rates of interest that are far higher than for loans without this flexibility. In these cases borrowers may be better off with an overdraft.

As with many types of financial product, what should in theory be very simple is now increasingly complex.

- Different rates are charged depending on how much is borrowed. The higher the loan, the lower the rate.

- Preferential rates can be given to existing customers – so check before borrowing.

- As with credit cards, outstanding debts can be transferred. The Halifax cuts its rate for the first six months to less than half its standard rate.

- Some lenders repackage their loans under different names. Car loans are a prime example. In most respects they are no different to standard loans other than that low-cost breakdown insurance or car-buy inspections may be offered as incentives to take out a loan with a particular company.

- Redemption penalties are common. In most cases two months' interest is charged if the loan is paid off early.

- Those applying via the Internet are often rewarded with a reduced rate.

- Rates can depend on a customer's credit rating or credit history with a particular bank or lender.

In addition, rates vary widely. It can cost £850 more to borrow £5,000 over three years with an expensive lender compared to the best buy, according to financial comparison guide MoneyFacts.

Rates now compete with those charged on credit cards and are often lower than those charged on overdrafts. Yet loans – partly because of their inflexibility – remain less popular. Four in ten of us have a credit card and three in ten have a mortgage, but only two in ten have a loan.

A major pitfall to watch out for is payment protection insurance. This is sold by most lenders and covers monthly repayments in the event that the borrower is made redundant or cannot work through sickness. The insurance is added to the loan instead of paid upfront, and as such the cost of protecting a £5,000 loan for three years can total £1,000.

These policies have exclusions and some borrowers may find that they cannot claim because they have moved jobs recently, only work part-time or have a pre-existing medical condition.

However, as the small print is not usually pointed out when the insurance is purchased (at the same time the loan is agreed), borrowers may be unaware that they do not even qualify for the expensive cover they have been sold.

SECURED LOANS

Personal loans are unsecured, which means the borrower does not have to put up any security – such as the family home. Secured loans, despite their name, are less secure for borrowers as if they fail to keep up with monthly repayments their home could be repossessed to pay off the debt. Loans can also be secured on endowment policies (against the surrender value) but only if the endowment is not already used to secure a mortgage.

Although secured loans used to be cheaper than personal loans, this is no longer the case. Borrowers should only opt for secured loans as a last resort. In most cases, there should be no need to put the family home at risk. Those with poor credit ratings (see the section later in this chapter) may, however, have no option. A cheaper alternative may be a further advance (i.e. increasing the size) of your mortgage.

CONSOLIDATION LOANS

Consolidation loans are another form of loan. They enable borrowers to put all their debts into one larger loan and cut the monthly costs by increasing the term of the loan. However, the longer the loan, the greater the total amount of interest paid (as interest is paid for longer). So although the monthly costs are lower, the total costs may be higher.

Firms offering debt consolidation have come under attack for charging high rates and arrangement fees. Often borrowers are advised to stop paying interest on existing debts. However, until the new lender has paid off these debts interest is still incurred and the existing lenders can credit-blacklist borrowers for failing to meet their monthly repayments.

The reason why so many debt management companies can offer these loans to those with a poor credit history or uncertain income (such as the newly self-employed) is that the loans are often secured on a property and are called 'home-owner loans'. Failure to pay the monthly repayments can mean that borrowers can lose their home.

Consolidation loans offered by debt management companies are often unnecessary. Any borrower can consolidate their debts themselves by taking out one larger – unsecured – loan at a competitive rate and using it to repay credit card borrowings, overdrafts, store credit and other loans. In order to reduce their monthly outgoings, they simply extend the term of the loan.

Often the cheapest way (in terms of monthly repayments, but not necessarily total interest costs) of consolidating debts is to remortgage and take out a larger home loan to cover all debts. This is because mortgage rates are far lower than even the cheapest personal loan rate.

STORE CREDIT

Store cards, cards that let shoppers buy goods on credit at one particular shop or chain of shops, tend to have much higher rates of interest than are charged by credit card companies so they are not an ideal way to borrow. However, if you shop regularly at a particular store, pay off your balance in full each month and take advantage of perks given to cardholders (such as free catalogues, special shopping days or 10 per cent off first purchase) store cards are a worthwhile addition to your wallet or purse. The four in ten store cardholders who fail to pay off their balance in full each month should consider other, cheaper forms of credit.

Interest-free credit on large purchases is worth having, however. Even those who have enough cash to cover the cost of the purchase should consider taking up these offers. They can earn interest on the cash while they are repaying the credit and should remember that the finance costs are built into the price anyway.

'Nothing to pay for a year' deals also sound good. They are if the borrower repays the entire amount owed at the end of the year. If they do not, penal rates of interest are usually charged.

CREDIT VERSUS DEBT

There is a fine line between credit and debt. All it takes is a sudden downturn in the economy or a hike in interest rates (and therefore borrowing costs) for increasing numbers of borrowers to find that they no longer have sufficient income to repay their credit or that the costs of borrowing are too high.

The first point to remember is that just because a lender will lend money to an individual it does not necessarily mean that person can afford the credit or should borrow the money.

Many borrowers make the mistake of thinking they can afford the minimum monthly payments (for example, just 5 per cent of the outstanding balance on a credit card) rather than considering how they will repay the entire amount borrowed.

Borrowers should also take precautions to ensure any credit can be repaid in the event of their circumstances changing. Insurance against accident, sickness and unemployment is one option. See Chapter 7: Insurance.

CREDIT SCORES AND CREDIT RATINGS

Those who struggle to meet their monthly repayments can quickly find that they run into trouble with their lender and this can lead to them being credit-blacklisted. Although there is no blacklist as such, all borrowers are credit-scored. This credit rating is a score awarded by lenders and credit reference agencies to determine whether or not an individual is creditworthy.

Credit reference agencies give lenders a whole range of information including:

- An individual's record of borrowing and repaying money

- Any County Court judgment awarded against them for non-payment of debts in the past

- Electoral roll details

This information is combined with details asked for by the lender such as the borrower's:

- Income

- Employment history

- Address

- Home-ownership

Those who have not been in employment with the same employer or at the same address for at least a year or two are less likely to be given credit as are those with poor credit histories and low incomes.

Those refused credit because of information supplied by a credit reference agency can ask for the name of that agency and write to them asking for a copy of their credit information file, enclosing £2, details of their surname, first names and title and any addresses they have lived at during the past six years. Any incorrect facts can be amended or removed. However, these cases are rare.

Borrowers may be unaware that they have had a County Court judgment awarded against them (perhaps because they failed to reply to correspondence from a lender). These judgments remain on their file for six years, after which they should be removed.

Credit repair agencies claim to be able to get a good credit rating restored but they can charge high fees and are not always successful. If there are any errors on file, anyone can ask for their files to be amended without having to pay an agency a fee.

It is possible to improve your credit rating. It may seem bizarre that someone with a massive debt such as a mortgage may be perceived as a better bet than someone with no credit cards or loans, but lenders feel that if someone has proven they can handle credit and meet monthly repayments they will be less of a risk than an unknown quantity. Also, if someone owns a property (even if their mortgage is large), they are more likely to be secure and want to remain that way by avoiding getting into debt.

Case Study 13

PROBLEM: TOO MANY BORROWINGS AND NOT ENOUGH INCOME OR SAVINGS

Vital Statistics
Name: Fiona Jamieson
Age: Thirty-seven
Location: Cheltenham, Gloucestershire
Occupation: Personal assistant
Income: £12,000 p.a.
Savings: £500 in the Halifax
Pension: None
Investments: 200 Halifax shares; thirty shares in Danka
Mortgage: £29,000
Borrowings: £900 to Girobank; £900 NPI loan; £2,400 owed on two
    credit cards; tax bill
Insurance: NPI life assurance

Animal-lover Fiona Jamieson quit her dream job as personal assistant to the Director of London Zoo, to live in the country in her dream house near Cheltenham in Gloucestershire.

Fiona, who has no dependants apart from her two cats, came up with the idea after spending a week in the Cotswolds celebrating her mother's sixty-fifth birthday. 'On the last morning, I sat looking down the garden across the fields and felt a strong impulse not to go back to London. I started making plans in my head.'

Since mid-January, Fiona has been employed on a temporary contract in the information systems department of insurance company Eagle Star's head office in Cheltenham. After tax, she earns £860 a month, £445 of which goes on the rent for her cottage in Bredon, a village nine miles away. The rest is swallowed by other overheads and payments into life assurance policies and Fiona is left with just £180 a month to live on.

Fiona said: 'When I lived in London, on a salary of £1,200 a month, I spent quite erratically, never knowing what was in my account until my statement arrived. Now that I don't have a guaranteed income, I keep records of my cash flow, something I never used to do.'

Fiona's job at Eagle Star is about to come to an end, and she does not know where her next job will be. Although this presents problems, she is not panicking, having had experience of going for ten weeks without work when she moved last summer.

She said: 'I am always aware of the fact that I can't afford to be ill; if I had a major emergency, I do not know where I would get the cash from.'

Fiona also has income from renting out her one-bedroom flat in north-west London, which she bought with the assistance of her local housing authority in 1996. She has a £29,000 Nationwide mortgage on half of the flat, while the housing authority owns the other half. She pays the authority £162 a month in service charges and rent and the Nationwide £196 in mortgage repayments. Her tenants pay her £625 a month, which is below the market average, but Fiona said she likes and trusts them and does not want to have to deal with an agency.

Fiona said she would like to switch her mortgage to a lower rate but knows she would have to pay £1,100 in early redemption penalties. 'My major concern is what I will be charged, and when, in terms of tax on the income from my London flat. I did write to the tax office asking for guidance on this, but never received a reply. I have been making no provision for paying the tax bill.'

Fiona also owes £900 to Girobank through a 'rolling credit' account. She also has her current account there and pays at least £40 a month to pay off the loan. When she runs short she is able to borrow again.

There is a £900 loan from NPI which Fiona took out, secured against a life policy she has with that insurer, in 1985. She pays £46 in interest twice a year and Fiona has never made an effort to repay this loan as she is required to give six months' notice before doing so.

More seriously, Fiona owes a total of £2,400 on two Visa credit cards – 'both of which were supposed to be just for emergencies'. One is with the Co-op Bank, the other with Girobank.

On the savings side, Fiona has £500 in a Halifax Liquid Gold account and has kept the 200 shares she received when the Halifax demutualized in 1997. She also has thirty shares in Danka.

Fiona pays £18 a month into two ten-year life policies with Family Assurance Friendly Society – she has done so since 1993 – and £10 a month into an endowment policy with NPI which is due to mature, after twenty-five years, in 2007. There are no other savings or investments and more worryingly, there is also no pension.

WHAT THE EXPERTS SAY

Fiona needs to restructure her debts as a matter of urgency, the advisers to Cash Clinic said.

Mark Bolland, of independent financial advisers (IFAs) Chamberlain de Broe, said: 'Fiona is paying very high rates of interest on her credit cards and it would make sense to try to clear these debts as quickly as possible. There are many credit card companies around now that offer relatively low interest rates but Fiona's difficulty may be in obtaining these cards on her current income.'

He said that she should try to amalgamate her debts while she is working and can show a steady stream of income. 'Without this, it will be very hard to do because her credit score would not be favourable.'

Peter Bridges, of IFAs Rickman Tooze in Cirencester, Gloucestershire, said: 'Fiona should be looking to remortgage for £33,000. Even if rates average 6 per cent over the term of the mortgage, the repayments would still only be £165 a month. This saves her at least £190 a month, so even if she pays Nationwide a penalty of £1,100, this is made back within six months.'

Mr Bolland said: 'If the Nationwide is happy with the current arrangement, Fiona should perhaps speak to them first because they might be able to remortgage reasonably quickly and cheaply and add the penalty to the loan.'

Adrian Shandley, of IFAs Balmoral Associates, advised Fiona to take out income protection insurance: 'Though her flat is producing a very modest income while rented out, it would not take many months as a vacant flat to threaten to sink Fiona financially.'

To insure an income of £7,500 to age sixty-five would cost just over £31 a month with Canada Life, which would refund 50 per cent of the premiums paid if no claims are made by expiry age.

Although Fiona should ideally have permanent health insurance in place, Mr Shandley recognized that she is unlikely to be able to afford this at present.

He said: 'Fiona has a number of endowment policies which should remain as they are. However, against a backdrop of insecurity I would recommend that she consider saving in a flexible medium-term vehicle, such as an individual savings account (ISA) to provide a readily accessible cash fund if needed in a few years' time.'

Mr Bridges said Fiona must make it a priority to build up a cash reserve. He said: 'A cash ISA would not only be tax-efficient, it would make administrative sense too because she does not need to disclose ISA investments to the taxman.'

The third issue to address is Fiona's tax liability in light of the earnings from renting out her flat in London.

Mr Bolland said: 'Fiona needs to make up an account to show

her income and expenses and it would make sense to make this up to 5 April, the end of the tax year.'

LESSONS TO BE LEARNED

- If borrowers want the cheapest monthly repayments possible – as is the case for Fiona because of her low income – they will be better off increasing their mortgage to repay all other debts. This will cut their monthly costs – in Fiona's case by £190 a month – and ensure that they do not need to get further into debt.

- Even if borrowers have to pay a redemption penalty if they want to switch their mortgage, it can be worthwhile. Fiona will make back the penalties in just six months.

- Borrowers should always consider how debts will be paid if they suffer a drop in income. It is possible to buy insurance so that monthly mortgage and other repayments can be met if the borrower loses his or her job.

- Apply for credit when you don't need it – those in permanent employment with good salaries are more likely to get credit than those in Fiona's uncertain position.

Case Study 14

PROBLEM: SAVING FOR THE FUTURE AND BUILDING UP A CREDIT RATING

Vital Statistics
Name: Camilla Hammond
Age: Twenty-two
Location: Cornwall

Occupation: Small company administrator
Income: £8,500 p.a.
Savings: £3,500 in bank accounts and National Savings;
    £100 in Premium Bonds
Pension: None
Investments: None
Mortgage: None
Borrowings: None
Insurance: None

Camilla Hammond has given up a career working with horses in order to earn more and save towards buying a home of her own. 'I am still living at home, although I started working four years ago,' she said. 'My job wasn't paying enough to save anything, though, so I am now working as an administrator for a fax machines and photocopiers company near where I live. I don't get much time even to ride horses any more – I used to ride every day.'

After she finished school in 1994, Camilla went to college for an equine business studies course. This ended in 1996 and she has been working ever since. She earns £8,500 a year at the moment and aims to move out of her parents' home before she has had time to save a healthy deposit to buy somewhere of her own, so she will need to rent for a time. She expects this to cost about £300 a month for a one-bedroom flat.

She said: 'I would probably buy a flat with my boyfriend eventually, and we would most likely be sharing the rent on a flat from next year.'

Camilla is saving hard for her independence. Her salary – which comes to around £600 net a month – is paid into her Lloyds TSB savings account. She then transfers £350 each month to her Lloyds TSB current account, leaving £250 savings a month.

She currently has £3,000 saved in her savings account, and runs a £300 surplus in her current account. She also has £200 in a National Savings Post Office account and £100 in Premium Bonds.

However, she said: 'I have been surprised at how little interest I am earning on my savings in the Lloyds Flexible Savings account.

I got an account statement recently and the interest paid on my £3,000 was very low – I only earned a few pounds. My main aim is to start investing and saving my money properly so that I can get a better return on it.'

She is not sure if she will need to be able to access the money quickly in the next couple of years, before she buys her own home, and said: 'I am half thinking of changing my car quite soon. I would probably want to invest about half of my savings in this and keep the rest on cash deposit.'

Camilla has heard about individual savings accounts (ISAs), but is unsure if they are appropriate for her. She said: 'I want to know if it is worth paying into an ISA, or whether I should just be putting my monthly savings into the bank.'

Camilla has no debts at all. She said: 'I haven't even got a credit card.'

WHAT THE EXPERTS SAY

Making an exception to prove the rule, the advisers to Cash Clinic said Camilla should get a credit card.

Recognizing this would not usually be regarded as prudent advice, Maxine Harvey, of independent financial advisers (IFAs) Torquil Clark, said: 'When it comes to arranging a mortgage in a few years' time, she would get a better credit rating if she had a credit card which was well managed.'

She recommended the Visa card from Egg, if Miss Hammond is comfortable using the Internet, or Goldfish, if she prefers post. The next thing for her to do is start saving a deposit for when she buys her own place.

Warren Perry, of IFAs Whitechurch Securities in Bristol, said: 'Based on an income of £8,500, she is looking at a maximum mortgage of around £27,000, and so she's going to need as much cash as possible as a deposit which will probably be needed in a very short space of time. She already has £3,000 saved and can commit another £250 a month. Over two years that equates to

£9,000, excluding interest. Either way, with a full mortgage, she is going to need every penny to be able to afford somewhere.'

The advisers felt she should keep her £3,000 savings intact and within easy reach, rather than spending it or investing in the stock-market.

Mr Perry recommended that Camilla open a mini cash ISA with her £3,000 savings. He said: 'If she has Internet access, Smile Bank is worth a try.' He also suggested she close one of her current accounts and open a higher-yielding savings account to put further cash savings into. If she has Internet access, an Egg account would be preferable, he said.

Clive Scott-Hopkins, of IFAs Towry Law in Bracknell, Berkshire, agreed that she should put her £3,000 into a mini cash ISA. He said she could then use half the £250 a month that she can save to add to her cash savings and half to invest. He said: 'Herein lies a dilemma, since, if she wishes to aim for outperformance, especially in the short term, she will have to take a risk.'

He also urged Camilla to consider investment trusts, rather than unit trusts, as they tend to have lower charges. Both are a form of pooled investment which allows investors to spread their money over a wide range of companies and/or sectors and share the cost of professional fund managers.

Ms Harvey preferred unit trusts and suggested that Camilla go for an equity ISA with a fund manager that offers a wide range of funds. She can invest up to £3,000 in a stocks-and-shares mini ISA each year as well as £3,000 in a mini cash ISA.

LESSONS TO BE LEARNED

- Without any existing credit, it is harder to get further credit or take out a mortgage. To build up a credit rating, young people – like Camilla – should take out a credit card and use it wisely. They can repay their balance in full each month so it will not cost them a penny.

- When saving up for a mortgage – or for any purpose – always shop around for the best rate. Miss Hammond has been earning a pitiful rate of interest on her hard-earned savings whereas, by switching to a cash ISA, she can earn ten times as much interest – and it will be tax-free.

Case Study 15

PROBLEM: SHOULD THEIR LOANS AND MORTGAGE BE PAID OFF?

Vital Statistics

Names: Robert and Maureen Nicol
Ages: Thirty-nine and thirty-eight
Location: Edinburgh and London
Occupations: Army Captain and Marks & Spencer sales adviser
Combined income: £45,000 p.a.
Savings: £4,200 in bank accounts, plus £5,000 to pay school fees
Pensions: Army defined-benefit scheme and Marks & Spencer
    company scheme
Investments: Three Standard Life unit-linked savings plans; two
    Standard Life with-profits endowment policies with total sum
    assured £90,000; Scottish Provident endowment with sum
    assured £42,000
Mortgage: £75,000 Halifax interest-only home loan
Borrowings: £7,500 loan
Insurance: PAX Army injury, accident and sickness insurance

After nearly two decades of following her husband around the world, Maureen Nicol decided to settle down to a job of her own in Edinburgh. She is now working as a sales adviser for Marks & Spencer, while husband Robert, an Army troop commander with the rank of Captain commissioned from the ranks, makes it home to his family twice a month from London, where he is posted.

This means that Robert must continue his career 'unaccompanied' by his wife and family and the Army will no longer pay 80 per cent of the children's school fees.

The couple's elder daughter, Louise, eighteen, has just started at Aberdeen University, but Caroline, sixteen, is still at boarding school in Edinburgh.

The couple earn £45,000 a year between them. Most of this – £36,000 – is earned by Robert. They share a joint current account with the Royal Bank of Scotland.

Robert said: 'We keep the current account in credit with a few hundred pounds surplus. There is quite a lot more in there at the moment. We have got £5,000 to pay the school fees, but will be paying it in instalments over the year. Perhaps there is a better way to save it.'

Maureen has £4,000 in a Halifax savings account and the couple have a cash-card Halifax account for their daughters to use; it has £200 in it at present. Robert said: 'We put the family allowance into that and Maureen uses it for clothes for Caroline.'

Robert is a member of the Armed Forces non-contributory pension scheme, which he believes will pay out around £9,700 a year when he retires. Maureen has been paying into the Marks & Spencer company scheme for a year and a half.

The couple do not have any stock-market investments, but have five investment policies with Standard Life. Two are unit-linked savings plans for their daughters – set to mature when they turn twenty-one – and the Nicols pay £25 a month into each 'to give them a lump sum for a deposit on a flat or a car – something to get them started.'

The couple have a joint unit-linked life insurance savings plan which they took out eight years ago. They pay £45 a month into this. The other two policies are twenty-five-year endowments in Standard Life's with-profits fund and are supporting the couple's mortgage. One was taken out in 1985 for £30,000 and costs £42 a month; the other was taken out in 1992 for £60,000 and costs £68 a month.

The couple also have a £42,000 Scottish Provident endowment, given to them as a wedding present by Robert's parents, which is set to mature this year.

They borrowed £75,000 from the Halifax to buy their home in Edinburgh in 1999 and pay £383 a month in interest on a three-year fixed rate of 5.6 per cent. The mortgage is a nineteen-year loan set to coincide with the maturity date of the second with-profits endowment.

Robert said: 'We would really like to pay down the mortgage early and keep the endowments as investments instead.'

There is also a £7,500 loan from Barclays Bank, costing £170 a month, with one year left to run.

WHAT THE EXPERTS SAY

The Nicols should pay off their Barclays personal loan as a matter of priority, the advisers to Cash Clinic said.

Clive Scott-Hopkins, of IFAs, Towry Law, said: 'At present, they have just short of £9,000 of net annual outgoings, but this would reduce to nearer £7,000 if they can clear the £7,500 loan.'

Mr Scott-Hopkins suggested they use part of the maturity value of the maturing Scottish Provident endowment to repay the loan.

David Wright, of IFAs Johnstone Douglas, agreed that the Scottish Provident endowment should be used for this purpose, but added that the Nicols should pay down the loan now and then replace their funds with proceeds from the endowment later in the year.

Mr Wright said: 'They might consider dipping into the Halifax savings account in order to pay off the Barclays loan.'

Philippa Gee, of IFAs, Gee & Co., pointed out that paying down the loan would free up money for additional investments each month. The couple should also decide whether they would like to pay part of the Scottish Provident endowment towards their mortgage as well.

Mr Scott-Hopkins said: 'The test is, can they earn more than 5.6

per cent net of tax (the rate of interest on their mortgage) on their savings instead?'

Mr Wright felt that it might not be beneficial to pay down the mortgage. He said: 'They would lose valuable flexibility – that is, have too many assets tied up in bricks and mortar. As I see it, they will have commitments of one type or another possibly for the next five years – for example, when their youngest daughter has finished boarding school and then goes to university.'

If the Nicols want their with-profits endowments with Standard Life to serve as investments rather than to support the mortgage, they could switch to a repayment loan instead, Mr Wright said. However, they should check if this affects their fixed rate and whether or not there will be penalties if they switch to a different deal.

Instead of paying down the mortgage, the advisers agreed that the Nicols should reinvest the money they receive from Scottish Provident.

They should first set aside enough of a cash fund to cover next year's school fees and university allowances for five years. Ms Gee said: 'A sum of around £10,000 could be invested in a top-paying building society account.'

The remaining cash from Scottish Provident – and the £170 a month freed up from the Barclays loan – could then be invested.

Mr Scott-Hopkins said: 'If the Nicols are prepared to take a five-year view, then they could go for a with-profits insurance bond with a financially strong insurer like CGU Life or Scottish Mutual, which is backed by Abbey National. They must hold it for five years to avoid a surrender penalty, and be prepared to invest for longer if investment markets have deteriorated over that period.'

Mr Wright preferred more direct stock-market investments for the couple. He said: 'The first port of call for reinvesting the £42,000 should be a Maxi ISA for each of them – i.e. a total of £14,000.'

LESSONS TO BE LEARNED

- There is no point in having savings earning a lower rate of interest than borrowings – borrowers will be paying out more interest than they earn. So, as the Nicols have been advised to do, use savings to repay any loans.

- Clearing debts frees up income – in this case £170 a month from repaying the £7,500 loan – which can be used to invest for the future.

- Think twice before repaying a mortgage. Those with other financial commitments – like the Nicols who need to fund school fees and further education for their daughters – may need their savings and investments so should not use them to clear their mortgage until they are sure they will not need the money.

Case Study 16

PROBLEM: REPAYING DEBTS INCURRED AS A STUDENT

Vital Statistics
Name: Stuart Tait
Age: Twenty-one
Location: Oxford
Occupation: Student
Income: £5,000 grant for next academic year
Savings: £2,500 in Post Office account
Pension: None
Investments: None
Mortgage: None
Borrowings: £900 overdraft; £6,000 student loans
Insurance: None

Determination and a degree of stamina are required to train as a lawyer. Law student Stuart Tait has already demonstrated these characteristics – swimming in a cross-Channel swimming race against Cambridge to raise funds for the Oxford University Swimming Club.

Stuart, who is from Manchester, said: 'It was scary at one point because the person swimming after me almost got run down by a very big boat.'

Although he has trained as a swimmer, he decided to go to university rather than try to make a living in the water as 'it is difficult to make money professionally as a swimmer.'

Stuart has just started the legal practice course at the Oxford Institute of Legal Practice. He will study there for one year before taking a six-month break to travel to Central and South America.

He is being sponsored by the City of London-based international law firm Clifford Chance, with whom he will start a two-year training contract, with the firm paying his £6,700 law school fees for the coming year and £5,000 to live on while he is a student.

Stuart said: 'They pay that in three tranches at the beginning of each term.' His parents have agreed to pay his rent while he is living in Oxford.

He can expect to command a fairly substantial salary when he starts work – trainee solicitors are beginning on salaries of £24,000. He said: 'Once I qualify as a solicitor after two years, the salary will go up to around £40,000, but it is by no means guaranteed that my contract will be renewed.'

Stuart has a Barclays student account, which is overdrawn by £900. There is a linked savings account, which has a balance of zero at present. He said: 'I will put my Clifford Chance grant into that account when it gets paid.'

He does have £2,500 saved in a Post Office account, which is earmarked to help with next year's expenses and pay for travelling.

On top of his £900 overdraft, Stuart has around £6,000 of student loans which he will have to begin repaying once he is working. He has no credit cards or personal loans.

He said: 'I will keep my overdraft as it is, because it is interest-free. I will be able to convert my student account into a graduate account once I finish my course next year. The overdraft will still be free for a while but I will pay it off immediately if I have to start paying interest on it, or they call it in.'

WHAT THE EXPERTS SAY

As Stuart can look forward to a relatively high salary when he starts his career, he need not worry too much about being able to repay his debts in the future, the advisers to Cash Clinic said. His main priority now, is to make sure he has enough to live on over the next twelve months.

Although it is better to avoid further debt, Richard Ogdon, business development director of the Careers Research Advisory Centre, suggested that Stuart should consider taking out a career development loan if he finds himself stuck for money.

Mr Ogdon said: 'A career development loan can be used to meet his living costs provided the course is full time and is vocational. He won't have to pay anything back until he has completed the course.'

The career development loan is administered by the major high-street banks – for more information call 0800 585 505.

Mr Ogdon said: 'Stuart could instead consider applying for an increase in his overdraft from its current limit of £900. He need not worry about making payments under his student loan until he starts his job. But given that he will be earning £24,000 when he does start, he will be required to start repaying the student loan at that time.'

The advisers agreed that Stuart should repay his overdraft as soon as the bank begins charging interest on it. Darius McDermott, of IFAs Chelsea Financial Services, said: 'You rarely earn as much interest on savings as you will pay out on loans and overdrafts, so he may want to repay his overdraft from his Post Office savings.'

The advisers agreed that Stuart should make his savings work harder, while keeping them accessible for the next year. Anna Bowes, of IFAs Chase de Vere, said: 'The Post Office account he has is paying a fairly low rate of interest. He could move £2,500 into a higher-paying account.'

All the advisers said Stuart should scan the Internet for high-interest savings accounts. Mr Ogdon said: 'Many of the Internet banks are paying higher rates even for the immediate-access accounts.'

Ms Bowes recommended Stuart should open a mini cash ISA. She said: 'Smile, the Internet bank, is currently offering a competitive rate with easy access to your money. That could make a difference of over £60 a year.'

She also suggested he should open a Nationwide Internet Account to manage his daily expenses. She said: 'This would be ideal for his £5,000 living expenses. It pays a very competitive rate of interest.'

LESSONS TO BE LEARNED

- Savers rarely earn more interest than borrowers pay, so it pays to use savings to repay debts unless – as is the case for Stuart – the debts are interest-free. Student accounts offer free overdrafts, so students should make the most of these while avoiding other forms of borrowing.

- Student loans, career development loans and student bank accounts are all there to help fund and spread the cost of education. Students should make the most of these accounts as they have special repayment terms to spread the burden of repaying debts and reduce the cost.

- Make the most of the Internet for banking and saving – rates are often far more competitive and access is easy, day or night.

- It is worth borrowing to invest for the future – whether in a career or a property. Without borrowing, successful careers, home-ownership, new cars and children's education may not be possible. Provided borrowers can repay what they owe – or, as in Stuart's case have the prospect of a good income in future – they should view borrowing as a means to an end, not a debt.

4 Property

Buying a property is probably the biggest financial commitment most of us will ever make. Investing in bricks and mortar is also seen, increasingly, as an alternative to pensions and other investments thanks to the advent of the buy-to-let mortgage. In addition, a property can be a vital source of income, particularly for the elderly who are often equity-rich but cash-poor and can use their home to pay for a better lifestyle using an equity release scheme.

With so much money tied up in property and so many billions borrowed against its value you would think that borrowers would take more care when choosing a mortgage. Yet, while they may spend months finding the right property, they often spend just a few hours choosing a mortgage.

It is not simply a case of saving a few pounds. In just two years it is possible to save more than £4,000 on a £100,000 loan by switching to a cheaper lender. Repay a twenty-five-year home loan over twenty years and the savings can be even greater.

BUYING A HOME

There are three main factors determining how much a home-buyer can borrow:

- Income
- Value of property
- Amount of deposit

How much you can borrow
Generally lenders will only advance a maximum of three times a buyer's annual salary, although some lenders do allow borrowers

up to three-and-a-half times their salary or even more. The income that is taken into account is basic salary before tax and other deductions.

Those taking out a mortgage together with another person can generally borrow three times one salary plus once the other. Alternatively, they can multiply their joint income by two-and-a-half or even two-and-three-quarters in some cases.

If part of a borrower's earnings is made up of commission or bonuses, this may be added to the main salary. However, this will only usually be the case if these payments are consistent, if not actually guaranteed.

Self-employed people like Peter Lawrence, in Cash Clinic Case Study 22 in this chapter, generally need to supply three years' accounts to prove their income, although two years' accounts plus a projection should suffice for many lenders.

Those who cannot provide proof can opt for what is known as a self-certification mortgage which requires the borrower to give details of their income but not proof. Borrowers also need a substantial deposit of 20 per cent or even 25 per cent of the property's value.

A poor credit history need not be a barrier to getting a mortgage. Several lenders will consider borrowers with what are known as minor debt cases: County Court judgments (preferably cleared) and small arrears cases. Those with more serious past debt problems can take out what are known as credit-impaired mortgages. These borrowers represent a much higher risk to lenders, and as such they must put down a substantial deposit in many cases, are charged a higher rate of interest than other borrowers, and are often locked into the loan with hefty redemption penalties.

The loan-to-value

Most lenders will advance no more than 95 per cent of the property's value, although once again there are exceptions, with 100 per cent-plus loans available in rare circumstances. This percentage is known as the loan-to-value.

However, those who can afford to put down a deposit of 20 per cent or even 25 per cent, will be able to take advantage of the cheaper deals offered by lenders which tend to be restricted to those with larger amounts of equity, who therefore represent less of a risk to the lender.

Saving for a deposit
The time-scale – usually one to three years – means that stock-market investments are not as suitable as savings accounts because of the risks.

However, savings rates are very low at the moment, leaving little room for capital growth. As such it is essential to shop around for the best rates and to save as much as possible free of tax by investing up to the maximum of £3,000 in a cash individual savings account (ISA). See Chapter 2: Savings, for tips and advice.

Budgeting for the costs
While saving a 5 per cent deposit may be difficult for many first-time buyers, it is not the only cost they need to consider. Other up-front costs can vary from £2,000 to £20,000 and include:

- Mortgage valuation (valuation for mortgage purposes)

- Survey (optional, but advisable – can be combined with the valuation)

- Mortgage arrangement fee

- Conveyancing (usually done by a solicitor)

- Local authority search fees and Land Registry fees

- Mortgage indemnity insurance (if borrowing more than 90 per cent of the value of the property. This can cost £1,000 or more, and even though the borrower pays the premium it protects the lender – not the buyer – should the mortgage default)

- Stamp duty – although there is no stamp duty on homes worth less than £60,000, for the tax year ending April 2003 it started at 1 per cent of homes selling for £60,000 or more, rises to 3 per cent for those worth £250,000 to £500,000, and increases to 4 per cent for homes worth £500,000 or more. Properties up to £150,000 in certain disadvantaged areas now escape stamp duty.

CHOOSING A MORTGAGE

With a bewildering choice of more than 4,000 mortgages on offer at any one time, it is no wonder that many borrowers simply take up the first mortgage they are offered or do not bother to shop around and approach their bank or building society. However, over the term of a twenty-five-year mortgage they could be losing £10,000 or more by selecting the wrong type of home loan.

Repayment mortgages

These do what they say – repay the mortgage. Each month borrowers pay interest on the amount outstanding and repay an element of their outstanding debt. The advantage of these loans is that borrowers do not have to worry about whether or not their mortgage will be repaid at the end of the term.

Interest-only mortgages

As the name implies, these only require the borrower to pay the interest on the debt each month. The outstanding loan is not repaid until the end of the mortgage term or when the mortgage is paid off. As a result, borrowers must usually pay into an investment scheme – such as an endowment policy or ISA – to build up sufficient capital to repay the mortgage at the end of the term. If the investment grows quickly, it may provide enough capital to repay the loan much earlier than with a repayment mortgage. However, there are no guarantees, as millions of home buyers with endowment mortgages have found to their cost. Although they are cheaper than repayment mortgages because there is no repayment element, once the cost of an investment is added endowment mortgages are usually more expensive. Also, borrow £100,000 today and you will still owe £100,000 in twenty-five years' time.

Endowments versus repayments

Thousands of home buyers are lumbered with endowment policies that will not repay their mortgages and as such have been forced to increase their monthly investments to meet the shortfall. At the same time, larger lenders have stopped selling these types of loan. The consensus today is that endowments are investments and investments carry risks and as such should not be used to repay a mortgage.

Although first-time buyers may not be sold endowments, that still leaves millions of home buyers with existing policies. As Gail Long-hurst, in Cash Clinic Case Study 20 in this chapter, is advised, borrowers may be better off remortgaging to a better deal, opting for a repayment loan and then keeping the endowments as investments.

Cashing in or surrendering an endowment is rarely a good idea as investors often suffer large penalties and maximum returns are usually only earned by those who keep their policy to maturity.

CAT standards

CAT stands for fair Charges, easy Access and decent Terms. The Government recently introduced this new standard to help borrowers identify mortgages that offer a fair deal.

However, the standard is voluntary and so not all mortgages meet it. To meet the standards lenders must:

- Make no separate charge for mortgage indemnity insurance (a high-lending fee)

- Disclose all charges up front

- Calculate interest daily

- Have an interest rate no higher than 2 per cent above the Bank of England base rate

- Impose no redemption charges for variable rate loans

- Charge no more than £150 in booking fees for fixed or capped-rate mortgages and have no extended redemption penalties on these loans (see below)

Hidden costs

Many mortgages – particularly those with special introductory rates – have additional charges, which can include:

• Arrangement fees – these can be as high as £400

• High-lending fee or mortgage indemnity guarantee – this is usually charged on loans above 90 per cent of the value of the property and can cost up to £1,000. It is an insurance policy to protect the lender if the buyer defaults on repayments

• Valuation fees

• Redemption penalties – see below

Some of these costs may be offset by the lender. For example, legal fees up to a certain limit (say, £200), cash back (for example, up to £300), free accident, sickness and unemployment insurance for six months or free valuations may be offered as incentives by lenders.

Redemption penalties

Borrowers who want the cheapest deals often pay a price – a redemption penalty. These are lock-in penalties and come in two types: extended and non-extended.

With an extended penalty, redemption penalties will be charged after a cheap rate ends. So borrowers may pay a low rate for one or two years but find they are locked in for three years. Non-extended penalties only last as long as the cheap rate.

Sometimes it is worth paying the penalty because the cost will be lower than the savings made from switching to a cheaper rate.

CHOOSING THE BEST RATE

Standard variable rate

This is what most existing borrowers pay and, as its name implies, the rate varies in line with rises and falls in the Bank of England base rate. Once special introductory rates end, this is what borrowers then pay. Borrowers can usually get a much better deal by switching to one of the special rates listed below.

Discount rate mortgages

These give a set percentage – say 1 per cent or 2 per cent or more – off the standard variable rate for a certain period of time, usually one to three years. However, if interest rates rise, so do the monthly repayments.

Fixed rate mortgages

These have a fixed rate of interest, usually for a limited period – the first one to five years of the loan. While they make budgeting easy, if interest rates fall, the fixed rate may be higher than standard mortgage rates.

Capped-rate mortgages

These come with the guarantee that whatever happens to interest rates during the capped-rate period, the rate charged will never rise above the cap rate. Borrowers benefit from falls in mortgage rates, but will see repayments rise if rates rise (up to the level of the cap).

Tracker mortgages

These have a rate of interest that is guaranteed to be no more than a set percentage above the Bank of England base rate. Thus borrowers will not see the margin between the base rate and their mortgage rate widen and the mortgage should remain competitive. However, if interest rates rise, so will the repayments.

FLEXIBLE AND ALL-IN-ONE MORTGAGES

In addition to a competitive rate, borrowers should also look at the flexibility of any mortgage and how interest is charged.

Flexible mortgages were until recently offered by only a few lenders. Today there are more than ninety flexible mortgages on offer with variable, discounted, capped and even fixed rates.

Most flexible mortgages have the following features:

- The ability to overpay – paying back more than the minimum enables borrowers to repay their mortgages far more quickly and cut the total interest charged as well as the term of the loan

- The ability to underpay or take payment holidays – provided you do not exceed an agreed borrowing limit

- A drawdown facility – the ability to withdraw lump sums provided the total amount owed does not exceed the initial agreed limit

- Daily interest calculations – every pound paid is used to reduce the amount owed and therefore the interest charged. With traditional repayment mortgages where the interest is based on the balance outstanding at the start of the calendar year, no account is taken of any repayments made during the year and so borrowers effectively pay interest on money they no longer owe

Current account, all-in-one or off-set mortgages go one step further. They maximize every penny home buyers have by using money held in a current account and savings accounts to reduce the amount owed on the mortgage (and in some cases on other debts such as loans and credit cards) and therefore cut the total amount of interest that is paid.

As savings reduce the amount owed, borrowers save rather than earn interest, which means they escape tax. And as they 'earn' interest at the mortgage rate, which tends to be far higher than savings rates, the rate is very competitive. A higher-rate taxpayer would have to earn 10 per cent on his or her savings before tax to receive the same benefit as savings in a current account, off-set or all-in-one account with a mortgage rate of 6 per cent.

At the same time borrowers pay one low rate – the mortgage rate – on all their borrowing rather than having to have an overdraft or loan which tends to cost far more.

CUTTING THE COSTS

There are three ways to cut costs:

- Switch to a cheaper interest rate
- Pay off the mortgage more quickly
- Combine all savings and borrowings in an all-in-one or off-set mortgage

Home buyers do not have to move home to move their mortgage. Anyone can remortgage at any time and usually make substantial savings. Before remortgaging borrowers should do their maths, taking into account savings over several years, the costs of switching (legal and valuation fees as well as any arrangement fees) and any redemption penalties.

The longer money is borrowed for, the more interest is charged. So the sooner a mortgage is repaid, the less interest is charged. It can therefore pay to use savings to pay off some of your mortgage – after all, the mortgage rate is usually much higher than the interest rate paid on savings.

However, some lenders limit the amount that can be repaid, requiring a minimum lump sum of £500 (rather than increases in how much you repay each month), and some do not credit these overpayments until the end of the year. Even so, lenders are being more flexible, allowing overpayments at any time to enable borrowers to reduce the term of their mortgage.

Most borrowers still take out a loan over twenty-five years. However, cutting the term of a £60,000 mortgage with an interest rate of 5.75 per cent from twenty-five years to twenty years will save £12,000 in interest and only cost an extra £43.79 per month. Cutting the term from twenty-five to fifteen years will save around £24,000 and cost only £120 extra per month.

BUYING WITH SOMEONE ELSE

Before taking on a joint commitment it is important to realize that each borrower is liable for the whole of the debt if the other buyer fails to pay their share of the monthly repayments.

Those buying with a joint tenancy will own half of the property each, and if one dies the other will inherit their share. This may be ideal for married couples, but not necessarily for everyone, particularly those with children from another relationship.

An alternative is to draw up a tenancy in common with a solicitor. This enables the ownership to be split in different proportions and also for each buyer to leave their share of the property to whomever they wish in their will.

RUNNING INTO PROBLEMS

Every year thousands of borrowers run into problems repaying their mortgages. Redundancy, divorce and sickness can mean that borrowers fall into arrears.

This is more of a risk today now that the state will no longer meet the mortgage interest for eight in ten home buyers for the first nine months after they have become unemployed.

Borrowers are advised to contact their lender before they run into trouble to agree a plan – either suspended or reduced payments for so many months. Borrowers should check that there are no additional penalties or higher rates of interest charged because they are in arrears.

Mortgage payment protection insurance

This should not be confused with mortgage indemnity insurance (this protects the lender). It pays the monthly mortgage bills if the borrower is unable to earn a living because of accident, sickness or redundancy for twelve or twenty-four months of payments and costs between £4.50 and £6 a month to cover every £100 of monthly mortgage payment. Home buyers who are self-employed, working part-time, about to change jobs or have previous medical problems should ask for a copy of the small print as these policies only pay out in particular circumstances and there are plenty of exclusions. As a result, this insurance may only be suitable for around half of all home buyers.

Negative equity

Less of an issue today thanks to rises in house prices in recent years, negative equity occurs when a buyer's outstanding mortgage debt is greater than the value of the property. So, if the property was sold, it would not repay the mortgage. As a result, lenders are only likely to agree to a sale of what is the security for the mortgage if there is an agreement on how this outstanding debt can be repaid.

Provided the borrower has sufficient income to support a larger mortgage, some lenders will advance more than the property value on a new home – but charge a far higher rate for this proportion of the loan, as Andrew and Sue Wagstaff, in Cash Clinic Case Study 19 in this chapter, found to their cost. A few lenders offer negative equity schemes to those who have their mortgage with another lender.

BUY-TO-LET

The advent of the buy-to-let mortgage in 1996 has been the real impetus behind the growth in private landlords, and now that it is possible to borrow at the same low rates as other home buyers, it is more economically viable.

How much can I borrow?

Buy-to-let investors need at least a 20 per cent deposit and in some cases 25 per cent or even 30 per cent. However, this is not the only lending criteria. Most buy-to-let lenders only take into account rental income, lending up to 75 per cent of the anticipated rent. So the monthly repayments should be easily covered by the rent.

Will it be profitable?

The mortgage is not the only cost to take into account. Using an agent to handle rent collection, repairs and advertising for and screening of tenants can cost between 10 per cent and 16 per cent of the rental income. Then there is insurance, service charges, ground rents and maintenance to pay for, and any periods when the property is not let. As a result, buy-to-let investors are advised to aim for a rent at least 130 per cent to 150 per cent of the monthly mortgage repayments, according to the Association of Residential Letting Agents.

What about tax?

Investors will only pay tax on any profit made – that is, the rent minus allowable expenses (which are tax deductible) such as interest on a buy-to-let mortgage, repairs, letting agents and accountancy fees, service charges, ground rent and buildings insurance. Although buy-to-let investors cannot claim the cost of furniture against tax, they can claim roughly 10 per cent of the rent as an allowance for depreciation of furnishing per year. If they rent the furniture they can deduct the entire cost.

When they come to sell they may also have to pay capital gains tax on the profit (what the property is sold for less the cost of buying and selling). The rate of tax depends on how long the property has been owned. Capital gains tax reduces the longer the asset is held, with an effective rate of 12 per cent after ten years.

Let-to-buy

This is similar to buy-to-let only the other way round – home owners let their existing home and then buy another. Let-to-buyers need substantial capital – 20 per cent of the price of the existing property for a mortgage and around 5 per cent as a deposit on the new home.

HOME INCOME PLANS

This is a dilemma faced by many older home owners. They are asset-rich but cash-poor with much of their money tied up in their property. So what is the solution? One option is to consider a home income plan or equity release scheme.

How much can I borrow?

Elderly home owners (who must generally be at least sixty-five years of age) can borrow around 30 per cent of their home's value, providing it is worth more than a certain amount. The loan is repayable from the proceeds when the home is sold or the owner dies or goes into long-term care.

How do the schemes work?

There are two ways the schemes work. Home owners can mortgage part of their property or they can sell all or part of their home to a 'reversion' company while retaining the right to live in it for the rest of their lives. Either way, they get a lump sum, which can be invested, or they get a monthly payment. Age Concern publishes a guide called *Raising Income or Capital from Your Home* (call 0800 009 966), which looks at the advantages and pitfalls and is easy to follow and comprehensive.

What should I watch out for?

Age Concern advises the elderly to read the small print carefully and always to ask about fees before making any commitment as they vary considerably between companies. Also ask: will the home income company let you sell your house if you decide you want to move and how will the income from the scheme affect any means-tested social security benefit? You might lose it all together.

The alternative is to sell the property – as Jean Tansley-Harris, in Cash Clinic Case Study 23 in this chapter, is considering – and to trade down to a cheaper home.

Case Study 17

PROBLEM: NO HOME OF THEIR OWN AT AGE FORTY

Vital Statistics

Name: Graham Mulvein
Age: Forty
Location: West London
Occupation: Conference organizer
Income: Business turnover £200,000 – he earns enough to be
    a higher rate taxpayer
Savings: A few thousand pounds
Pension: Two personal pension plans with Allied Dunbar
Investments: None
Mortgage: None
Borrowings: None – pays off credit card in full each month
Insurance: £100,000 life cover from London & Scottish

Graham Mulvein and his wife Lynn work and live in west London, where they rent a house for £1,000 a month.

'We are very happy where we are but we couldn't afford to buy a house when we moved here five years ago. We are unsure whether we should move and buy a house or consider buying a property to let out to someone else.'

The couple have owned and sold two places since they married in 1986. Graham said: 'We went back to renting at a time when we didn't have much money but we have managed to put ourselves back on a good economic footing now. We originally moved into our house with a view to looking for something else to buy but we loved it here and stayed.'

After twenty years of working in the entertainment industry as a stage manager for musicals and operas, Graham moved into corporate communications, organizing conferences, product launches and other events for international clients. He used the experience to set up his own business, Face to Face Communications, in 1991, taking a break in 1992 to produce the play *Scrooge*, which eventually went to the West End – his dream come true. His business is not set up as a limited company and he works from home.

The business turns over more than £200,000 a year on average and Graham is able to pay himself enough to make him a higher-rate taxpayer.

Graham's personal bank account is with Abbey National and he shares two savings accounts with his wife, Lynn. These each have a few thousand pounds in them and are with Abbey National and Bristol & West.

The Mulveins have no children and Lynn works for an RSPCA hospital in Putney, south-west London.

On the investments front, Graham has two personal pension plans with Allied Dunbar in place. He took out the first in 1983 and currently contributes £300 a month. The contributions are index-linked and there is life assurance attached, which is due to mature when he reaches sixty-five.

When the Mulveins married, Graham took out a second pension plan that is also index-linked and he currently contributes £200 a month to this. Again, there is life assurance attached, and the policy is due to mature when he turns sixty. The two insurance policies are for a total of £100,000 and cost £35 a month.

WHAT THE EXPERTS SAY

Buying a property should be the Mulveins' priority, the advisers to Cash Clinic said.

Adrian Shandley, of independent financial advisers (IFAs) Balmoral Associates, said: 'They do not currently own a property and I find this alarming for somebody who is aged forty and in London where property prices are rapidly outstripping wage rises. The long-term future must be considered, particularly with regard to whether or not Graham could continue to pay £1,000 per month rent on a pension income.'

Mr Shandley recommended that the Mulveins buy a property as soon as possible, either as a place to live in or from which to operate Graham's business. If he decided to buy offices rather than a home, he could sell them when he retired and use the capital to buy a home.

Tim Cockerill, of IFAs Chartwell Investment Management, said: 'At present they are paying £1,000 a month in rental and this level of payment would provide for quite a substantial mortgage.'

On the subject of buying a property to let, Mr Cockerill said: 'With the rise in house prices, the net yield on this type of arrangement has fallen substantially. The Mulveins should also take into account that there are agency costs, there may be periods of time when there are no tenants, and this could dramatically affect the annual return. Another factor to consider is that a buy-to-rent arrangement tends to allow a loan of up to 75 per cent of the value of the property, which means a 25 per cent deposit.'

Mr Shandley recommended that Graham draw money from the company to raise the deposit for a property, otherwise he will have to gather savings to pay for it.

Mr Cockerill said: 'The Mulveins have joint savings accounts but, from a tax point of view, amalgamating these two accounts into Lynn's name only would make sense.'

He added: 'Before long-term savings can be considered, the Mulveins must decide about a property purchase because there is no point in saving in stock-market-based investments if you are going to want to call on the money in two or three years' time. Any investment in the stock-market should be considered on a minimum of a five-year view.'

On the pensions side, Mr Cockerill said that Graham should pay close attention to his two personal pensions as they are quite old and may not have the most favourable terms.

Mr Shandley recommended that Graham consider converting his personal pensions into a self-invested personal pension (SIPP). He said: 'He could use his pension fund to purchase a premises from which the business could trade. This could be very tax efficient as at retirement it would be sold free of tax.'

LESSONS TO BE LEARNED

- They say rent money is dead money. At least with a mortgage, borrowers own something at the end of the term. In addition, rental incomes rise each year, whereas those with repayment mortgages see the amount they owe fall each year. And, as Graham has been warned, how will he afford the rent once he retires?

- Investing in the stock-market is not always the ideal place to save for a deposit on a property. Stock-market investments are long-term and most home buyers plan to buy within just two or three years so should opt for a safer savings account.

- If renters like the Mulveins cannot afford to buy where they want, they can consider buy-to-let so that they can still get a stake in the property market. However, as they have been advised, there is no guarantee they will make a profit and they will have to put down a 25 per cent deposit.

- Purchasing business premises also makes economic sense. Instead of paying rent and owning nothing, the business has a valuable asset. Buy it through a pension fund and then it can be sold on retirement free of tax, with the proceeds used to fund a pension.

Case Study 18

PROBLEM: HOW TO GET ONTO THE PROPERTY LADDER WHEN UNABLE TO AFFORD TO BUY IN LONDON

Vital Statistics

Name: Kitty Johnson
Age: Twenty-seven
Location: London
Occupation: Freelance wine writer
Income: £20,000 a year
Savings: £6,000 in bank and building society accounts
Pension: None
Investments: PowerGen and National Power shares
Mortgage: None
Borrowings: None
Insurance: None

Kitty Johnson does not think she can afford to buy a home in London because property prices are so high, but is prepared to move to the country. Fortunately, she has no debts and is prepared to save between £300 and £400 a month towards a deposit.

'I want to buy my own place,' Kitty said. 'I think I am in the minority, not having bought my own flat already, but I will do that in the next few years.'

After trying her hand at the stage, Kitty, who lives in Clapham, south London, decided to become a freelance wine writer because she was not making enough money.

'I was working in a bar and wine shop, and I have an interest in wine,' she says. After working as a researcher for Robert Joseph, wine writer for the *Sunday Telegraph*, for two years, she was approached by Handbag.com, a joint venture with the *Daily Telegraph*, to write about wine for the website. She now writes for three websites on a regular basis and has also appeared on television.

Although her income can fluctuate because she is a freelance, she estimates that she is currently earning around £20,000 a year.

She has a Coutts current account, in which she keeps several thousand pounds, and has £2,000 savings in a Scarborough Building Society account. She added: 'I have to keep the Coutts account in credit or there are hefty charges.'

On the investments side, Kitty has 140 PowerGen shares and 224 National Power shares but no pooled investments. She said: 'My dad bought me those shares a few years ago and I occasionally get a £30 cheque from one or the other of them. I do not have any individual savings accounts (ISAs), but I would like to make some investments. I realize that I have got to look more seriously to the future.'

WHAT THE EXPERTS SAY

Kitty's priority is to save for a home of her own, so she should focus on this for the time being, the advisers to Cash Clinic said. She is in a good position, having already made a start with cash savings and avoiding debt.

Mark Bolland, of independent financial advisers (IFAs) Chamberlain de Broe, said: 'In principle, if she can put down 10 per cent of the purchase price as a deposit, she may well be able to take advantage of better offers on mortgages.'

Kevin Minter, of IFAs David Aaron Partnership, said: 'The timescale for buying a house is unlikely to be longer than three years and I would have concerns with regard to investing in equities over such a short period.'

Brian Dennehy, of IFAs Dennehy, Weller & Co., in Chislehurst, Kent, agreed that Kitty should move money out of her current account, which is likely to be earning no interest. However, as Coutts charges a £45 per quarter fee if balances drop below £3,000, she may need to reconsider her account.

To save towards a property, the advisers also recommended that Kitty sell her shares. Mr Bolland said: 'I would suggest that these be sold and added to the cash on deposit for safety. Clearly, at the moment, every penny will help to build up the required amount of cash to buy a property.'

Mr Dennehy said: 'She should sell the shares now. Otherwise, there is every risk that if she only sells once she has found her property, the prices will be lower than now.'

The advisers said that as Kitty has no dependants, she will not need to buy life insurance. However, as a self-employed person she could consider critical illness cover, to provide a regular income if she is unable to provide for herself. Mr Minter said this should be set up to pay out after a deferment period of just one month. 'This does make the policy more expensive but is necessary in her situation. Swiss Life can provide this cover at a premium of £48.71 a month.'

LESSONS TO BE LEARNED

- Borrowers should aim to save up a deposit of at least 10 per cent of the purchase price – as Kitty has been advised – as they then have a wider choice of cheaper mortgages.

- The self-employed are vulnerable. If they should fall ill and be unable to earn a living, they do not have an employer to rely on who can pay them generous sick pay. As such they need to consider either permanent health insurance or – as Kitty has been advised – critical illness cover.

- Play safe. Save for a deposit in a savings account. Shares are risky and could fall in value.

Case Study 19

PROBLEM: PAYING OFF NEGATIVE EQUITY FROM A PREVIOUSLY OWNED PROPERTY

Vital Statistics

Names: Andrew and Sue Wagstaff
Ages: Thirty-two and thirty-three
Location: Yeovil, Somerset
Occupations: Naval Petty Officer and hospital administrator
Combined income: £27,500 p.a. rising to £37,500
Savings: £1,700 in savings accounts
Pension: Forces final-salary pension, NHS final-salary pension
Investments: £1,700 in PEP; £900 in mini equity ISA
Mortgage: £83,000 Nationwide mortgage divided between
    endowments and repayment loan on house in negative equity
Borrowings: None
Insurance: None

Andrew Wagstaff and his wife Sue, have been haunted by the spectre of negative equity for the past five years. As a result, they have a particularly complicated mortgage arrangement with the Nationwide, which is divided into three tranches.

Andrew said: 'We had £18,000 of negative equity on our house in Plymouth when we moved, so we had to borrow more than the value of our new house. We have a mortgage of £83,000 on a house we bought for £65,000. I believe it is now worth around £72,000.'

The first tranche of the mortgage is covered by two endowment policies totalling £48,000: a £40,000 endowment from Standard Life and an £8,000 endowment from Lloyds TSB. Then there is a £17,500 slot covering capital in the new house and a £16,250 slot to cover negative equity – the couple chose to cover part of it themselves.

There is a higher rate of interest for the negative equity slot. This makes a total of £584 a month to cover the twenty-five-year loan due to run out in 2024.

Unsurprisingly, Andrew is keen to try to pay down the loan earlier. He said: 'My priority is to pay off the negative equity slice of the mortgage and then maybe pay down the mortgage early. Should I take out an individual savings account (ISA) in order to be able to pay off the mortgage in fifteen years rather than twenty-five?'

Andrew, who has served in the Navy for thirteen years, earning £22,500 a year, is about to be promoted from his position as Petty Officer to one of Supply Officer at Britannia Royal Naval College in Dartmouth, Devon which will give him a £10,000 pay rise. He is serving on HMS *Chatham*, moored in Plymouth Harbour, but is able to spend weekends with his wife and twin sons Matthew and Christopher, aged five, whom the Wagstaffs would like to educate privately when they reach secondary school.

Sue works part-time as a hospital administrator in the physio-therapy department of Yeovil Hospital, earning £5,000 a year.

Andrew says: 'I also want to arrange some proper life insurance now that we will be able to afford it. The Navy would pay out to my wife if I died, but I think it is pretty inadequate. It pays out more if I die in service as well.'

In their favour, the couple have no other debts besides the mortgage. However, they have little in savings – £400 in a Bradford & Bingley account in Sue's name, a further £1,300 in a second Bradford & Bingley account, and two Halifax savings accounts into one of which they pay £150 a month. The couple save £25 a month for each of their sons in two Halifax children's accounts. Andrew said: 'We buy them 100 Premium Bonds every five months and they have 300 each now.'

On the investments side, Andrew has £1,700 saved in a Prudential Prudence Gold personal equity plan (PEP). He said: 'I'm just leaving that to grow now. I used to save £80 a month but switched the payments into a Prudence Gold mini equity ISA when ISAs were launched.'

WHAT THE EXPERTS SAY

An extra £10,000 pay a year results in around £580 a month in extra income after tax and National Insurance, the advisers to Cash Clinic pointed out.

The first thing to address with the extra money is paying off the negative equity part of the Wagstaffs' mortgage.

Tony James, of independent financial advisers (IFAs) Ashton House, based in Dunstable, Bedfordshire, said: 'The Wagstaffs are paying over the odds in interest, so there is no reason to delay. I would suggest making overpayments on this part of the mortgage as quickly as possible.'

Philippa Gee, of IFAs Gee & Co., said: 'They are suffering from a high interest rate of 9.25 per cent on the negative equity loan, which is even worse than many unsecured personal loans, so paying that off is better than investing elsewhere.'

Ms Gee said that to reduce the repayment period from twenty-five to fifteen years would carry an additional monthly cost of around £30.

She added: 'However, if the Wagstaffs are prepared to take a more aggressive approach and repay this loan as quickly as possible, their costs would be increased by £210 a month to repay within five years or £75 to repay within ten years. The very short-term option would have the advantage of their outgoings reducing substantially after five years, to help towards either education or pension funding at that time.'

As far as the main mortgage is concerned, Ms Gee suggested the couple consider negotiating with their existing lender to move to a more competitive rate – this would probably be less expensive than a full remortgage.

Mr James pointed out that only part of the mortgage is covered by two endowment policies. He said: 'Since life cover at their ages is going to be quite cheap, I would advise them to cover the whole mortgage amount for peace of mind. Joint life cover of initially £33,750, decreasing to zero over twenty-four years – to cover the repayment parts of the mortgage – would cost just £5.93 with Norwich Union.'

The next thing to focus on is building up the couple's savings. Brian McLean, of IFAs Chartwell Investment Management, said: 'An obvious method of saving for the Wagstaffs is to take advantage of their allowance for ISAs, which are very flexible and tax efficient. Contributions can be made by lump sum but they may wish to start making higher regular contributions from the increase in income.'

Mr McLean pointed out that ISAs are ideal for saving for the medium to long term and would be good for saving for school fees or to build funds to reduce the mortgage in about fifteen years' time. He added: 'As Andrew is already contributing to the Prudential ISA, Sue should consider an equity-based maxi ISA with some exposure to an overseas market.'

Mr James also suggested that the Wagstaffs consider using up their 'friendly society allowance' for their children rather than buying Premium Bonds. He said: 'Any individual, including children, can pay up to £25 a month into a friendly society bond, and investment growth is not taxed.'

Ms Gee pointed out that the Wagstaffs should also be increasing their cash savings. As Andrew only has a mini equity ISA, he is also entitled to take out a mini cash ISA this tax year and can invest up to £3,000.

LESSONS TO BE LEARNED

- Cutting the term of a mortgage can cost very little in additional monthly repayments but can save thousands of pounds in the long run. The Wagstaffs will only need to pay an additional £30 a month to reduce their mortgage from a twenty-five year loan to a fifteen-year one and an extra £210 a month to repay it in just five years.

- Negative equity may not be a problem today, but many borrowers, including the Wagstaffs, are still repaying the losses they suffered in the last property price slump. Negative equity loans enable borrowers to sell a property for less than the mortgage debt and transfer the additional outstanding debt to a new property. The catch is the high rate of interest. Anyone with a negative equity loan should make it a priority to repay this as quickly as possible.

Case Study 20

PROBLEM: MORTGAGE PROBLEMS AFTER BUYING OUT AN EX-PARTNER

Vital Statistics
Name: Gail Longhurst
Age: Thirty-three
Location: Guildford, Surrey
Occupation: Beautician
Income: £25,000–£30,000 p.a.
Savings: £13,600 in bank and building society accounts
Pension: Royal Life personal pension; Friends Provident personal
  pension
Investments: Tunbridge Wells savings plan; £420 a month into
  Henderson ISA; £6,000 in Fidelity PEP; £6,000 in Invesco PEP;
  £75,000 twenty-five-year Friends Provident endowment; £64,000
  twenty-five-year Royal Life endowment
Mortgage: £75,000 West Bromwich Building Society interest-only
  home loan
Borrowings: None
Insurance: None

Beautician Gail Longhurst was able to fall back on her family when she needed assistance to buy out the other half of her home when she separated from her partner.

Gail, a thirty-three-year-old divorcee, who has lived in Guildford, Surrey for fourteen years, bought her house a year ago with her last partner. Her desire now is to save enough over the next few years to pay back her family for helping to buy the other half of her home.

The mortgage she now shares with her family is with West Bromwich Building Society and each half is for £75,000. To complicate the situation further, the two loans are not straightforward repayment mortgages, but are each supported by an endowment policy from Friends Provident.

'I also have another endowment policy with Royal Life for a sum assured of £64,000 which is due to mature in 2020,' she says. 'I kept that on from a previous mortgage as an investment, it costs £71 a month.'

She earns between £25,000 and £30,000 a year, depending on commission, as a business manager for a cosmetics company in Harrods.

'I definitely need to be in a position in five years' time where I can take on the rest of my mortgage,' she said. 'I think I may need to rearrange the savings and investments I already have in order to achieve this.'

Gail has £1,000 saved in an account with Egg, the Internet banking arm of the Prudential. She also has £1,000 in an account with Bradford & Bingley and is also three years into a Bradford & Bingley tax-exempt special savings account (TESSA) and has invested the maximum – a total of £6,600 to date. She can invest a further £2,400 over the next two years before the TESSA matures. There is £5,000 saved in a Flemings account as an emergency fund.

She also saves £37 a month in a Tunbridge Wells ten-year savings plan which she started four years ago and saves £420 a month – by far her largest savings – in an ISA with Henderson Investors, investing in the fund manager's Global Technology unit trust.

In 1996, Gail invested £6,000 in a Fidelity personal equity plan (PEP), dividing the money equally between the manager's European and Special Situations unit trusts. She has also invested in the Invesco European fund – £6,000 through a PEP in the first year and £7,000 through an ISA.

Gail has been contributing £40 net a month to a Royal Life pension she has had since she was twenty-one and £130 net a month into a Friends Provident pension.

WHAT THE EXPERTS SAY

Kim North, of independent financial advisers (IFAs) Calkin Pattinson, said: 'Ideally, Gail would like to have £75,000 in unfettered cash to repay her family's share of the mortgage. If this is not achievable, she should be able to remortgage in five years' time to cover any shortfall.'

Tracey Case, of IFAs Dover Financial Services in Dover, said that Gail ought to be able to pay down most of the other half of the mortgage without too much difficulty in five years' time: 'Assuming 7 per cent growth on the existing PEPs and ISAs – and continuing her contributions – they could be valued at over £50,000 in five years' time. In addition, Gail will have funds on deposit and her TESSA, which should be transferred to a TESSA-only ISA at maturity.

'Therefore, in five years' time, she could take on around £30,000 of the mortgage and use £45,000 of her investments to repay her family. This will still leave her with capital for an emergency fund.'

Ms Case recommended, therefore, that Gail consider remortgaging with another lender to £105,000 in five years' time, as she felt this should be affordable if she is still earning £30,000 a year.

Ms Case said Gail should consider switching to a repayment loan in five years' time and Vivienne Starkey, of the IFAs Equal Partners, said: 'Personally, I am not a fan of endowment mortgages because of their inflexibility and high-charging structure. However, Gail did the right thing in continuing the Royal Life policy she already had.'

The next thing Gail needs to consider is how to rearrange her investments to make sure she makes the maximum over the next five years.

Ms Case said: 'I would suggest that Gail thinks about contributing to a less volatile fund for next year's ISA allowance. Technology funds, which she has, are pretty risky, and for shorter-term investments, could produce losses rather than gains.'

Mrs Starkey said: 'The addition of a UK growth, smaller companies and perhaps a UK equity income fund would help to give a more balanced portfolio of investments.'

LESSONS TO BE LEARNED

- Divorce or the ending of a relationship is one of the major reasons for falling behind on mortgage repayments or getting into debt. Gail was lucky that her family could help her out – in many cases borrowers have no option but to sell the property and split the proceeds.

- Before buying a property with a cohabitee it is vital to draw up an agreement – either a tenancy in common or a joint tenancy. That way both parties know what will happen in the event of a split or on death.

Case Study 21

PROBLEM: BUYING A HOME LATE IN LIFE

Vital Statistics
Names: John and Jill Fearn
Ages: Sixty-seven and sixty-six
Location: Hereford
Occupations: Retired priest and medical receptionist
Income: £27,000 p.a.
Savings: £17,800 in bank and building society accounts
Pensions: Both are drawing their pensions
Investments: Two endowments totalling £89,500; range of unit

trusts, some held in personal equity plans (PEPs); shares in BT
    and CGNU
Mortgage: None
Borrowings: None
Insurance: None

The Rev. John Fearn and his wife Jill are in the unusual position of
being in need of a mortgage later rather than earlier in life.

John was a priest for thirty-eight years – he was the curate at
Bladon, Oxfordshire, in 1965 when Winston Churchill was buried
there. He said the Church of England always provided accommodation for him and his wife when he was working.

The couple, who have lived in Berkshire, Hertfordshire and
Hereford, have about £45,000 from selling their current home to put
down on the house they wish to buy.

However, they will still need to borrow around £85,000, a move
John describes as 'moving financially out of the Church of England
world and into the real world'.

He said: 'My wife is retired from her job as a nursery school
teacher but she still works part-time as a medical receptionist. We
want to move nearer to her job and this place we are living in now
is too big.'

The couple, who have grown-up children, have two endowments
which could be put towards repaying the home loan when these
policies mature in a few years' time. One is a £60,000 policy with
the Ecclesiastical Insurance Group and is due to mature in three
years' time. Jill has a £29,500 Norwich Union endowment which
matures in 2010.

The couple have a joint annual income of about £27,000. John's
Church pension generates £1,000 a month, and he receives another
£312 monthly from the state pension. His wife earns £273 a month
from her job and receives around £450 a month from her teacher's
pension.

The couple keep separate Barclays current accounts and Nationwide Invest Direct Postal accounts. There is £1,800 saved in John's
account and £1,000 in Jill's. John also has a Nationwide Flex

Account. He said: 'We try to keep about £250 in the current accounts.'

Each has £4,800 in an instant-access individual savings account (ISA) with Nationwide, John has £3,000 saved in a Barclays cash ISA and there is £100 in a Post Office savings account.

The couple have some stock-market-based investments. There is £5,500 in a Barclays Managed Income fund personal equity plan (PEP) and £11,000 in a Barclays Global Investors Gilt and Fixed Interest Income fund.

John also has nearly £7,500 in the M&G Income Fund, while Jill has money saved in the Barclays Income Trust and the Barclays General Fund.

John said: 'We also have 950 BT shares that we have held for years. My wife also has 490 CGNU shares which she got from holding her endowment with Norwich Union.'

WHAT THE EXPERTS SAY

The Fearns may have difficulty raising an £85,000 mortgage on their current income, the advisers to Cash Clinic said.

Warren Perry, of independent financial advisers (IFAs), Whitechurch Securities, said: 'I fear that mortgage providers would discount Jill's earned income on the basis that it will not continue.'

Kerry Nelson, of IFAs Deep Blue Financial, said: 'As a general rule of thumb, mortgage companies will lend around two-and-a-half times joint income, and will not lend beyond retirement age. However, certain lenders have a very flexible approach and will view the mortgage on an affordability basis.'

The couple could consider realizing some of their stock-market investments to meet the difference they need to buy a new property if they cannot get a large enough mortgage, Mr Perry said.

Anna Bowes, of IFAs Chase de Vere, suggested the couple consider selling some of their investments to raise a larger deposit for their new property. She said: 'They should start by looking at the investments that are not in a PEP wrapper in order to use up their capital gains tax (CGT) allowances of £7,700 a year each this tax year (the 2001/2002 tax threshold). For example, they could sell the BT shares and CGNU shares and the Barclays General unit trust holding.'

Ms Nelson recommended the couple use their endowments to repay their loan as soon as they mature instead. She said: 'In total, they are targeted to mature at £89,500. This will allow them to make a significant reduction in their mortgage within the next three years using the first endowment which matures in 2004. In these circumstances, an interest-only mortgage would be appropriate.'

The advisers urged the Fearns to rejig their stock-market investments. Mr Perry said: 'They have a good deal in equity investments but, across the board, the quality is poor.' He recommended that the Fearns transfer their PEPs to new providers and Ms Nelson suggested the Fearns transfer their investments in funds that are not currently within a PEP wrapper into an individual savings account (ISA).

Although John has already taken out a mini cash ISA this tax year, he can still invest up to £3,000 in a mini equity ISA. Jill has not yet used her ISA allowance at all, so she can invest up to £7,000 in a maxi ISA. After the end of the tax year, each will have a new £7,000 ISA allowance to make use of.

LESSONS TO BE LEARNED

- Age need be no barrier to property ownership provided the borrower has enough equity to put down as a deposit. More than a dozen lenders now offer interest-only age-related mortgages to those aged fifty-five and over, with the maximum loan to value varying from 50 per cent to 75 per cent. However, lenders will usually require that life cover is in place (and assigned to the lender) to repay the mortgage in the event of death. John and Jill Fearn already have a significant amount of life cover in the form of endowment policies.

- All borrowers – not just those past pension age – benefit from putting down a larger deposit. In most cases it results in cheaper mortgage rates as there is more security for the lender.

Case Study 22

PROBLEM: LETTING EXISTING HOME TO BUY ANOTHER

Vital Statistics
Name: Peter Lawrence
Age: Thirty-nine
Location: Bristol
Occupation: Human resources consultant
Income: £20,000 p.a.
Savings: £3,000 in bank and building society accounts
Pension: Barclays personal pension plan
Investments: £3,750 invested in shares, Norwich Union savings plan; Friends Provident savings plan
Mortgage: None
Borrowings: £3,000 Egg credit card debt; £6,000 First Direct home improvement loan
Insurance: None

Peter Lawrence is looking to make his way up the property ladder by renting out his home and buying another.

A self-employed human resources consultant, Peter bought his home in Bristol outright, in an auction a year ago. Through renovation, DIY and hard work, he has succeeded in nearly doubling the value of his house in just a year, from £35,000 to £65,000.

Peter, who lives alone and has no dependants, said: 'I would like to be able to do the same thing again somewhere else. My old boss has four or five properties and it works well as a way of building up a retirement income for the future.'

He expects to need to borrow around £60,000 for a new house, although he has £2,000 saved in a First Direct high-interest account, which is earmarked for a deposit. However, he will need to find a mortgage suitable for him, as he is self-employed.

Peter said: 'As well as getting a mortgage, I want to clear my credit card debt and build up my savings because I am self-employed. I think I need to have three months' income in the bank for emergencies.'

Although he has £1,000 saved across a range of building societies, he also has substantial debts. There is £3,000 outstanding on his Egg credit card and a £6,000 home improvement loan from First Direct. This loan is a year old, and is due to run for another three years. He repays £156 a month.

He said: 'I have recently applied for a Cahoot credit card. I pay off around £60 a month.'

He is regularly up to £600 overdrawn on his current account, as well as having the credit card debts and loan payments. Peter, who earns around £20,000 a year, has found it difficult to make long-term savings since he has been self-employed. He has two ten-year £3,000 savings plans, into which he invests £25 a month each, £20,000 in a pension – although he no longer makes contributions – and £3,750 in shares.

WHAT THE EXPERTS SAY

Peter will have to look to his existing savings and investments to repay his credit card debt as soon as possible, the advisers to Cash Clinic said.

Tim Cockerill, of independent financial advisers (IFAs) Chartwell Investment Management, urged him to sell some of his shares to reduce his credit card debt. He said: 'He will have to sell three out of the four to do this.'

If there is still an outstanding balance, he should switch cards, the advisers recommended. David Hollingworth, of London & Country Mortgages in Bath said: 'RBS Advanta is offering an introductory annual percentage rate (APR) of only 1.161 per cent on balance transfers, and this offer lasts until June 2002.'

The advisers said Peter would have to continue repaying his First Direct loan. Mr Cockerill said: 'The loan is at a competitive rate and Peter has little option but to continue paying it because there isn't any capital available to pay it off.'

On the subject of buying a new property, Maxine Harvey, of IFAs Torquil Clark, said: 'The trap is capital gains tax. If Peter has a property other than his main residence, then come the sale of this property, he will be liable for CGT on any gain in the proceeds. He also has to be careful, as a landlord, of the regulations regarding renting out a property. Although he may receive a rental income sufficient to cover his own mortgage payments, he may need to spend money on the upkeep of the rental property.'

Mr Hollingworth said that Peter may need to go for a specialist mortgage because of his self-employed status: 'He will need evidence of his income by providing audited accounts to the lender. Lenders will want to see three years' accounts, although two years' accounts plus a projection should suffice in many cases.

'Peter has a deposit of £2,000 and will be looking to borrow about £60,000, which will give a loan-to-value of more than 96 per cent. Most lenders only lend up to 95 per cent.

'There are schemes that will go up to 100 per cent, but be aware of the mortgage indemnity guarantee. This covers the lender if it cannot recoup the full loan amount in the case of sale on repossession, and could amount to more than £950.'

Mr Hollingworth therefore recommended that Peter use any remaining investments after clearing his credit card to increase his deposit.

He could also consider using some of the equity in his current home by taking out a buy-to-let mortgage against part of it. Mr Hollingworth said: 'He will generally have to borrow at least £25,000 and so could clear his other debts this way as well. The rental income will have to cover the mortgage interest by 125 per cent typically.'

LESSONS TO BE LEARNED

- To buy a property with a competitive mortgage borrowers generally need to put down at least 5 per cent of the purchase price as a deposit. Not only will the interest rate be lower but borrowers with larger deposits can escape expensive mortgage indemnity guarantee (a high lending fee) which, in Peter's case, could amount to £950.

- A buy-to-let mortgage can be a good idea even if the owner owns the property outright (as Peter does with his existing home). This is because the interest charged on the mortgage can be offset against the rental income, reducing the amount of income that is taxable.

- Owning two homes generally means capital gains tax is payable on the sale of the house the individual is not living in, with this tax charged at up to 40 per cent. This cost should be factored in when calculating whether or not buy-to-let is worthwhile.

Case Study 23

PROBLEM: RELEASING MONEY FROM A HOME TO BOOST INCOME

Vital Statistics
Name: Jean Tansley-Harris
Age: Seventy-two
Location: Frinton, Essex
Income: £6,200 p.a.
Savings: £1,500 in Nationwide postal account
Investments: £64,000 in Barclays managed fund
Mortgage: None

Borrowings: None
Insurance: None

Jean Tansley-Harris is facing a problem increasingly common among
the elderly; she is asset-rich and cash-poor. She lives in a house she
bought three years ago and did up herself. She said: 'It is a detached
bungalow and its value seems to be rushing up by the day – I think
it is about £120,000 at the moment. It does gall me slightly that I
have so much tied up in my home.'

She said: 'I get the state pension and have some savings, which
bring in a trickle. In total it's about £6,200 a year, which is enough
to scrape by on. But all my friends have lovely holidays and I
would like to find some way to make the rest of my life a bit more
fun. At present it is even hard to afford a hair-cut. I am tired of
penny-pinching.'

As a result, Jean is considering the option of living on a boat as
this would allow her to sell her home in Frinton, Essex and live
on the proceeds. It would also allow her to move back to London
where she would have access to theatres and galleries. She said: 'All
I can do otherwise is buy down, but that doesn't appeal. I thought
about a caravan, but that is a bit grim and I don't want to live on a
claustrophobic site with lots of strict rules.

'The idea of living on a boat is a sort of a desperate last resort.
I can't swim and I've certainly never lived on one, but I thought it
might be more open and free. I could go into a flat, but then I would
have people living above me and I'm not used to that.'

Jean has already considered the option of releasing some or all of
the equity in her home through an equity release scheme provided
by insurance companies. However, she has rejected this idea as she
feels it presents poor value for money.

She said: 'The interest being charged would add up so fast. Some
offered me £2,000 a year for the rest of my life – much less than the
annual increase in the market value of my home.'

She has two sons and three grandchildren but does not think that
they will be relying on an inheritance from her.

Jean said: 'I want to find out if I can release the capital tied up in my home without doing an income-release scheme with an insurance company. The profits for the companies in those schemes are huge.'

She has a current account with Barclays with telephone banking and a Nationwide postal account with £1,500 saved for emergency expenses.

The bulk of her savings is tied up in a Barclays managed fund, which includes an individual savings account (ISA) from last tax year and personal equity plans (PEPs) for two earlier years.

Jean invested £58,000 three years ago when she sold her previous home in Brighton. She said: 'The investment is worth around £64,000 now, and would be more except I have had to take money out of it to pay for work on the house.'

WHAT THE EXPERTS SAY

Living on a boat is by no means a cheap option, the advisers to Cash Clinic said – even if it allows Jean to release capital from her home.

Vivienne Starkey, of independent financial advisers (IFAs) Equal Partners, said: 'She should also consider that she would be trading in the convenience of a bungalow for a boat with stairways and gangplanks, which may present a problem in a few years' time. There are also the costs of maintenance, mooring and services such as water, electricity and drainage.'

The advisers urged Jean to reconsider an equity release scheme, as an interest-only mortgage will need to be paid for during her lifetime. Janine Starks of IFAs Case de Vere said: 'If she were to take a traditional interest-only mortgage, then the downside is that, although she could raise around three times her income, she would have to service the loan interest every month. This route would ensure that the equity in her property would not be eroded but the net income gain might be very small after the interest has been paid.'

Bearing in mind Jean's reservations about costs, the advisers recommended her to consider schemes provided by well-established insurers such as NPI and Norwich Union. Mrs Starkey said: 'Understandably, she would like to pass on as much as she can to her children when she dies. However, it is important to remember that she worked and saved hard all her life to be as comfortable in retirement as possible.'

Jean could also consider altering her savings and investments to boost returns.

Ms Starks said: 'More competitive rates are available than the one she is earning on the Nationwide postal account. It is also possible to keep this money tax-free by using a mini cash ISA with a bank or building society.'

However, Jean must remember that she cannot invest in a mini and a maxi ISA in the same tax year and she may want to use the maxi ISA allowance for her investments.

Ms Starks said that it is wise to diversify investments. She said: 'It's a good idea to spread your investments between different fund management groups – that way your risk is not all with one company. What Jean does need to bear in mind, though, is that the investments are only three years old and charges will be incurred, therefore she should consider moving, say, £20,000 away to other investment groups, and keep a good proportion with Barclays.'

Mrs Starkey said: 'Jean could increase her income by transferring to the Perpetual Monthly Income Plus fund. This income would be tax-free on the part of her investment that is held in PEPs and ISAs.'

Ms Starks recommended that Jean consider with-profit bonds or corporate bonds, both of which pay good rates of income.

LESSONS TO BE LEARNED

- It takes a lot of capital to provide a decent income. With interest rates and gilt yields as low as they are today, even if a homeowner releases £50,000 of equity that may give an income of just over £2,000 a year. Jean may think this is poor value but this is an income for life.

- Moving home is expensive. Also, if equity is to be released, it will mean a substantial move down the property ladder to a much smaller home in a less desirable area. So staying in your home – even if it means giving up some of the equity to a home income company – may be a better option.

- Some elderly home buyers have, in the past, suffered as a result of taking out home income schemes that left them nursing bigger and bigger debts or suffering from a falling income. These schemes are no longer offered. However, elderly home owners are recommended to use only those companies that are members of the Safe Home Income Plans (SHIP) organization.

Case Study 24

PROBLEM: RELEASING MONEY FROM A PROPERTY TO PAY FOR HOME IMPROVEMENTS

Vital Statistics

Name: Xandra Bingley
Age: Fifty-eight
Location: North London
Occupation: Landlady
Income: £30,000 p.a.
Savings: £16,800 in building society accounts
Pension: None
Investments: £50,000 in CGNU and Sun Life with-profits bonds; £6,000 in CGNU personal equity plan (PEP); £1,800 in Groucho Club shares
Mortgage: None
Borrowings: £16,000 Bank of Scotland personal loan secured against CGNU bond
Insurance: Equitable Life insurance sum assured £6,000

Xandra Bingley stopped working as a literary agent several years ago in order to spend more time raising her daughter, who is now seventeen, and lives on the money she earns from renting out a flat at the top of her north London home, where she has lived for the last thirty-two years.

Money is tight, however, and Xandra is faced with the increasingly common dilemma of having a valuable home that she is unwilling to give up. She lives in Primrose Hill, one of London's most expensive areas. 'I want to stay, but I have rain coming through the roof and the central heating system is on its last legs,' she said. 'I need to find a good way to raise some capital to spend on the house.'

Xandra said she had thought about an equity release scheme to draw down some capital tied up in her home. She said: 'So far I've called Saga and Norwich Union for advice on raising capital on the house. Both say I have to be in my sixties, but I am only fifty-eight. By the time I am sixty-five, the house will have fallen down.'

Xandra has a total gross annual income of just under £30,000, most of which comes from renting out the flat and a room to a lodger in her own part of the house. She said: 'My income looks so huge to me but it disappears on this old house. I seem to spend most of my time with a hammer in my hand.'

She also has a small amount of income from savings and investments. There is £10,000 in a Bradford & Bingley savings account, £6,800 in a Nationwide savings account and £25,000 in a CGU (now CGNU) Life Portfolio Bond, which is 75 per cent invested in the with-profits fund and 25 per cent invested in the guaranteed fund. She also invested £25,000 in a Sun Life deferred distribution bond. Both provide monthly interest.

A further £6,000 was invested in a Commercial Union monthly income personal equity plan (PEP) in 1997 and she has £1,800 tied up in Groucho Club shares. Xandra has never contributed to a pension.

She has no mortgage, but she does have a £16,000 personal loan from the Bank of Scotland, secured against the CGNU life bond. She took the loan out in April 1999 and pays interest of 8.5 per cent.

Xandra said: 'I have had some life assurance since I was a child, which costs £10 a year and is due to mature next year at around £8,000. I thought I would use that to pay down most of the loan.'

WHAT THE EXPERTS SAY

Equity release would be the most effective method of raising capital from Xandra's home, the advisers to Cash Clinic said.

Liz Lyke, of independent financial advisers (IFAs) Options for Women, based in Witney, Oxfordshire, said Xandra has two choices: a mortgage or an equity release scheme. Ms Lyke did not feel that mortgaging the property would be the best course. She said: 'The main problem is that part of the house is used for commercial purposes and lenders will not be willing to offer their usual plans.'

However, Ms Lyke found the equity release company Home and Capital Trust would be willing to make an offer to Xandra on an equity release-type scheme now. She said: 'Home and Capital's usual lending criterion is to people over sixty-five years of age. However, as the value of property in London is high, even though Mrs Bingley is only fifty-eight, Home and Capital would be willing to offer an equity release scheme on a maximum of 25 per cent of the property.'

There is an arrangement fee of 2 per cent of the value of the part of the house being sold and an additional 1 per cent on property over £250,000. She would also have to pay legal fees.

The catch is that although Xandra's home may be worth £1 million, the company will not give her £250,000 for 25 per cent of it: they may only give her around £100,000. This is to take into account the fact that they will not get their money back until her death. When she does die, the house is sold and 25 per cent of the value paid to the company.

Ms Lyke said that if Xandra decided to release capital from her home in this way, it would provide her with ample funds to do up her house and invest for the future. She said: 'Assuming that she raised £100,000 and her capital requirements were met with £50,000, this would leave £50,000 that could partly be invested in her CGNU Life Portfolio bond, using different funds to those in which she is currently invested.'

Kevin Minter, of IFAs David Aaron Partnership, agreed that insurance bonds would be a sensible option: 'Single-premium life bonds, such as those she already has, would be tax-efficient for her as they avoid the need to declare most of the income tax for a twenty-year period.'

Kim North, of IFAs Calkin Pattinson, advised Mrs Bingley to take some exposure to stock-market investment vehicles such as unit and investment trusts as well as corporate bond funds for higher income through an individual savings account (ISA) to shield some of her investments from tax.

Ms Lyke noticed that both of Xandra's with-profits bonds provide the option of increasing the income she takes from them to 10 per cent of the original investment at no extra penalty. This means that she can draw up to £5,000 from both a year, which would go towards enabling her to stop renting out the room in her part of the house.

Ms North said Xandra should also pay off her personal loan as a matter of priority. She said: 'The only way she can do this is by equity release from her property.'

LESSONS TO BE LEARNED

- Home owners who need to release equity from their property, but who do not meet normal lending criteria, should talk to an IFA or broker. As Xandra Bingley has found, there is often a way to get the loan you need.

- Properties are expensive to run. Even if there is no mortgage, homes need regular maintenance. Those approaching retirement should take these extra costs into account.

5 Pensions

There are two sides to the pension problem – the first, pre-retirement planning and the second, making the most of your pension at and after retirement. If you do not get the first right, it will be much harder to achieve the second.

INVESTING FOR RETIREMENT

The first thing to bear in mind is that you do need to invest. Relying on the state will only provide you with a very basic income. However, when calculating how much you need to invest you should first find out how much you will get from the state and then aim to boost this to at least half your final salary.

Basic state pension
Contrary to popular belief, not everyone qualifies for the full pension as individuals need to pay national insurance contributions for at least 90 per cent of their working lives to qualify. If there is a shortfall it is possible to make additional contributions to boost the amount of basic state pension paid on retirement.

SERPS
The state earnings-related pension is based on earnings between a lower and upper earnings limit (the same as the National Insurance limits and for the 2002/2003 tax year £75–£585 a week) during an individual's working life, and gives a current maximum pension of around £100 a week, although many get substantially less. The self-employed do not qualify for SERPS and some employees are contracted out of the scheme through their employer's pension. All other employees build up a SERPS entitlement unless they earn less

than the lower earnings limit of £75 a week, or have opted out of SERPS using a personal pension, in which case they receive national insurance rebates. As from April 2008 the maximum pension will be cut. Younger workers (under forty-five for a man and forty for a woman) earning at least £12,000 a year should considering opting out of SERPS – if they have not done so already – and having the rebates invested in their pension plan. When they get over these age thresholds they can consider contracting back (opting back) into SERPS again. This will maximize their pension.

Second state pension

SERPS was reformed in April 2002 with the introduction of the Second State Pension. Anyone working as an employee will automatically be covered by the new scheme if they earn more than the lower earnings limit. However, unlike SERPS, which benefits those who earn more, the Second State Pension will benefit those with low or moderate earnings or broken work records who will be able to build up a bigger pension than under SERPS. Those earning £23,600 or more (the 2001/2002 level) will receive the same pension as under SERPS.

To find out how much you will receive from the state you can ask for a retirement forecast by filling in form BR19 available from social security offices.

NO PENSION PROVISION

Those who have no private pension provision at all – including non-earners, stay-at-home mothers, the self-employed and employees with no occupational pension scheme – should consider taking out a stakeholder pension. They can invest up to £3,600 a year and as with all pensions they will get tax relief (see below).

OCCUPATIONAL SCHEMES

Over 10 million people are members of occupational pension schemes or have built up a pension entitlement from a former employer's scheme. Generally, anyone who has a chance to join an employer's scheme should do so as employer schemes often give extra benefits such as life insurance (of up to four times salary) and widow's pensions, and most employers contribute to the scheme and pay the running costs.

There are two main types:

- Final salary: these pay a pension based on the number of years of service and salary in the final years before retirement. To earn the maximum pension – two-thirds of final pay – most employees have to work for the same employer for forty years. As few do, they will not get anything like the maximum pension. Even so, these are the best pensions on offer as they have guarantees and are not linked to stock-market growth or annuity rates (see below).

- Money purchase schemes: these pay a pension based on the amount of contributions paid in (by both the employer and employee), how well these contributions are invested and annuity rates at retirement. Employers tend to pay less into these schemes and they rely on stock-market growth, so the pension may not be as generous.

In addition, all companies that have no company pension scheme and have five or more employees must now offer stakeholder pensions to staff. In many cases the employer will contribute – but does not have to.

Some employers have also, in the past, offered group personal pension plans – a cluster of plans arranged by the employer, who often contributes.

As with all pensions, occupational schemes qualify for tax relief at the individual's highest rate (see below) and on retirement individuals can take a tax-free lump sum in addition to their pension.

PAID-UP PENSIONS

When calculating how much you will receive on retirement, it is important to take into account pensions left behind with former employers. Many people leave their pensions behind, but they keep growing (they have had to be preserved since 1986) and can still provide a reasonable pension on retirement.

It is important to track any past pensions down. To do this contact the trustees or if you do not know where to write to call the Pension Schemes Registry (0191 225 6316).

PERSONAL AND STAKEHOLDER PENSIONS

Some 65 per cent of low-earning employees have no private pension arrangements, which is why the Government introduced stakeholders in April 2001. In addition, stakeholders can be taken out by those with no earnings from employment or self-employment who now qualify for tax relief for the first time.

Stakeholders offer better value and are more flexible than previous personal pensions as the annual management charges are capped at no more than 1 per cent of the fund value. Contributions can start from as little as £20 per month and can be increased, reduced or even stopped without penalty. Those with existing personal pensions do not necessarily lose out. Many life companies have guaranteed that the charges on older-style plans will be no higher than for stakeholders.

However, those with high-charging personal pensions should consider switching to or taking out an additional stakeholder pension because of the low charges and flexibility. Only those with

even older-style pensions – known as retirement annuity contracts
– should consider keeping them as the tax breaks are different (see
below).

The pension paid out on retirement depends on how much is
paid in, the charges deducted, how well the money is invested and
annuity rates on retirement. Pensions can be invested in:

- With-profits funds – these smooth out rises and falls in the stock-
market

- Unit-linked funds – these invest directly in the stock-market and
rise and fall as it does

- Unitized-with-profits funds – a mix of the two above

- Self-invested schemes – the individual manages his or her own
investment and can invest in either insurance company funds,
individual shares, gilts or bonds

TAX RELIEF ON PENSIONS

Tax relief on pension contributions is given at the highest rate an
individual pays, which means a basic-rate taxpayer investing £3,600
in a stakeholder pension needs to part with only £2,808. The remaining £792 is tax relief, which is invested in the plan by the Inland
Revenue (without the individual having to claim it).

Higher-rate taxpayers, however, must claim higher-rate tax relief
– in this case an additional £648.

Members of occupational schemes do not have to claim higher-
rate tax relief as it is given automatically (contributions are made
out of gross pay).

The tax breaks do not end there. Pension funds grow free of tax
and on retirement it is possible to take a tax-free lump sum.

Everyone is allowed to contribute a maximum percentage of their
earnings to a pension plan each year.

Occupational schemes

Employees in occupational pension schemes can contribute a maximum of 15 per cent of pay.

Personal and stakeholder pensions

The maximum amount that can be contributed from earnings either from employment or self-employment rises with age from 17.5 per cent aged thirty-five or under to 40 per cent aged sixty-one or over.

Earnings cap

These percentages are subject to an earnings cap which rises each year. It is set at £97,200 for the 2002/2003 tax year. So an employee can pay in a maximum of 15 per cent of £97,200, or £14,310, in the current tax year and receive tax relief at the highest rate.

Retirement annuity contracts

These are pre-July 1988 pensions. They have lower contribution limits than personal pensions, but are not subject to the earnings cap.

Tax relief

Those with no earnings can now get tax relief too. As from April 2001, non-earners can invest up to £3,600 a year in a stakeholder and receive tax relief. So that means that husbands can get extra tax relief by taking out a stakeholder for their non-earning wives and parents can even invest for their children (although they will not be able to get their hands on the money until they retire, which can be from age fifty).

Investors in personal pensions can maximize tax relief by back-dating (carrying back) contributions to the previous tax year if they did not invest the maximum allowed in that tax year.

Tax relief is not the only tax break. Those in company schemes can take a tax-free lump sum on retirement (generally at age sixty-five although some schemes allow early retirement and older female employees may still be able to retire at age sixty) of one-and-a-half times final pay, up to the earnings cap.

Those with personal and stakeholder pensions can take 25 per cent of their fund at retirement as a tax-free lump sum.

HOW MUCH DO I NEED TO INVEST?

A decent pension should cost about as much as the family home –
yet most people spend far more on mortgage repayments than they
ever invest in a pension.

First find out how much pension you will receive if you do
nothing, including pensions from past employers and the state.

Then decide how much you want when you retire. Most aim to
retire with a pension that is at least half of their salary, two-thirds
being the ideal. Those hoping to retire before state pension age need
to invest more.

As a rough guide, those who expect an annual investment return
of 6 per cent should take the shortfall in annual income – say £6,000
– and multiply it by $\frac{100}{6}$ the investment return) to give the additional
capital sum they will need. So £6,000 $\times \frac{100}{6}$ = £100,000.

Another way to calculate how much should be invested is to
invest a set percentage of earnings – the longer you leave it before
starting to invest, the more a decent pension will cost.

AGE WHEN STARTING PENSION	PERCENTAGE OF EARNINGS THAT SHOULD BE INVESTED
20	10 per cent
30	15 per cent
40	22.5 per cent
50	25 per cent

The cost of delay

If you want a £10,000 pension and start investing at age thirty-five
it could cost around £132.8 a month. Wait until ten years from
retirement and you will have to invest almost £800 a month. The
longer money has to grow and the more monthly contributions are
made, the lower those contributions need to be.

RETIREMENT PLANNING

As you approach retirement it is time to check that you have sufficient invested to provide for a comfortable old age.

For many the answer will be that they have invested too little – but it is not necessarily too late. It is relatively easy to boost the amount of pension an individual receives. The options depend on what existing arrangements are in place.

Members of occupational schemes have two main choices:

1. Top up the employer's pension by investing in an additional voluntary contribution (AVC) either offered by the employer's scheme or run by a separate pension provider, known as a free-standing AVC. The former usually offers better value. Those with group personal or stakeholder pensions can simply increase their monthly contributions.

2. Invest in a stakeholder. Until April 2001 it was not possible to be a member of a company scheme and pay into a personal pension (unless the employee had additional earnings from self-employment). However, the introduction of stakeholder pensions means that employees who are members of their employer's scheme can also invest up to £3,600 a year in a stakeholder (provided they earn less than £30,000 a year and are not a controlling director of the company that employs them). Even if they earn more than £30,000 a year, provided they have additional earnings from their main employment – even if it is the odd piece of freelance – they too can contribute up to £3,600 a year into a stakeholder.

Stakeholders are more flexible than AVCs as they can be taken with you when you move jobs and you can have a tax-free cash lump sum when you retire, which you cannot with an AVC as all the money must be used to provide a pension. Also with an AVC you may be required to retire at the same time as the occupational scheme.

The next step is to reduce all outgoings. Pay off the mortgage, loans, credit cards and any other debts so that less income is needed and more income is freed up to invest in the last few years before retirement.

In addition to a pension – which must generally be used to provide an income rather than taken as a lump sum – opt for more flexible tax-efficient investments such as individual savings accounts (ISAS) as well as some emergency cash savings.

Investments should be reassessed. Younger investors may be able to take risks with their money, older investors should not. Switch investments away from risky funds into safer stock-market funds, investment or with-profits bonds and cash savings.

ANNUITIES

Those in final salaries have their pension pre-determined by length of service, salary in the last few years before retirement and any additional voluntary contributions they have made. Those with money-purchase schemes, personal and stakeholder pensions, however, must rely on annuities – policies sold by life companies to provide an income for life.

At least 75 per cent of the fund on retirement must be used to buy an annuity and it must be purchased before the age of seventy-five.

The amount of pension is a percentage of the fund and is known as the annuity rate. Rates are very poor as a result of low interest and gilt rates and it may take a fund of £100,000 to provide an income of £8,000.

Do not forget inflation. Even in these low-inflation times it will have an impact. A man retiring at age sixty has a life expectancy of about twenty-two years. After that amount of time, £10,000 will be worth just £5,117 in terms of spending power if inflation rises by 3 per cent a year.

So as part of pre-retirement planning it is vital to look not just at how big a fund has been built up, but also at what level of income it will provide.

The annuity rates depend on life expectancy based on:

- **Age**: The older you are, the lower your life expectancy. As the life company will probably have to pay out less in total, it will give you a higher annuity rate (a larger income).

- **Sex**: Women tend to live longer, so get lower annuity rates.

- **Health**: Those who smoke or have a poor history of health will receive more than someone with a longer life expectancy. Ask about so-called impaired life annuities.

There are several different types of annuity:

Index-linked or level: Level annuities have payments that remain the same throughout your lifetime. With index-linked annuities the pension is linked to the retail prices index (RPI) to preserve its purchasing power. But this peace of mind comes at a price – initial payments can be cut by as much as 25 per cent to pay for a 3 per cent annual increase.

Single or joint life: The annuity can be related to the life of one person or two.

Widow(er)'s benefit: The drawback with annuities is that they die when you do – even if this happens only a few weeks into retirement. Buying a spouse's or dependant's pension can be expensive.

Guaranteed: To get round the fact that the annuity dies with you, you can buy a five- or ten-year guarantee. If you die within this period the annuity will continue to be paid until the end of the period.

This peace of mind comes at a cost. Buying an index-linked

pension with a five-year guarantee and 50 per cent widow's benefit can cut the pension paid out by almost half.

Income can also be affected by how often the annuity pays out.

Investment annuities

Low gilt yields mean low annuity rates. To get round this problem it is possible to opt for an investment annuity. The payments are linked to underlying investments. The most common type are with-profits annuities which aim to iron out peaks and troughs in the stock-market's performance. However, these annuities are riskier and income can vary.

Boosting your annuity

The easiest way to boost the amount of annuity paid is to take the open-market option. That means shopping around for the best annuity rate instead – as three-quarters of all people do – taking the easy option and buying it from the company that managed their pension fund. The difference for a sixty-five-year-old man with £100,000 to invest can be as much as £13,000 over the rest of his life. Remember, once an annuity is bought that is it – it is a once-in-a-lifetime decision and you cannot change your mind.

Income drawdown

Annuities die with you (unless you buy a widow's pension), are inflexible and the returns are poor. So why buy one? The answer is, because you have to. However, you do not have to buy one until the age of seventy-five. In the meantime, you can opt for income drawdown and take an income from the fund equivalent to the income that would be paid by an annuity. The fund is then invested and should, in theory, grow to provide a much larger fund by the time an annuity has to be purchased. Most investors in these schemes do not draw the maximum allowed (often in early years of retirement when they have less need for the money) in order to boost returns. However, charges and risks mean that only those with at least £100,000 should consider this option.

Boosting retirement income

Always take the maximum tax-free cash allowed on retirement as it gives you more flexibility and options. The capital can be spent or invested as you like rather than going to purchase an annuity. By investing it in tax-free individual savings accounts (ISAS) the returns are likely to be greater than from an annuity.

Case Study 25

PROBLEM: HOW TO MAXIMIZE EXISTING PENSION PLANS

Vital Statistics

Names: David and Anita Preece

Ages: Sixty-two and fifty-one

Location: East Sussex

Occupation: Retired baker and baker

Combined income: Anita £84 a week, plus £12,000 p.a. from leasing
  their bakery

Savings: None on deposit other than money set aside to pay for
  daughter's wedding, £2,500 in Premium Bonds

Pension: Seven different plans

Investments: 2,330 BT shares; 250 Rolls-Royce shares; 400
  Eurotunnel shares; 187 Vickers shares and 450 Woolwich shares

Mortgage: None

Borrowings: None

Insurance: All pensions have life assurance policies linked to them

David and Anita's pension arrangements – all seven of them – are more complicated than usual because they ran their own business for almost thirty years. Both hold policies with Allied Dunbar, Clerical & Medical – now part of Halifax – and Norwich Union. David also holds a Time Assurance policy – a company now part of the Axa Group. David has stopped paying into his pensions, but has yet to start drawing down from them. Anita is still paying into hers. All seven plans have life assurance policies linked to them.

David says: 'We never made extra payments in years when we could have done. I wish we had now. I am concerned that if I do not leave it long enough before I start drawing down my pension, my wife will not benefit from it after I die, especially as she is quite a bit younger than me.'

He added: 'We really want to know what to do with all these pensions. Is there any way to consolidate them, for example?'

David said he thinks his pensions are worth around £95,000, while Anita's are projected to be worth around £130,000 when she turns fifty-five.

Luckily, the couple were able to pay off the mortgage a year ago when they received a windfall from the flotation of Norwich Union.

In addition to their pensions, the couple have other financial priorities – paying for their daughter Samantha's wedding (for which they have enough savings, but nothing extra) as well as having enough left over to pay for repairs to their roof. David added: 'We would like to replace our car at some point as well.'

The couple, who live in East Sussex, are retired bakers, having sold their business in Heathfield to a French family for £40,000. The buyers paid £15,000 up front and are paying the balance in monthly instalments over five years plus interest of two points above the base rate. Anita and David bought the business from David's father for £5,000 in 1970.

Anita continues to work in the bakery three mornings a week, earning £84 a week. They also lease the bakery building, for which they receive £12,000 a year.

The couple hold £2,500 in Premium Bonds and some shares in Anita's name. They have 2,330 BT shares, 250 Rolls-Royce shares, 400 Eurotunnel shares, 187 Vickers shares and 450 Woolwich shares which they received as a windfall.

Anita said: 'We don't often review our shares but I quite like looking in the papers to see what they are worth.'

WHAT THE EXPERTS SAY

The advisers to Cash Clinic focused on the Preeces' lack of cash funds. Gaynor Lyth, of the North Wales-based independent financial advisers (IFAs) David Allsup Investment and Insurance Services, said: 'Money in a deposit account is essential – it is important to have an emergency fund available.'

The Preeces' next priority is to look at immediate demands on their money. Adrian Shandley, of IFAs Balmoral Associates, said: 'There are two key events on the horizon. First, the wedding of their daughter, and second, money to fix the roof and buy a car. Both these events must be paramount in capital planning.'

Income is the next challenge. In order to ensure adequate income, the couple should consider raising the rent on their old bakery building when it comes up for review shortly. Mark Bolland, of IFAs Chamberlain de Broe, said Anita and David should not lift the rent too high, however: 'They clearly need to be realistic and not over-egg the cake. They do not want to put the tenants in a position where their business may be threatened.'

Then they need to look at their pensions. David's four pension plans can be transferred into one personal pension draw-down plan, the advisers said. Gaynor Lyth explained: 'This will enable him to take a tax-free cash sum of up to 25 per cent of the overall value of his combined fund and then to draw a percentage of the fund as income each year.'

The advantage of such a plan is that the fund can remain invested in a tax-efficient environment until David turns seventy-five, when he will be obliged to buy an annuity based on his and Anita's ages and health at that time. Gaynor Lyth recommended a plan from Scottish Widows.

Before he transfers his policies, however, David should check whether any of them carry guaranteed minimum annuities. If so, it may be better to stick with the ones that do, as annuity rates are low at the moment, Mr Bolland advised.

He said: 'A fund of £95,000 would produce a tax-free cash sum of £23,750. If David were to take an annuity now, he generates about £5,400 annual income which would be on his life only, with no escalation and nothing to Anita on his death. If he were to add some protection for Anita, the income would fall to about £4,500. Adding escalation (to take into account inflation) would greatly decrease the annuity further.'

Mr Shandley said: 'A drawdown facility would enable the Preeces to meet the three expenditures of the wedding, the roof and the car which could not apparently be met out of current funds on deposit.' His favourites for drawdown plans are NPI and National Mutual Life.

It would be prohibitively expensive to move or aggregate Anita's pensions, so it will be important to review the funds she is currently investing in to make sure all are doing well, Mr Bolland said.

Anita could continue to pay £100 a year into her Norwich Union plan, but it is hardly worth it, he added. 'Depending on affordability, it might be worth considering increasing the premiums for long-term capital growth.'

In the past Anita would have had to be very careful that her pension contributions did not exceed her personal allowances of 20 per cent of her income for retirement annuities or 30 per cent for personal pensions. However, the introduction of stakeholder pensions in April 2001 means that anyone can pay in up to £3,600 a year regardless of earnings.

On the investments side, all three advisers agreed that the National Savings Premium Bonds had turned out to be a poor investment. Instead, the couple should cash them in and put the money towards the wedding, roof and car expenses.

The couple should hold their shares in a tax-free individual savings account (ISA) (they have a £14,000 allowance each year between them) and review their holdings.

Mr Bolland said: 'As far as the portfolio is concerned, it is clearly overweighted towards BT. If they wish to boost income, they should invest £6,000-worth of shares each in corporate bond or high-yield ISAs, using a share exchange scheme to cut the costs.'

LESSONS TO BE LEARNED

- It is vital to review the performance of pension plans regularly, as Anita has been advised to do, to ensure that they are performing well.

- Personal pensions can be taken from any age between fifty and seventy-five so they offer flexibility. Also, it is no longer compulsory to buy an annuity on retirement – this can be deferred until age seventy-five. David has been advised to use this flexibility to take a lump sum now and a regular income.

- If David dies before buying an annuity (if he takes the income drawdown option), all of the money in his pension fund will go to Anita. If, however, he dies after buying an annuity, she will only receive a widow's pension.

- If a pension has a guaranteed annuity – keep it. The guaranteed rates are usually far higher than the rates on offer today. That means foregoing the income drawdown option.

Case Study 26

PROBLEM: NOT ENOUGH SAVED FOR RETIREMENT DESPITE HAVING FOUR PENSIONS

Vital Statistics
Name: Fiona Lindsay
Location: Central London
Occupation: Celebrities' agent
Income: £70,000–£80,000 p.a.
Savings: Enough to pay tax bill but nothing else

Pension: Personal pension plans with Scottish Widows, Axa Sun
    Life and Friends Provident; a fourth pension with Axa Sun Life
    supporting her mortgage
Investments: None
Mortgage: £140,000 pension mortgage from the Royal Bank of
    Scotland
Borrowings: Loan from the Royal Bank of Scotland
Insurance: Term assurance to cover the mortgage; health insurance
    from Norwich Union

Fiona Lindsay represents celebrities who work in food, gardening,
interior design and antiques. Her clients are often writers, but she
also represents television presenters as well, including Antony
Worrall Thompson and James Martin, both chefs on *Ready, Steady,
Cook*, as well as wine expert Oz Clarke.

Fiona, whose income varies between £70,000 and £80,000 a year,
wants to retire to the South of France and is thinking about buying
a house there now, so that she can get to know the community
before she moves there permanently. Her ambition is to spend half
the year there and half in Africa working on conservation projects,
something she has been planning with a friend.

Fiona has a total of four pensions, although one of these is
supporting her mortgage. She said: 'I did my first pension about ten
years ago, putting £86 a month into a personal pension with Scottish
Widows – I'm still doing it.'

Fiona also picked a high-risk, aggressive investment plan through
a pension with Axa Sun Life to which she contributes £100 a month.
She has been doing that for five months.

There is a small pension with Friends Provident of £30 a month,
with only £1,500 invested, and Fiona's fourth pension is also with
Axa Sun Life and is supporting her current mortgage. She has paid
£150 a month into that for almost two years.

Her £140,000 mortgage is with the Royal Bank of Scotland and
she pays £1,000 in interest each month. Also on the borrowings
front, Fiona has a personal loan from the Royal Bank of Scotland for
her car and pays £150 a month.

There are no other loans and Fiona pays off her MBNA credit card in full every month, explaining: 'It's because I am Scottish. I can't stand paying them interest.'

Fiona has no life assurance because she has no dependants, but pays £10 a month for term assurance to cover the mortgage. She pays £14 a month for permanent health insurance from Norwich Union.

She has a Royalties Gold current account and a thirty-day notice account with the Royal Bank of Scotland in which she keeps enough money to pay her tax bill at the end of the year. There are no other savings.

WHAT THE EXPERTS SAY

Fiona will have to work hard at her savings if she expects to enjoy the same life-style in retirement as she does now, the advisers to the Cash Clinic said. Some might think four pensions more than sufficient. But the advisers said that despite the diversity of managers, Fiona is not putting enough into these plans to make the most of tax reliefs available to high earners. Another worry is that, in addition to the usual compulsion to spend three-quarters of the pension fund on an annuity, Fiona is committed to using part of her retirement fund to repay her mortgage.

Susan Rodrigues, of independent financial advisers (IFAs) Millfield Partnership in Croydon, south London, said: 'Based on Fiona's income, her current pension funding levels are inadequate and need urgent attention.' As Fiona's income varies from month to month, Ms Rodrigues said she should consider using single contributions to boost her provisions.

Ms Rodrigues said: 'As she is a higher-rate taxpayer, this will mean she is able to claim tax relief of 40 per cent on these contributions.'

Martha Catterall, of IFAs City Independent in London, said: 'Although Fiona is currently contributing £366 a month net, this is only 7.13 per cent of her income. She needs to be closer to her 20 per cent maximum. I would recommend an increase in pension con-tributions of £500 a month.'

Ms Catterall said a pension contribution of £866 a month net from now until age fifty-five would produce a fund of £252,000 and a maximum tax-free lump sum of £63,200.

The advisers noted that Fiona is intending to repay her £140,000 mortgage from one of her pensions.

Ms Catterall said: 'This means from the tax-free cash of the pension, which is limited to 25 per cent of the total fund. Therefore it means that the total fund needs to be at least £560,000. This would leave no tax-free cash for Fiona once her mortgage was repaid.'

Ms Rodrigues said Fiona must keep an eye on pension investment returns to make sure the fund is on target to meet the mortgage repayment at the end of the term of the loan.

She said: 'I suggest that she obtain projections from the relevant providers to ensure that her funds are still on target. It is important to remember that as growth assumptions have been reduced, this will have an impact on the projected returns, making them lower than originally anticipated.'

On the mortgage front, the advisers thought that Fiona should carefully consider finding a loan with a better rate. Ms Rodrigues said: 'Fiona's mortgage interest payment seems very high. I would advise that she contact the Royal Bank of Scotland to see if she is on a fixed rate, and if so, what the penalties are for switching to a vari-able rate.'

On the savings front, Fiona needs to make the most of tax-free savings if she intends to buy a property in France and retire there. Karen Wright, of IFAs Options for Women, based in Kent, said: 'Fiona needs to assess the current market situation in France – that is, are the property prices high at the moment, do they fluctuate as they do in the UK? She needs to consult a specialist estate agent who would be able to advise her. If she ties her money up in pro-perty now, she may need the capital for other purposes, so this is an important decision.'

Ms Wright recommended that Fiona retrieve the £5,000 she lent to her business when it started up and put this towards her future savings. She also said Fiona must put the maximum allowance, £7,000 each year, into an individual savings account (ISA), which can protect her investment from tax.

On the cash savings side, Ms Rodrigues said: 'If Fiona was to move her money to a Standard Life bank account, she would receive a far higher rate of interest with instant access.'

LESSONS TO BE LEARNED

- Pensions cost more than you think. Even with four policies, Fiona is not saving enough, putting in just over 7 per cent of her income when this should be nearer 20 per cent.

- Using a pension to back (repay) a mortgage means there is less available when you retire.

- Higher-rate taxpayers gain most from pension investments as to have £1,000 invested in their pension costs them only £600, with the remaining £400 coming in tax relief.

- Pensions are not the only way to fund retirement. Making the most of ISA tax breaks (although they do not qualify for tax relief, they are tax-free) gives greater flexibility. With a pension, not all of the fund can be taken as a tax-free lump sum. This will suit Fiona who wants to retire to a house in the South of France.

- Those whose income varies should consider single-premium investments rather than committing to regular amounts each month.

- Investment returns have fallen in recent years so anyone with a pension – particularly one that is linked to a mortgage – should review it to ensure that it will provide a sufficient lump sum and income on retirement.

Case Study 27

PROBLEM: SHOULD HE INVEST IN A PENSION?

Vital Statistics
Name: Paul Belk
Age: Twenty-three
Location: Bath
Occupation: Professional swimmer
Income: £15,000 p.a. tax-free
Savings: £1,500 in Abbey National savings account
Pension: None
Investments: 400 shares
Mortgage: None
Borrowings: £3,000 student loan
Insurance: None

Swimming for a living is a dream come true for Paul Belk, but he knows it may not pay the bills forever. Paul who lives in Bath where he graduated from university in material science and engineering last year, took part in the last Olympics and is training for the next in 2004.

He said: 'I wouldn't go beyond the next Olympics. I might go back to university after that to study for a Master's in management, but I am not sure yet what I will do for a living after I stop swimming professionally.'

Paul lives in a rented flat with a friend in Bath, which costs £250 a month each. He is paid a tax-free grant from the National Lottery of £15,000 a year.

He said: 'My life-style is quite expensive – I have just had to buy a new car and I have to follow a special diet which I need to pay for.'

Paul is able to earn extra cash on top of his Lottery grant. He said: 'I can earn money doing demonstrations for children at swimming clubs. I am also hoping to look for sponsorship.'

He has a current account with Lloyds TSB into which his grant is paid. He said: 'I keep a few hundred pounds in that for the month and transfer the rest into my Abbey National savings account, which has £1,500 in it at the moment.'

Paul has some longer-term investments – shares given to him by his parents including 333 Railtrack shares (which have been suspended since he was interviewed, although shareholders are due to receive compensation) and 81 National Grid shares.

He said: 'I have never invested in pooled funds such as unit trusts or investment trusts, but I am very interested in shares and stock-market investments. I would like to invest in an individual savings account (ISA).

'I also want to take out a pension as soon as possible but my income is being reviewed at the moment and I'll have to wait to see how much I will be getting before I know how much I can afford to save.'

Although he is renting a flat at the moment, Paul would like to buy his own home when he can afford it.

He also has student loans totalling £3,000, which he has not yet had to start paying back.

WHAT THE EXPERTS SAY

While Paul is swimming professionally, he is missing the opportunity to start saving for a home and the future.

Until April 2001 he could not start a pension as he had no earnings (Lottery grants do not count). However, the introduction of stakeholder pensions means anyone – even those who do not have any relevant earnings – can pay up to £3,600 a year into a pension and get tax relief.

Graham Bates, of independent financial advisers (IFAs) Bates Investment Services, said: 'He could make a start with £50 a month and reassess this level of contribution every year.'

Kim North, of IFAs Pretty Technical Partnership, said: 'A stake-holder can be opened with as little as a one-off £20 payment. As he is young, he can top up his pension when he can afford to for any amount over £20.'

Paul is also keen to start saving for a deposit on a house. The advisers to Cash Clinic said he should put as much as possible aside into a deposit account at the end of each month for this purpose. Anna Bowes, of IFAs Chase de Vere, said: 'The larger the deposit, generally the more flexible the mortgage that you can get.'

Mr Bates said: 'As he is interested in buying a house, he should aim to build up a deposit of at least 5 per cent. He should also keep this money on easy access so that he can get his hands on the money at short notice.'

Ms North said Paul should check in which Abbey National account he now has savings. She said: 'One of the instant-access accounts pays only 0.2 per cent gross.' Mr Bates added: 'A better option would be the Scottish Widows Instant Transfer account, which can be operated via post or phone.'

If Paul is determined to stay with Abbey National, Ms Bowes suggested switching to the bank's Saver account, which is paying a far higher rate of interest, or could consider saving for a deposit into a mini cash ISA, which has an annual investment limit of £3,000.

The advisers said Paul should concentrate on building up his savings rather than repaying his student loan, which he is not required to do yet, as the interest on the loan is less than the interest he can earn on his savings.

Paul should be thinking about medium- to longer-term savings as well. He has already indicated an interest in stock-market savings, so the advisers suggested he consider taking out a stocks and shares based ISA.

He should remember, however, that if he has already taken out a mini cash ISA, he cannot take out a maxi ISA in the same tax year and will have to go for a mini equity ISA instead.

Mr Bates said: 'Paul's investments are exposed to the fortunes of just two shareholdings in Railtrack (since this interview the shares have been suspended) and National Grid. Most investors should seek greater diversification and I think this is something he should address.

'One option would be to sell the shares and reinvest the proceeds into a collective investment fund held within a stocks-and-shares ISA. A collective investment fund such as a unit trust, open-ended investment company (OEIC) or investment trust provides a professionally managed exposure to a portfolio of equities. A dedicated fund manager makes the day-to-day investment decisions.'

LESSONS TO BE LEARNED

- Starting a pension in your twenties means less has to be invested each month to provide a decent pension on retirement. Leaving retirement planning until later will cost far more.

- Stakeholder pensions are ideal for young workers and those with no, low or variable earnings such as Paul, as contributions can be stopped and started at any time without penalty.

- Diversify investments and do not put all your eggs into one basket. Paul had most of his investments in Railtrack, the shares of which have been suspended.

- Get the right balance – a mix of cash savings for short-term requirements (Paul is saving to buy a home), stock-market ISAs for the medium-term and pensions for the long-term future.

Case Study 28

PROBLEM: FORCED TO GO BACK TO WORK AFTER UNSUCCESSFUL EARLY RETIREMENT

Vital Statistics

Names: John and Susan Shorey
Ages: Fifty-five and fifty-three
Location: South Wales
Occupation: Post Office owners
Income: £30,000 from Post Office
Savings: £30,920
Pensions: NPI personal pension (Mr Shorey) and Standard Life
    personal pension (Mrs Shorey)
Investments: Nationwide one-year fixed rate bond and three-year
    reward bond, Halifax TESSA ISAs and Halifax Save As You
    Earn accounts
Mortgage: None
Borrowings: Co-op Bank business loan
Insurance: NFU Mutual joint-term assurance to cover £40,000
    business loan

After an unsuccessful retirement, John and Susan Shorey were forced to go back to work to save up a second time. Having sold their hundred-cow dairy farm and bought a bungalow in Cornwall to retire to, it soon became clear that the couple would not have enough to live on.

John said: 'Despite some savings and no mortgage or borrowings, we had no actual income and the bungalow represented a lump of money earning no interest. So we sold it and invested our savings, plus a small inheritance, in a Post Office and newsagent's in a lovely part of south-east Wales in June this year.'

The Post Office has been in the village of Penperlleni for fifty years and the Shoreys, who have two daughters of thirty-two and thirty, bought the freehold, including a house to live in, for £145,000.

John is the postmaster and earns £18,000 a year from the Post Office, minus 25 per cent in the first year under the terms of their contract. The couple are running the newsagent's business in Susan's name, and they expect it to turn over £75,000 in its first year, producing a net profit of about £12,000 a year.

John said: 'We had most of the £145,000 we needed to buy the business, but we still had to take out a Co-op Bank ten-year business loan for £40,000.'

The loan is interest-only for the first year to allow the couple to get the business up and running and is repayable at a rate of £230 a month. For the remaining nine years, the couple will repay £500 a month. There is joint life-term assurance from NFU Mutual to cover the loan and this costs £35 a month.

The Shoreys have a joint current account with the Halifax which is always in credit. Their business account is with the Co-op Bank and all the bills are paid from there.

On the savings side, the couple have £5,850 each in a tax-exempt special savings account individual savings account (TESSA ISA) with the Halifax. These allow you to roll over your maturing TESSA into an ISA on top of the normal cash ISA allowance for the year.

The Shoreys' TESSAs matured in April this year and they both added the £3,000 ISA allowance for the year. They also each have a Halifax Save-As-You-Earn account and both are due to mature, giving £1,760 each.

There are two easy-access savings accounts – one with £3,000 in it and one with £1,700. John had a small inheritance last year and put £5,000 of it into a one-year fixed-rate bond with Nationwide. He also put £5,000 into a three-year Reward Bond with Nationwide.

On the pensions front, both have a personal plan, but neither is making contributions at the moment. John has a plan with NPI which is worth around £11,000, and his wife's is with Standard Life and holds £2,400.

As for other investments, John holds 750 shares in Genus, a

privately owned company. Apart from this, neither holds any stock-market investments.

The couple have private medical cover from Guardian Health which costs £117 a month. They have held this for twelve years.

There is no mortgage and no borrowings apart from the business loan, and the task facing the Shoreys now is to save enough for retirement and to generate income.

John said: 'Our daughters are self-sufficient and they don't need to be supported any more. I don't think we need to put money aside for them; we need to look after ourselves now. We are workaholics and have to get up at 5.15 every morning. We don't want to do that for too much longer.'

WHAT THE EXPERTS SAY

Tracey Dell, of independent financial advisers (IFAs) Vine House Financial Planning in Northampton, urged the Shoreys to make a realistic estimate of how much income they need in retirement. She said: 'It may be that in five years' time the business will be worth enough, with the investments they have made, to provide them with the level of income they want.

'At fifty-five and fifty-three, they have a little time to make amends but their money will need to work very hard for them to achieve an income of £30,000, which is what they would normally expect to earn from the business.'

Ms Dell said the Shoreys should immediately consider switching their business account in order to save money. She said: 'They should consider changing to one with free business banking for the first one to two years. This may save them between £500 and £1,000 a year. The Co-op does pay interest if in credit but with the standing charge and charges for cheques, the interest is quickly eaten up.'

She also recommended that the Shoreys move their savings from the Halifax easy-access account in order to get a better rate of interest. She liked the Northern Rock Base Rate Tracker account, which is a no-notice account, but only allows three withdrawals a year.

Steve Buttercase, of IFAs Maddison Monetary Management in Surrey, said that the Shoreys should also think about investing for growth. He said: 'I have a rule of thumb for people with an average attitude to risk. It is that whatever your age is should be close to the percentage of your assets that is invested in interest-earning investments, such as bond or gilt funds.

'As the Shoreys have an average age of fifty-four, they should consider having 54 per cent of their medium-term savings in interest-earning vehicles, and around 46 per cent in equities or share-based funds to hedge against inflation and provide some growth over the medium term.'

As the Shoreys have already used up their cash ISA allowance for the year, they cannot open maxi ISAs until the next tax year. However, they still have the option of opening mini equity ISAs this year.

Mr Buttercase said: 'They both have a £3,000 allowance to invest in equity ISAs for this tax year. They can choose to invest this anywhere in the world.'

Ms Dell agreed that the Shoreys should have some exposure to equities. She said: 'As their current account is always in credit, they have money left at the end of the month. They should commit this to a unit trust, something with volatility, to build into an additional lump sum.'

She urged the Shoreys to consider a Skandia unit trust, which allows investment in not only Skandia funds but also other companies' funds. Ms Dell said: 'This allows a spread across the market.'

Harris Frazer, of IFAs Assured Benefit Consultants, suggested that the couple consider pensions as well. He said: 'The £5,000 Nationwide bond that is due to mature should be used towards John's personal pension with NPI.

'It is worth mentioning, though, that it could be placed in a maxi ISA, where the benefits of the fund can be taken as 100 per cent tax-free cash, as opposed to a pension, where only 25 per cent can be taken as tax-free cash and the rest must be used to purchase an annuity.'

Ms Dell agreed that the Shoreys might be more attracted to maxi ISAs, saying: 'They should commit a monthly figure to an ISA from next April. Choose a high-yield ISA that includes gilts and corporate bonds for some security.'

Steve Buttercase preferred pensions, however, saying: 'The most tax-efficient form of saving, especially for the over-fifties, is personal pensions. Every penny will get tax relief at 22 per cent so it may be worth restarting contributions to NPI and Standard Life to try to increase the funds that will be available when the Shoreys retire.'

LESSONS TO BE LEARNED

- Retirement can last a long time – even if you do not retire early like John and Susan Shorey. In fact, retirement can last half as long (twenty years) as your working life (forty years).

- Although overheads tend to be lower (the retired have usually paid off their mortgage), it still takes a substantial amount of capital to provide an income. In some cases as much as £200,000 may be needed to give an annual income of £12,000.

- Those who face a pension shortfall as they approach retirement have little time to make this up. For greater flexibility – although at the expense of tax relief – they should consider ISAs.

- Don't take too much risk as retirement approaches. Keep close to your age the percentage of assets that is invested in interest-earning investments, such as bond or gilt funds. So, if you are aged sixty, 60 per cent of your assets should be in these safe investments.

Case Study 29

PROBLEM: HOW TO GET BY ON ONLY AN ARMY PENSION AND NO STATE PENSION

Vital Statistics

Names: Peter and Jenny Wilkins

Ages: Fifty-one and fifty-seven

Location: Oswestry, Shropshire

Occupations: Semi-retired caravan site attendants

Combined income: £22,000 p.a.

Savings: £10,500 in bank and building society accounts

Pension: Mr Wilkins is drawing his pension

Investments: £35,800 in personal equity plans (PEPs) and
    individual savings accounts (ISAs); £26,000 in friendly society
    retirement fund; two endowments totalling £25,000 maturing
    2004; one endowment for £40,000 maturing 2014

Mortgage: £37,000 interest-only home loan

Borrowings: None

Insurance: £6,600 Equity & Law life cover (Mr Wilkins)

Peter and Jenny Wilkins retired from their careers three years ago but, through a need for income, continue to work part of the year as caravan site attendants.

They hope to be able to retire completely in four years' time when Peter's army pension is expected to rise by about 50 per cent when he reaches age fifty-five.

Up until their semi-retirement, Peter was a store manager, while his wife was a nurse.

Peter, who served as a Captain in the Royal Hussars, said: 'We move on to the caravan site in March and live there until November, maintaining and looking after the site as well as doing all the accounts.'

The couple have three children, the youngest of whom looks after their home when they are away, as he is an electronics engineer with the Royal Air Force, stationed nearby.

When they retire, the couple will need to start generating more income, as they want to travel. Peter said: 'We went to Kenya on safari last year and to Egypt the year before. We also want to see more of Europe, especially Italy.'

His Army pension currently pays out £6,500 a year. The couple make this up to £22,000 a year with their seasonal job. They elect to have 60 per cent of their salary paid to Jenny.

Peter said: 'We will get a rise in salary when we become fully fledged wardens – it can go to £18,000 a year shared salary.'

Jenny keeps her share of the salary – £9,300 this year – for a big holiday in the winter and other expenses. She has her own Lloyds TSB current account.

Her husband pays his share of their income – a total of £12,700 this year – into the couple's joint account at Lloyds TSB. He said: 'I try to keep around £1,000 in that account at any one time and I have a Lloyds deposit account with £2,400 emergency money.'

Jenny has a Coventry Building Society mini-cash individual savings account (ISA) containing £4,100. The couple also have substantial investments, with a total of £35,800 saved in PEPs and ISAs. Jenny has £17,400 of this invested in a Legg Mason UK Emerging Growth PEP and Invesco European Smaller Companies PEP. Peter has £18,400 invested in a Gartmore European Select Opportunities PEP, Jupiter UK Income PEP and Gartmore UK Techtornado ISA.

The rest of the Wilkins' investments are life assurance-related. They have £26,000 in a Homeowners Friendly Society retirement fund and also have three endowments. Two of them, both from Legal & General, are due to mature in 2004, for a total assured sum of £25,000. They hope there will be enough to pay down their £37,000 interest-only mortgage from Cheltenham & Gloucester, covered by a £40,000 Scottish Widows endowment, due to mature in 2014.

Peter said: 'We want to pay down the mortgage earlier than that, and at the moment, with projected bonuses the Legal & General endowments should cover it. Then we would keep the Scottish Widows endowment for investment purposes.'

WHAT THE EXPERTS SAY

The Wilkins are going to have to consider carefully how they will get by on an Army pension when they retire in 2004, the advisers to Cash Clinic said. Kay Lowe, of independent financial advisers (IFAs) Equal Partners, said: 'My concern is how they will cover the short-fall in income when they retire – Peter will be fifty-five and his wife over sixty. They will have a reduced income of around £9,750 but will not have to meet mortgage costs any more, saving them £2,880 a year.'

Mrs Lowe pointed out that the couple will have to wait another ten years before Peter can draw his state pension for them both and their Scottish Widows endowment matures. They will have to find some way of bridging this gap. One answer would be to switch away from capital-growth investments to income-yielding ones.

Brian Dennehy, of IFAs Dennehy Weller & Co., recommended this course of action – particularly as the Wilkins' current investment strategy is rather risky.

He said: 'As they move closer to retirement, the level of investment risk they take should reduce. At the moment, the choices of PEP and ISA funds have a higher risk bias. They should be considering having more mainstream UK stock-market funds or lower-risk corporate bond funds.

'More generally, having only £10,000 in cash and more than £60,000 in risk investments feels a bit unbalanced.'

Kay Lowe agreed that the couple's spread of investments was on the risky side. She said: 'To provide additional income in retirement, these funds could be gradually switched to lower-risk, high-income funds such as the Norwich Union High Income fund.'

Another way to generate more income in retirement would be for Jenny to save into a pension for the next four years, said Kevin Minter, of IFAs David Aaron Partnership. Mr Minter said: 'It looks as though Mrs Wilkins will be a non-taxpayer when the couple do retire, and as such they should try to use up this allowance. Stake-holder pensions attract tax relief and if she is unable to afford the

maximum amount she can contribute into her pension, she should
consider taking some of the money out of the Homeowners Friendly
Society fund and moving that across to make the most of tax relief
available.'

Likewise, the couple should use money from this fund to pay
down any of the mortgage not covered by the maturing Legal &
General endowments in 2004, the advisers suggested.

LESSONS TO BE LEARNED

- As you approach retirement, take less of a risk with capital. The
  Wilkins have just £10,000 in savings and £60,000 in stock-market
  investments so they are taking too big a risk with their capital.
  Also, they are going to need income, not growth, so should
  adjust their portfolio accordingly.

- Retiring before the state retirement age means you will need an
  even larger private pension. Some company schemes pay out a
  pension with a deduction made for what is paid by the state, so
  retirees should take this into account.

- Pay off mortgages as early as possible to leave more disposable
  income to invest for retirement.

- The tax breaks on pensions are generous. Jenny could take £780
  out of her other investments and turn it instantly into £1,000
  invested in her stakeholder pension because she will receive £220
  in tax relief.

Case Study 30

PROBLEM: BRIDGING THE INCOME GAP IN RETIREMENT

Vital Statistics

Names: Brian and Jill Smith

Ages: Sixty-two and fifty-eight

Location: Swansea

Occupations: Retired analytical chemist and Inland Revenue employee

Combined income: £25,252 p.a.

Savings: £19,250 cash savings

Pensions: Mrs Smith is contributing to the Civil Service occupational pension; Mr Smith is drawing a pension income

Investments: Properties worth £180,000; £136,300 in PEPs, ISAs and pooled funds; shares in Morgan Crucible, Ninth Floor and Egg; £2,000 Legal & General endowment; £10,000 Prudential Gold Bond

Mortgage: None

Borrowings: £600 Barclayloan; Fiat interest-free loan

Insurance: £100,000 life assurance policy written in trust for children; £2,000 Eagle Star term assurance

Brian and Jill Smith have set themselves up well for retirement, but face an income gap if they follow their dream of retiring to Spain soon.

Last year, Jill and her husband bought a villa in Spain outright with money they had inherited. While Brian has already retired from his career as an analytical chemist, his wife is still working part-time for the Inland Revenue and is wondering if she can afford to do the same.

Jill said: 'It is like a role reversal – I work and he's retired. It would be nice to be at home with him as well. We would like to winter in Spain and spend the rest of the year in Wales. We don't want to move away entirely – it is wet but beautiful here.'

The couple believe they need to generate around £4,000 extra income a year until they start receiving their state pensions. They do not wish to rent out either of their properties.

They have three grown-up children and have set up a discretionary trust, with a £100,000 life policy, to help their children with inheritance tax. They own both their homes outright and the properties are worth a total of £180,000.

Jill earns £11,500 a year, while her husband has invested his £250,000 pension fund in an Eagle Star income drawdown scheme, which he started in March 2000. Jill said: 'He is not happy about the idea of buying an annuity. Hopefully by the time he gets to seventy-five, when he has to buy an annuity, the Government will have changed the rules.'

Brian receives income from the fund monthly and is drawing down 70 per cent of the Government Actuary maximum of 8.5 per cent of the fund a year. This equates to £13,752 a year, of which £8,000 is tax-free to take account of the 25 per cent tax-free lump sum he is allowed to take from his pension fund as well as his personal tax allowance. In total, the couple have an income of £25,252 a year.

They have a joint Barclays current account which they run to zero each month. They do not drift into overdraft. There is £1,000 in a joint Egg account and £1,000 in Bank of Bilbao in Spain for use when they are there.

They each have £8,627 in a Norwich & Peterborough tax-exempt special savings account (TESSA). Both are due to mature in April 2003.

The couple have substantial investments. However, Jill has missed out to some extent on her pension.

Although she worked for the Civil Service for twelve years before raising children, she has lost the contributions she made to the Civil Service Pension Scheme during that time. She said: 'So now I only have nine years' service from when I went back to work in 1992. I have also put £6,500 into the Scottish Widows additional voluntary contribution (AVC) through work.'

She has a total of £78,365 invested in pooled stock-market funds. Some of these are wrapped in PEPs, some in ISAs, including funds from Skandia, Direct Line, SG Asset Management, Henderson and the Woolwich.

Jill's most successful investment is in the Skandia Multifund, into which she invested £30,000 in October 1997. This is now worth £43,310 and will produce income when she elects to receive it.

She has a fifteen-year £2,000 Legal & General endowment which matures in April 2004 and also has £10,000 invested in the Prudential Gold Bond.

Brian also has an impressive array of investments. He has a total of just over £40,000 in pooled stock-market funds, including ones from Henderson, Woolwich and Legg Mason. The couple hold direct shares in WPM Barclays – old Woolwich windfall shares – Morgan Crucible, Ninth Floor and Egg. Jill said: 'My husband worked for Morgan Crucible and built up his 1,144 shares over fifteen years.'

The couple have a £600 Barclayloan debt and an interest-free Fiat car loan.

WHAT THE EXPERTS SAY

There are various ways in which the Smiths can generate additional income when Jill decides to retire, the advisers to Cash Clinic said.

The simplest would be for Brian to increase the level of income he takes from his income drawdown scheme. James Dalby, of independent financial advisers (IFAs) Bates Investment Services, said: 'There should be scope for this as he is currently only taking 70 per cent of the maximum allowed.'

Tim Cockerill, of IFAs Chartwell Investments, felt, however, that it might be more prudent to find the extra income elsewhere. He said: 'This seems a reasonable sum to take, because the growth the fund should achieve over the coming years should be more. However, there is always a danger that the fund may not grow at a fast enough rate and, if it does not, this will leave Brian with less money to purchase an annuity when he is forced to at seventy-five.'

Darius McDermott, an IFA and managing director of the discount broker Chelsea Financial Services, pointed out that the couple will have £283 more net income a month once their car loan is repaid later this month. This equates to £3,859 a year gross income.

Mr McDermott said that additional income can be generated from their current investments. He suggested they split about £80,000 of their investments into new funds – some investing for income and some for growth.

For income funds, Mr McDermott recommended Norwich Union Higher Income Plus, a corporate bond fund, Aberdeen Fixed Interest, Henderson Preference Bond, and M&G Corporate Bond. Spreading £60,000 over these funds, more heavily in the first two, would produce a reasonable income but not quite £4,000 a year. The rest should be invested across growth funds.

Mr Cockerill said: 'I would suggest selling the Skandia Multifund to find £8,000 to put on deposit for emergencies and placing the balance, £35,000, into two equity income funds – Credit Suisse Income and ABN Amro Equity Income. This would generate an income to help supplement their outgoings.'

Mr Dalby recommended that the Smiths at least tidy up some of the worst-performing funds in their portfolio and consider transferring their ISAs to Fidelity's Managed International fund ISA which gives a 'one-hit' exposure to world markets.

LESSONS TO BE LEARNED

- Income drawdown – where the purchase of an annuity is delayed – gives retirees like Brian Smith more flexibility. But, as has been pointed out, relying on investments rather than annuities has risks, so, like Brian, it is advisable to withdraw less than the maximum allowed.

- Track down lost pensions when calculating what income will be received in retirement. However, note that it was not until 1986 that preserved pensions were introduced. Pensions built up before then in company schemes are usually lost – as is the case for Jill Smith.

- Annuities and pensions are not the only way to generate income in retirement. A carefully balanced portfolio of income-generating investments can meet any income gap.

- Retirement planning should go hand-in-hand with inheritance tax planning. Mr and Mrs Smith have wisely bought a £100,000 life policy written in trust so that their children will not be left with a hefty inheritance tax liability.

- One of the easiest ways for members of occupational schemes to boost their pension is to pay into an additional voluntary contribution (AVC).

6 Investments

Although the last two years may have painted a different picture, the stock-market has historically been the best place for long-term investments. Yes, there can be ups and downs and there are no guarantees (well, unless you buy an investment with guarantees built in). However, that does not mean stock-market-based investments should not be part of your financial portfolio.

You can reduce the risks of equity investment by diversifying into a wider range of shares – usually through collective investments such as unit trusts – and by investing for the longer term so that your money can ride out any rises and falls in the stock-market. You can also invest tax-free through investment schemes such as individual savings accounts (ISAs).

SHARES VERSUS COLLECTIVE INVESTMENTS

The Internet has brought down the cost of trading in individual shares and made it far more accessible. On-line stockbrokers enable individuals to open accounts with just a few hundred pounds and buy and sell whenever they want. The only drawback is that you have to know what shares you want to buy or sell, and for many understanding the stock-market and keeping track of it day and night is a responsibility they would rather devolve to an expert. Advisory stockbroking services often require an initial investment of at least £10,000 to make them worthwhile because of the costs.

The other pitfall of direct share investments is that it is difficult to spread your risks across a wide number of shares – and even different stock-markets around the world – unless you have vast sums of money. Even with the cheapest on-line broker, someone investing the £7,000 ISA allowance could only buy twenty or so companies. Some investors get round these problems by forming investment clubs. There are usually up to twenty members who pool their money and ideas to given them greater buying power and expertise.

However, for most investors there is a better alternative to individual shares.

Collective investments, such as unit trusts, investment trusts and open-ended investment companies, collect together the money of hundreds – if not thousands – of investors so that a wider range of shares can be bought than each individual could afford. The other advantage is that costs are shared, bringing down the charges.

In addition, investors need far less money to gain access to the stock-market – as little as £30–£50 a monthly or £250–£500 as a lump sum.

Collective investments include:

Unit trusts

Investors buy units of equal value which rise and fall depending on how well the money in the fund is invested. They are split into sectors, according to the type of investments they hold and the investment aims. Some are more specialist – Japanese or technology funds – and some more general – UK growth. There are over 1,000 different unit trusts and performance varies widely.

Investors who want advice on which trusts to buy can go to an independent financial adviser (IFA). The cost of advice is built into the charges, with the adviser being paid a commission.

Buying through a discount broker – who does not give individual advice but usually provides recommendations – can cut the costs significantly – from 5 per cent of the money invested to nearer 1 per cent. Buying through a fund supermarket also cuts the costs but widens the choice. Investors buying unit trusts and holding them in a tax-free ISA can mix and match different funds from different providers, instead of being limited to the funds offered by just one fund management company.

Unfortunately unit trust sales tend to follow investment fads. Just before the Internet-bubble burst, technology funds were the flavour of the month and investors who poured millions of pounds into these funds were left nursing losses.

Some of the more popular funds include:

- **Tracker funds**: These aim to track a particular stock-market index, such as the FTSE 100 index of the leading 100 shares by stock-market value or the FT All Share index. They have low charges but when the stock-market falls they fall too, as there is no active fund management.

- **Corporate bond funds**: These have become popular because of falling stock-markets and low interest rates. Companies can issue shares to raise money or bonds – these bonds pay a set rate of interest and are bought back at the initial price after so many years. Bonds pay an income which is higher if the company issuing it is considered risky. The capital value of bonds can also go down. This is because they are traded (bought and sold) and can be bought for more than the initial price. So while they can be low-risk funds, they are by no means no-risk.

Charges: While some unit trusts still charge up to 5.25 per cent as an initial charge and 1.5 per cent or more of the fund as an annual charge, others have no initial charges and only a 1 per cent annual charge. These charges are built into the bid-offer spread. This is the difference between the price at which shares are bought (offer) and sold (bid).

Investment trusts

These are stock-market-quoted companies and investors buy shares in these trusts as they would shares in any other company. However, unlike other companies that provide goods or services, investment trusts are set up solely to invest shareholders' money. The value of shares rises and falls according to supply and demand. Although this is broadly in line with the value of the underlying assets owned by the investment trust, many trusts trade at a discount – which means that the value of the shares is less than the value of the assets. These discounts can widen, making investment trust shares riskier than many unit trusts. In addition, investment trusts can borrow to invest, which adds additional risk.

Trusts have varying investment remits – some very general and others more specific. There are also different type of shares – capital shares and income shares – to cater for different investment needs.

Zeros: Zero dividend preference shares, to give them their full name, have become increasingly popular in recent years. They are a type of investment trust share that pays no income (no dividend), but on redemption (on maturity) a return equivalent to a competitive rate of interest each year is paid out along with the initial investments, which is returned – although this is not guaranteed. As these pay no income, there is no income tax.

Charges: Investment trust charges are far lower than for unit trusts – often only 0.5 per cent of less a year. As with the purchase of all shares, there is 0.5 per cent stamp duty to pay. Investment trust shares can be bought from stockbrokers or direct from the companies (this option is usually cheaper). As with all shares, there is a difference between the buying and selling price (bid-offer spread).

Open-ended investment companies (OEIC)

Pronounced 'oik', these are usually unit trusts that have converted to a company. Some fund managers prefer this structure as they can simplify their trusts. Instead of managing dozens of unit trusts, they only have to deal with one umbrella OEIC with several different sub-funds. Investors can switch more easily from fund to fund. In addition there is no bid-offer spread, only a single price. As a result, charges are paid separately instead of being built into the price. In all other respects, OEICs are the same as unit trusts.

INVESTING AND TAX

Income from investments that pay dividend distributions – including individual shares, investment trusts, unit trusts and open-ended investment companies – is treated as being paid net of tax at 10 per cent. This is known as a *tax credit* and it should be shown on the dividend or distribution voucher.

Only higher-rate taxpayers need pay more tax and are required to pay a further 32.5 per cent. However, non-taxpayers cannot reclaim the 10 per cent tax deducted.

Note, however, that some unit trusts or OEICs may pay interest distributions (if they invest in gilts, bonds or money markets) rather than dividend distributions and as such the income is classed as interest and tax is deducted at 20 per cent.

In addition, investors may be liable to capital gains tax on the sale of shares if the gains – including the profits from the sale of all other assets in that tax year – exceed their annual allowance, which is £7,700 for the 2002/2003 tax year.

In addition, when shares are purchased investors must pay stamp duty of 0.5 per cent on the purchase price.

TAX-FREE INVESTING

Stocks-and-shares ISAS

Individual savings accounts (ISAs) enable savers to invest up to £7,000 in each tax year (until April 2006 when the limit will be reviewed) free of income and capital gains tax (although after 5 April 2004 ISA investments that earn dividends will attract tax on these dividends at the 10 per cent rate, which the ISA provider will pay).

Savers can hold three different types of investment:

- **Cash deposits**: Savings accounts

- **Stock-market based investments**: These can include unit trusts, investment trusts, open-ended investment companies, government bonds or gilts, corporate bonds and individual shares.

- **Life insurance investments**: There is no life cover as part of these investments, instead they are investment funds run by life insurance companies.

The amount that can be invested in an ISA (within the £7,000 overall limit) depends on the type of investment and the type of ISA.

Maxi ISAs: These allow investors to invest the maximum ISA allowance of £7,000 with just one ISA provider. Investors cannot shop around for the best rates on savings and buy these from one provider and then find the most suitable investment fund and buy it from another provider. They have to buy all their investments from the same company – unless they go to a fund supermarket where they can mix and match unit trusts from different fund managers. The investment limits (with a £7,000 overall maximum) are:

- Up to £7,000 in stocks and shares-based investments

- Up to £3,000 in cash savings

- Up to £1,000 in life insurance investments

Mini ISAs: Investors can have up to three mini ISAs provided each invests in a different type of allowable investment. So that could be one cash ISA, one share-based ISA and one life-insurance ISA. It is not possible to have two cash ISAs – even if the investor does not exceed the overall £7,000 ISA investment limit. And if an investor has a mini ISA, he cannot have a maxi ISA. The maximum that can be invested in each type of investment through a mini ISA is:

- Up to £3,000 in cash savings

- Up to £3,000 in stocks and shares

- Up to £1,000 in life insurance investments

Choosing a stocks-and-shares ISA: Those who want to invest in a cash savings ISA with perhaps a small amount in a stocks-and-shares ISA should look primarily at mini ISAs. Those who want to maximize stocks and shares investments should buy a maxi ISA.

If you need help in selecting an ISA, ask an IFA who should give impartial advice and will be paid a commission out of the charges of the fund. Alternatively – if you have a sizeable portfolio – you could find that paying the adviser a fee and in return having any commission rebated may be more cost-effective.

Those who simply want a bit of guidance can look at the many guides on offer from execution-only (which means no advice) discount brokers and fund supermarkets. Some even put together model portfolios – say, for growing income – so that investors only need select the portfolio that matches their investment goals.

For those who really want to go it alone there are self-select ISAs. These enable investors to manage their own money and are offered by stockbrokers. They allow the investor to chose individual shares or even a combination of shares, investment trusts, unit trusts, open-ended investment companies, gilts and bonds.

Past performance: When selecting which unit trust, investment trust, OEIC or share to hold within an ISA it is tempting to look at past performance and simply pick the best performer over the last one, two or five years. However, there is no guarantee that this performance will be repeated (look what happened to technology trusts – they soared in value and then, in the following eighteen months after the Internet-bubble burst, fell by up to 70 per cent).

Charges: It is also tempting to opt for the ISA with the lowest charges. However, sometimes funds with higher charges perform much better – you get what you pay for. To find the lowest-charging ISAs, look for those that are CAT-marked. This stands for low Charges, easy Access and fair Terms. For stocks-and-shares ISAs to be CAT-marked, the charges cannot total more than 1 per cent of the investment and the minimum saving must be no more than £500 as a lump sum per year or £50 per month.

If you are not happy with your ISA: Investors who are not happy with the performance of their ISA should not be tempted to cash in their investment. They will lose the tax breaks. Instead, they should consider switching to another fund or another ISA provider.

However, only the same components of an ISA can be switched. So an investor cannot move a stocks-and-shares ISA into a cash ISA or vice versa. Transfers must be made directly from one ISA provider to another – investors cannot cash in their investment and then reinvest this money with a different provider.

PEPS

There is more cash locked up in personal equity plans (PEPs) than there is in ISAs, which is why it is even more important for PEP investors to check the performance and suitability of their investments. Far too many of the Cash Clinic case studies in this chapter have poor-performing PEPs that no longer meet their investment goals. Although PEPs were withdrawn from sale on 6 April 1999, when ISAs were launched, they did not cease to exist. Any PEP investments made before that date can continue to grow free of tax. However, no additional investments can be made.

Investors should not cash in any PEP investments unless there are no other options. Once a PEP is sold, the tax breaks offered by these schemes are lost forever. Remember, PEP investments are in addition to any ISA investments – so they increase the amount that can be invested free of tax. Instead, investors who are unhappy with the performance of their PEP should consider making a transfer to another PEP provider (this retains the tax breaks) but should check if there are any penalties or charges for switching. Under new rules, PEPs investing in single shares (single-company PEPs) can be transferred to collective investments such as unit trusts and still retain the tax breaks.

Friendly societies

Friendly societies (which are mutual organizations like building societies but offer investments like life insurance companies) offer tax-free savings plans but investors can only invest up to £25 per month (a total of £300 a year) or £270 as an annual premium. Only one plan is allowed per saver. Premiums must be paid for seven-and-a-half years on a ten-year term policy or for ten years on any longer-term policy to be tax-free.

However, as investors are restricted to paying small premiums, costs are disproportionately high and the investment rules make these investments very inflexible. For this reason, investors who fear they may not be able to keep up regular payments to a friendly society investment should think twice before investing. Early encashment penalties are often hefty and there is no guarantee that investors will get back what they have paid in, particularly in the early years of the policy.

These schemes can, however, be good savings vehicles for children and most friendly societies offer baby or children's bonds.

Insurance company investments

Endowments: Compared to unit trusts, investment trusts and OEICs, life insurance investments tend to be inflexible (there are fixed investment terms and penalties for early encashment of the policy), expensive (charges are usually far higher than for many other forms of investment) and complicated. However, many of those interviewed for the Cash Clinic are lumbered with these investments. The penalties mean you are usually better off sticking with your endowment rather than cashing it in (surrendering it). In terms of tax the proceeds from most 'qualifying' life insurance policies (investments which also offer life insurance), such as endowments, are tax-free.

With-profits bonds: These iron out the rises and falls in the stockmarket, with investors earning regular bonuses which are their share of any profits. In addition, investors may also qualify (usually after five years) for a terminal bonus when they cash in the policy. As bonds do not provide any life insurance, they are taxable, although the life company already pays basic rate tax so this is only a problem for higher-rate taxpayers.

Each year up to 5 per cent may be withdrawn as a return of capital and is therefore tax-exempt. There is no personal capital gains tax liability from these bonds and they are therefore attractive for basic-rate taxpayers who are already using their capital gains tax allowances.

Investors should be aware that if they cash in a with-profits bond before five years are up, there could be a hefty exit penalty to pay. Also, if the stock-market is falling, the life company can introduce a market value adjuster (MVA), which means it will not pay out the full value of declared bonuses. Charges can also be high and include a bid-offer spread (the difference between the buying and selling price of units), annual expense costs and allocation rates.

Distribution bonds: These are similar to with-profits bonds in that they are run by life insurance companies and invest in equities and fixed-interest investments. However, while a with-profit bond will increase in value, the value of a distribution bond can fall as well as rise. To compensate for the additional risk of a distribution bond, there is additional growth potential.

The investment is structured so that the capital growth and income can be separated from each other. Income can either be paid out or distributed – hence the name of these bonds – or reinvested to purchase extra units. As with other life insurance investments, the returns on a distribution bond are paid net of basic rate tax, so only higher-rate taxpayers have any tax liability on encashment or regular withdrawals.

Offshore funds and bonds

If investors want to earn income gross from a life insurance company income bond they should consider offshore bonds, as Malcolm Ettridge, in Case Study 40 in this chapter, has been advised to do. This is because all life insurance funds are taxed and this tax cannot be reclaimed by non-taxpayers.

Higher-rate taxpayers can also benefit from offshore investments. Investors planning to retire in the near future, or even take a career break, should consider investing in one of these tax-delaying schemes

so that they can pay tax at a lower rate when they retire, instead of
up to 40 per cent today.

Offshore roll-up funds are like unit trusts and accumulate any
income and reinvest it. Investors do not have to declare these
earnings until they cash in the scheme. However, as the charges of
these funds are often much higher than for ordinary unit trusts, the
tax breaks may only be worthwhile for higher-rate taxpayers –
provided when they come to cash in the scheme (when the earnings
must be declared) they no longer pay tax at the higher rate.

Offshore insurance bonds work on the same basis with the added
advantage that investors can take out 5 per cent of their investment
each year without having to pay any tax until they cash in the bond
– usually after five to ten years. These bonds are offered by most of
the major UK life companies.

Low-risk investments

Investors who want greater returns than from a savings account,
but who do not want to be exposed to the full risks of the stock-
market, are often advised to consider bonds. Bonds are loans made
to companies or even the Government, and include British Government securities known as gilts, corporate bonds and permanent
interest-bearing shares.

Income from bonds is taxed at the same rate as interest – with 20
per cent deducted. However, this tax can be reclaimed by non-
taxpayers whereas the 10 per cent tax deducted from dividends
cannot.

To spread the risks, as the value of bonds can rise and fall, and
keep income tax-free, most investors buy them through a unit trust
ISA. Corporate bonds tend to pay interest of around 0.5 per cent to
1.5 per cent more than gilts as there is a higher risk of these
companies defaulting than the Government, with the riskiest companies paying as much as 5 per cent more than gilts to attract
investors. However, your capital can fall in value and the income is
not guaranteed.

MEETING YOUR INVESTMENT NEEDS

Now that we have covered what investment products are available, it is important to look at how they can be used to meet an investor's needs. The first step in any financial review with an adviser is 'know thy customer'. The adviser will ask what investments you already have, how much you have saved, how much you can spare to invest, what your short-, medium- and long-term goals are and what is your attitude to risk. Your tax position is also important.

Investing for growth

Long-term capital appreciation is the aim of most younger investors who do not need an income from their capital but want it to grow – as fast as possible. The younger an investor, the more risk he or she can usually afford to take as there is more time for the investments to recover if a particular market falls.

The golden rules are to diversify and regularly monitor investments. Some funds perform badly consistently and there is no point in holding on when your money could be growing faster elsewhere.

Collective investments are an ideal choice as they are flexible and low-charging and investors can easily diversify into international and specialist markets.

Watch out for capital gains tax. Although this falls the longer an asset is held, it is easily avoidable if you invest via an ISA.

Investing for income

Bonds – particularly corporate bond funds – are recommended to many of those in the Cash Clinic case studies looking for income.

However, those wanting income over a number of years are advised to invest some of their capital for growth so that they can use this in later years to provide an income.

In addition, with-profit bonds are recommended – particularly for taxpayers – along with distribution bonds. Both are offered by life insurance companies.

Lump sum versus regular savings

Some of the people in our Cash Clinic case studies have been lucky enough to inherit large lump sums, but for most it is a case of investing little and often in regular savings plans.

Those who do not have much to spare can invest in:

- Investment trust savings plans

- Unit trusts

- OEICs

These can all be held in ISAs.

- Friendly societies

- Corporate bond funds

However, with-profits bonds, distribution bonds, venture capital trusts and enterprise investment schemes all require lump-sum investments.

Making regular contributions rather than a one-off lump sum investment can have its benefits, as it has had for Siu-Fai Lam and Emma Lawrence in Cash Clinic Case Study 33 in this chapter. Regular contributions smooth out the volatility of a fund thanks to what is known as 'pound cost averaging'. When the price falls, you buy more shares or units for your money and then when prices rise, you benefit from the growth on a larger number of shares.

Medium versus long term

Investors are advised only to put money into the stock-market that they can afford to lose/leave for at least three to five years.

However, with collective investments and ISAs there are no penalties if you need your money in a hurry.

There is less flexibility with investments such as friendly society schemes, with-profits bonds, distributions bonds and endowments – as Nick and Kathryn Hollings in Cash Clinic Case Study 32 in this chapter, found to their cost. These must be kept for the full term, to earn maximum returns and avoid penalties.

Case Study 31

PROBLEM: WHERE TO INVEST A LUMP SUM

Vital Statistics

Names: Michael Sherwin and Angie Smith

Ages: Thirty-nine and thirty-eight

Location: Hitchin, Hertfordshire

Occupations: Role-play business for corporate training

Combined income: £50,000 p.a.

Savings: £17,000 in Egg account

Pensions: £56 net a month each into CGU personal pension plans

Investments: £12 a month each into ten-year savings plans with
    Axa Sun Life; £700 in Premium Bonds

Mortgage: £50,000 HSBC endowment mortgage with endowments
    from Standard Life and HSBC; £12,000 equity release loan from
    HSBC

Borrowings: Loan from First National

Insurance: None

A tide-me-over between acting jobs turned into a business for
Michael Sherwin and Angie Smith, a married couple who provide
role-play courses for corporate training programmes. Their business,
which supplies actors to companies such as Bass Brewers and BT,
helps people to learn how to handle situations ranging from inter-
views to telling staff they are redundant.

Michael is currently appearing in a major play in London, so
Angie is concentrating on the business which turned over £60,000
last year. They each earned around £25,000 before tax with their
acting jobs included. The couple pay their earnings into a joint
Halifax savings account, and then transfer enough to pay bills into
an HSBC joint current account.

The couple hold their tax money along with their savings in an
Egg savings account. This currently contains around £17,000, £7,000

of which is to pay tax. Angie said: 'The acting profession is very precarious and we have always worked on the idea that it is nice to have that money there.'

Both contribute £56 a month net to a unit-linked personal pension plan from CGU. They have been doing this for ten years and their contributions rise with inflation.

Angie said: 'I know they are probably not worth very much but I am not very trusting of pensions at the moment as interest rates are low and you can't buy a decent annuity. I want to look into other ways to invest for the future.'

Each pays £12 a month into an Axa Sun Life ten-year savings plan, taken out two years ago, and Angie has £700 in Premium Bonds and has won £50 in three years.

The couple have a £50,000 mortgage from HSBC, which will be repaid by two endowments in thirteen years' time and have also taken out a £12,000 equity release loan on their £130,000 home in Hitchin, Hertfordshire, which they bought for £58,000 five years ago.

There is also a loan from First National to improve the couple's bathroom but there is only around £400 outstanding on this loan and the couple are repaying it at £110 a month.

WHAT THE EXPERTS SAY

Michael and Angie should not be too concerned about having a great deal of spare cash available, the advisers to Cash Clinic said. Instead, they should consider investing £10,000 of their Egg savings and rebuilding a cash reserve as soon as possible after this.

Angus Millen, of independent financial advisers (IFAs) Millen Financial Management in Southport, said: 'They should contribute £5,000 each into an individual savings account (ISA), using their Egg account funds.' He said they could opt for fairly speculative funds if they felt they could afford to invest for five to ten years.

Philip Harper, of IFAs Philip Harper Financial Management, favoured investing in a technology fund, while Harris Frazer, of IFAs Assured Benefit Consultants, based in Manchester, preferred the Fidelity Money Builder fund, which could also be wrapped into an ISA as it would 'provide the couple with a gentle introduction to a pooled investment.'

Mr Frazer also suggested that the couple might consider with-profits bonds for a lump-sum investment if they would prefer something less risky than investing directly into the stock-market. For a lower-risk investment, Mr Harper preferred corporate bonds and recommended the corporate bond fund provided by Aberdeen Asset Management. He said: 'Keeping around £10,000 as liquid cash would seem an adequate level, given their circumstances.'

He noted that their pension contributions are insufficient to provide income at retirement similar to their income now and suggested investing in an ISA as an alternative to supplement their retirement provisions.

He said: 'ISAs offer a far more flexible method of funding for income in retirement than pensions and although savers receive no tax relief on contributions made, the income from ISAs is free of tax, unlike pension benefits, which are taxed in an identical manner to earned income. ISAs also permit investors to stop, start, reduce and increase contributions at any time with no penalty.'

Mr Frazer pointed out: 'An ISA will allow either of them to retire when they wish to do whereas a pension has to be taken between the ages of fifty and seventy-five.'

To save on outgoings, the couple could consider remortgaging to a cheaper lender.

LESSONS TO BE LEARNED

- If you can afford to tie up money for five to ten years, you can afford to speculate and take a little risk. Higher-risk funds tend to be more volatile (the rises and falls are greater), however their aim is to produce greater returns over the longer term. Anyone who needs money in a hurry should not consider these funds as they may be forced to cash them in when the price is at a low rather than a high.

- ISAs are tax-free, can be cashed in at any time and the contributions varied, making them an ideal alternative to pensions. And unlike a pension, all of the cash can be taken as a tax-free lump sum – it does not have to be used to buy an annuity (a policy that provides a pension income for life).

Case Study 32

PROBLEM: INVESTING TO MEET A MORTGAGE SHORFALL

Vital Statistics

Names: Nick and Kathryn Hollings
Ages: Thirty-four and thirty-one
Location: South London
Occupations: Doctor and housewife
Income: £41,000 p.a.
Savings: None
Pension: Nick is contributing to the NHS superannuation pension
    scheme
Investments: RNPFN ten-year investment plan; Standard Life
    fifteen-year endowment
Mortgage: £150,000 Alliance & Leicester part-endowment, part-
    repayment home loan
Borrowings: None
Insurance: £225,000 Scottish Widows life cover for Nick; £100,000
    Legal & General life cover (Kathryn); Standard Life income
    protection cover (Nick).

Dr Nick Hollings and his wife Kathryn lives in a £210,000 house in south London. Kathryn has stopped work as a language teacher to raise the couple's two children, Madeleine, nearly two, and Monty, five months. Nick is finishing training in radiology and is now look-ing for a consulting post.

The couple need to start investing to pay off the part of their mortgage that is not covered by an endowment policy after recently cashing in two endowment policies because they had performed so badly. 'I had paid about £3,500 into them and I surrendered them for £2,500 – I had to take a big hit,' said Nick.

These endowments were taken out to support the couple's mort-gage, alongside a Standard Life endowment which is due to mature in 2016 at a sum of £32,500.

'We have had a letter saying that provided the fund grows at 6 per cent a year, then it will mature at the correct amount,' said Nick. 'I plan to put the £2,500 I have from the other endowments into an ISA to support the rest of the mortgage so we will need good growth for that.'

The couple's £150,000 mortgage is with the Alliance & Leicester, but only £67,000 of it is on an interest-only basis and nearly half of this is covered by the Standard Life endowment – so they will need to build up a similar amount from other investments.

'I know that I will have to make regular contributions to the ISA to cover the rest of the interest-only part,' Nick added.

He said: 'I am earning about £41,000 a year at the moment and this will rise to £48,000 when I start as a consultant. Salaries go up annually after that and the maximum is around £60,000.'

The couple have no savings accounts or short-to-medium-term investments such as ISAs. Their joint current account swings from being £500 in credit to £1,000 overdrawn.

However, Nick has longer-term savings – a ten-year investment plan with the Royal National Pension Fund for Nurses and two pension funds. He said: 'My contributions to the NHS superannu-ation fund comes out at source – I put in the maximum amount I can and I have been in it since I qualified as a doctor in 1991. The other fund is a free-standing additional voluntary contribution (FSAVC) scheme. However, with this I do not quite contribute 15 per cent of my salary to my pension.'

Nick switched this second scheme from Lincoln National to the

Royal National Pension Fund for Nurses when he became dis-
illusioned with his original provider – the same company from
which he bought the poor-performing endowments.

He has £225,000 life cover, arranged with Scottish Widows, and
his wife has £100,000 cover, obtained from Legal & General. Nick
added: 'I also have an income protection plan from Standard Life
which would pay me £7,900 a year and I would get an NHS pension
if I was injured.'

WHAT THE EXPERTS SAY

Nick and Kathryn Hollings' two priorities are to make short- and
medium-term savings and to cover the rest of the mortgage, the
advisers to Cash Clinic said.

Adrian Shandley, senior partner of independent financial advisers (IFAs) Balmoral Associates, said: 'The investment plan with
RNPFN is a ten-year investment plan which seems strange as the
couple have planned almost totally for the long term without any
medium- or short-term planning. Possibly, future investments
should go into less restrictive investments such as ISAs or unit and
investment trusts on a monthly basis.'

When looking for ISAs, the couple can keep in mind the need to
save to repay the mortgage as well as the need for medium-term
savings. Brian Dennehy, of IFAs Dennehy Weller & Co., said: 'There
is currently a shortfall for repaying £34,500 of the mortgage and this
probably requires an ISA.'

Warren Perry, of IFAs Whitechurch Securities, said: 'If Dr Hollings puts the £2,500 into an ISA and starts monthly savings, then I
would suggest something fairly aggressive.'

Mr Shandley said: 'The couple might like to consider either
extending their existing endowment with Standard Life or taking
out an ISA with one of the more dynamic investment providers
such as Henderson, Framlington or Fidelity. An ISA can provide a
flexible way of repaying a mortgage.'

He added, however, that the couple should not start stock-market investments until they have sorted out short-term savings for emergencies. He said: 'Before investing the proceeds of the Lincoln National endowments into an ISA, I would ask the couple to consider carefully where their contingency funds are.'

Mr Dennehy recommended paying a monthly sum into a savings account for this purpose. He said: 'I would recommend a low-risk deposit account. If they have Internet access, the best of the bunch is the e-savings account from Nationwide.' Mr Perry recommended savings accounts with Smile, the Internet arm of the Co-op Bank.

Although Nick does not save the maximum he is allowed into his pension scheme, Mr Shandley said that he should be focusing more on shorter-term savings anyway. He also pointed out: 'Does he realize that an FSAVC can only ever provide extra income and does not provide extra tax-free cash at retirement? The income from the FSAVC will also be dependent on annuity rates, which are particularly poor at present.'

LESSONS TO BE LEARNED

- Prioritize. Nick and Kathryn Hollings have no short-term savings and no medium-term investments – all their money is locked up in long-term investments and pensions, so in an emergency they will have no savings to fall back on.

- Endowments are expensive, inflexible and do not always perform that well. If looking for an investment to repay a mortgage, consider a stocks-and-shares ISA – the money invested grows tax-free, it can be cashed in at any time (so if it performs well the mortgage can be repaid early), the contributions can be varied and there are no hefty surrender penalties.

- Before cashing in or surrendering an endowment, think twice. As Nick and Kathryn found to their cost, there is no guarantee you will even get your money back. If you are determined to get rid of a policy, consider selling it through a traded endowment policy (TEP) company.

Case Study 33

PROBLEM: TRANSFERRING PEPS
TO PRODUCE BETTER GROWTH

Vital Statistics

Names: Siu-Fai Lam and Emma Lawrence

Ages: Both thirty-four

Location: Huddersfield, West Yorkshire

Occupations: Both quantity surveyors

Combined income: £45,500 p.a.

Savings: £3,200 in building society accounts

Pensions: Both have frozen pension schemes from previous
   jobs; Mr Lam currently contributes to employer's final salary
   scheme

Investments: £4,000 in personal equity plans (PEPs) and individual
   savings accounts (ISAs); £500 in unit trusts; twenty-year Scottish
   Widows endowment; £1,540 in shares; two ten-year Scottish
   Friendly bonds

Mortgage: £100,000 Yorkshire Building Society repayment loan

Borrowings: £15,000 Tesco car loan

Insurance: Life cover under pension scheme; mortgage protection
   policy; permanent health insurance

Emma Lawrence and her partner Siu-Fai Lam bought their £115,000
home in Huddersfield, which they share with their son George,
seven months, and Emma's mother, Enid, sixty-one, following the
death of Emma's father when she was five months pregnant.

   Now that they have a new home, the couple would like a larger
family and plan to marry when they have the money to do so. That
means they need to start investing for the future.

   'We want to build up some cash and investments and put at least
£100 a month each away into a fund,' said Emma. 'However, we do
not want to take too much of a risk.'

Emma has returned to work part-time after maternity leave and is earning £17,000 a year. Siu-Fai earns £28,500 a year.

The couple, both quantity surveyors for the same company, have a joint Lloyds TSB Classic current account which they keep in credit. Emma has £200 in a Scarborough Building Society account and saves £15 a month into it.

The couple keep £3,000 in a Smart 2 Save Nationwide children's account in their son's name and have a £100,000 Yorkshire Building Society repayment mortgage fixed at 5.59 per cent for two years. Emma said: 'After the two years, we will look for another lower rate.'

Both have frozen pension schemes with previous employers, and they are unsure if they should leave them where they are or transfer them. Siu-Fai only is contributing to their employers' final salary scheme but Emma said: 'I will join that once I have been back at work for six months. We put in 2 per cent of salary and our employer puts in 6.3 per cent. We also get life cover.'

The couple have some investments already. Emma invested £2,000 in the Lloyds TSB UK Growth personal equity plan in 1998. She said: 'It has not done well and I am considering moving it.'

Siu-Fai has a Royal & Sun Alliance Portfolio Accumulation ISA which he took out as a PEP in 1996, investing £2,000. He also has £500 in the Jupiter Global Technology fund.

Both have a Scottish Friendly Society ten-year bond, investing £25 a month each tax-free.

Sui-Fai has a Scottish Widows Versatile twenty-year endowment which matures in 2016. Emma said: 'He pays £100 a month into that and it is worth £6,000 now. In 2006 we will have the option to withdraw ten years' contributions.'

The couple have some shareholdings, with £800 in Abbey National, £600 in Electronics Boutique and £140 in Artisan.

Besides the mortgage, they have a four-year £15,000 Tesco car loan which they took out eighteen months ago. They have life insurance worth £100,000 for Sui-Fai and £70,000 for Emma. They also have a mortgage protection policy and permanent health insurance which would pay out £197 a week.

WHAT THE EXPERTS SAY

The couple have planned their finances well so far, the advisers to Cash Clinic said, but there is scope for more effective saving.

Emma should certainly move her Lloyds TSB PEP, they agreed, as it has not performed well. Kevin Minter, of independent financial advisers (IFAs) David Aaron Partnership, said: 'I would suggest a move to ABN Amro UK Growth.'

Maxine Harvey, of IFAs Torquil Clark, said: 'Emma should transfer to something like the M&G Managed Growth Fund which is a fund of funds built up from a selection of M&G's range of UK funds. The benefit of this is that the fund manager makes all the switching decisions and the peaks and troughs of one fund's performance are smoothed out by the other funds held.'

The couple have not used their ISA allowance for this year and should consider this for the £100 a month they each want to invest.

Ms Harvey was in favour of funds of funds. She said: 'This would be an option for either to invest on a monthly basis as an alternative to an index tracker which, as we have seen over the last year or so, can be a fairly volatile investment.'

Mr Minter, however, favoured a tracker fund if the couple are risk-averse. He said: 'The Legal & General UK Tracker fund has the lowest charges in the market and comparatively good performance. I agree that tracker funds have not performed too well of late, but that may mean now is a good time to start investing.'

Vivienne Starkey, of IFAs Equal Partners, noted that some of the couple's existing investments were quite speculative even though they have declared themselves to be fairly risk-averse.

She said: 'The Jupiter Global Technology fund which Sui-Fai has invested in is a higher-risk investment and Artisan is listed on the Alternative Investment Market which is a more volatile market. I recommend that they plan their investments to fit their attitude to risk.'

Mrs Starkey suggested a tracker fund that follows the FTSE All

Share index rather than the FTSE 100 as it gives a broader spread of companies.

Ms Harvey said: 'If they wanted to be a little more adventurous, a European fund such as Gartmore's European Select Opportunities is a good idea, especially as making regular contributions rather than a one-off lump sum helps to smooth out the volatility of a fund.

'They will both be able to take advantage of their ISA allowances to invest in these funds. And as they each have an allowance of £7,000 for this tax year, they could also consider topping up their monthly contributions by using their shares in a share exchange with one of the fund managers.'

The advisers urged the couple to make sure that their wills are up to date, to ensure that their son and Ms Lawrence's mother could continue to live in the house if anything happened to them.

Mr Minter said: 'They should consider leaving the property to an 'interest in possession' trust, with Ms Lawrence's mother having a right to live there for her lifetime and their son having the right to the property on her subsequent death. They should also place any joint life cover in trust for their son.'

LESSONS TO BE LEARNED

- Make sure your investments meet your investment goals. Emma said the couple wanted low-risk investments but had money tied up in volatile shares and a higher-risk technology fund.

- If you don't use your ISA allowance, you lose it. Everyone should make the most of the £7,000 they are allowed to invest free of tax each year (even if they cannot afford to use up the full allowance).

- However young you are, pension and inheritance tax planning should form a part of financial planning – particularly if you have dependants.

Case Study 34

PROBLEM: INVESTING WINDFALLS FOR LONG-TERM GROWTH

Vital Statistics

Names: Dave and Helen Roberts

Ages: Thirty-eight and thirty-seven

Location: Longridge, Lancashire

Occupations: Royal Mail data controller and teacher

Combined income: £39,000 p.a.

Savings: £6,600 in bank accounts

Pensions: Both have personal pensions and company pension
schemes

Investments: £4,035 in personal equity plans (PEPs); £47,000
Scottish Widows endowment

Mortgage: £47,000 interest-only home loan

Borrowings: None

Insurance: None

Since having their third child, Dave and Helen Roberts have had to
tighten their belts financially – but they still find ways to save.

Helen a design and technology teacher at a local school, said: 'My
husband is in the middle of retraining. He was a quantity surveyor
and now he works for the Royal Mail on the accounts side – he is
in data control, doing accountancy exams.'

Helen herself retrained from architecture to teaching several years
ago after the couple were forced to move from London to Lancashire
because of financial pressures. She said: 'We are both from around
here and we moved back about ten years ago after being married
for three years. Now our careers are stabilizing, but we have the
extra financial burden of three children and having two of them in
full-time childcare.

'We would like to start saving as much as we can so that we can release it when we need it – and we are willing to make sacrifices to do that.'

The couple's children are Beth, eight, Ella, three, and Adam, eight months.

The couple have invested heavily for the future, making financial sacrifices for Dave to retrain so that he can earn a higher salary later.

Helen said: 'I earn £24,000 a year and I have applied to receive the Government performance-linked addition of an extra £2,000 a year. Dave earns £15,000 a year – we are investing in his salary more than in mine to get him retrained and earning more in the long run.'

The couple benefited from a Scottish Widows windfall of £4,751, which is sitting in a Scottish Widows VIP account. Helen said: 'We are getting a bonus on the interest rate for six months and then we want to reinvest that money.'

She believes they may need it to make up for a projected shortfall of £4,800 on their £47,000 Scottish Widows endowment. She said: 'We are not panicking about this, but we would like to be able to use the windfall to make up any shortfall we actually do have.'

The endowment is intended to repay a £47,000 interest-only home loan from Scarborough Building Society which is still within a five-year redemption penalty period that ends shortly. After the five years are up, the redemption penalty falls to one month's interest. Helen said: 'We will bite the bullet then and change to a better rate.'

The couple have two joint current accounts and pay £150 a month into a savings account for annual bills such as household and buildings insurance. They also have a joint Egg telephone savings account with £1,850 saved. Helen said: 'We are renovating the house and so £1,000 of the money is earmarked for that.'

The Roberts have £250 in National Savings children's bonds, which mature in January, and want to save more for their children, but will not be able to afford much until their elder daughter comes out of childcare next year. Helen said: 'We can only afford to save around £50 to £100 a month until then.'

The couple have an M&G single-company personal equity plan

holding 207 Halifax windfall shares. Helen said: 'We sold the other windfall shares and invested in a Jupiter European PEP, which is worth around £2,800 now – the Halifax shares in the PEP are worth about £1,200.'

For longer-term savings, both Dave and Helen have pensions.

WHAT THE EXPERTS SAY

The couple are wise to keep their Scottish Widows windfall to cover a possible endowment shortfall, the advisers to Cash Clinic said.

Iain Smith, an independent financial adviser (IFA) from Askfigaro, a website providing investment research including fund analysis, said: 'While it is not good to have a projected shortfall of their endowment, should there be a shortfall in 2013 they should have sufficient investments at that time to cover this.'

He said that after the six months of bonus rate on the Scottish Widows VIP account are up, the couple should consider making use of individual savings account (ISA) allowances for the next tax year and invest the windfall in a maxi ISA. They could combine regular savings with this lump sum and gradually increase the amount they contribute as their childcare costs diminish and once they have built up a larger cash fund for emergencies.

Mr Smith advised them to consider ISAs with investments focusing on Europe, the UK and North America, and added: 'The Jupiter PEP is currently invested in the Jupiter European fund and this has shown a good level of fund performance and should be left untouched for the time being.'

Warren Perry, of IFAs Whitechurch Securities, pointed out that the Jupiter fund, into which the couple put one set of Halifax shares, had done much better than the second set of Halifax shares they had retained. He said: 'The couple would be better off with an actively managed unit trust than with keeping the shares.'

The advisers also urged the couple to consider stock-market savings for their children rather than National Savings. Mr Perry said: 'They need to query why they bought those. If it is for higher education, then they are looking at investing for at least ten years. In this case, they need to look at investing this and any other regular savings into a good investment trust savings scheme. They should consider schemes from Hendersons, Aberdeen and Invesco.'

If the couple are not keen to risk their savings on the stock-market, they could try friendly society children's savings products instead.

Harris Frazer, of IFAs Assured Benefit Consultants, said: 'They should invest up to £25 monthly, the maximum allowed, in a friendly society baby bond – a ten-year tax-free savings plan. But it should be noted that the charges on these plans may be quite high and returns rather low. Tunbridge Wells Equitable Friendly Society offers both traditional with-profits and unit-linked baby bond plans with ten-year terms.'

LESSONS TO BE LEARNED

- Don't risk your fortunes on one or two shares. As the Roberts found, they sold one lot of windfall shares and this performed better in a unit trust than the second lot which they held on to. Although in some cases individual shares do better than pooled investments, for most investors there is too much of a risk and they should consider investing in a wide range of shares through a unit trust, investment trust or open-ended investment company.

- Make the most of tax-free schemes. The Roberts have been advised to invest in both ISAs and friendly society bonds.

Case Study 35

PROBLEM: INVESTING FOR LONG-TERM GROWTH, BUT NOT IN A PENSION

Vital Statistics

Name: Mike Stonehouse
Age: Thirty-two
Location: Windsor
Occupation: Management consultant
Income: £100,000 p.a.
Savings: £22,000 in bank accounts
Pension: None
Investments: £10,000 in Barclays Stockbrokers share-dealing
    account
Mortgage: None
Borrowings: Hire-purchase car loan
Insurance: None

Mike Stonehouse does not believe in making gains without pain – or at least the prospect of pain. A natural risk-taker, Mike, who is a self-employed management consultant in the engineering industry, prefers to take high risks on the stock-market in the hope of high returns.

His risk-taking has, so far, paid off. By his own account, he earns about £100,000 a year by being prepared to shoulder losses as well as benefit from the gains of working for himself.

However, an income five times national average earnings has yet to translate into many visible assets.

Mike, who lives in Windsor with his girlfriend in a rented house, said: 'I am not too worried about the future. I do not have a pension because I would rather do it my own way. Pensions are too rigid. I want to be able to access my money when I want it and not have to wait until I am fifty. I realize that I am missing out on tax relief, and yes, I want the tax relief, but not the restrictions of a pension plan.'

He has an aggressive investment plan for providing for his retirement: he intends to buy a string of properties and use the rental income to support himself.

With income as high as his, Mike should not have problems raising capital to buy the properties he wants. His plan is to buy two this year – both to rent out – and to think about buying a place for himself in a year's time.

Mike keeps his current account in credit all the time and said: 'I keep a running balance of around £6,000 or £7,000 which is why I haven't bought life insurance or income protection cover. I keep this float of money, which ought to keep me going for about six months anyway. Most income protection policies only seem to come in after around three or four months, so I don't see the point in spending money on that.'

He has a further £15,000 spread across 'carpetbagging' accounts with building societies that are likely to turn into banks and pay windfalls. He has already benefited from the conversion of the Woolwich and, more recently, the Bradford & Bingley.

Mike said: 'I sold my Bradford & Bingley shares straightaway. This money is my stockpile to pay my tax bills at the end of the year. I would love to find some ways to reduce my tax liabilities.'

Mike takes an aggressive stance when it comes to investments as well, putting his money into individual shares rather than lower-risk pooled funds or life insurance-related products. He said: 'I have been playing around with shares until last year – I stopped investing in shares for a while because the markets were looking a little too risky. I have, for the time being, sold off most of my shareholdings, but I keep an open balance of around £10,000 in my account with Barclays Stockbrokers.

'If I could find a decent managed or investment fund, then I would go for it. I would rather go for higher-risk funds because I believe that is where the returns are likely to be.'

Mike is still repaying a hire-purchase loan on his car, which costs him £400 a month. He will finish paying off the loan later this year.

WHAT THE EXPERTS SAY

Mike is prudent to consider ways of saving for retirement other than pensions, the advisers to Cash Clinic said.

Milena Atanassova, of independent financial advisers (IFAs) Rickman Tooze, said: 'There is a school of thought which advocates not putting all your retirement eggs in one pension basket and it seems Mike fully supports it. With pension contracts, investors cannot get any of their money before the age of fifty, with a few exceptions to this rule. They can only take a maximum of 25 per cent of their fund in cash, and if they survive to seventy-five, they are forced to buy an annuity, although by the time Mr Stonehouse reaches this age, the position could well be different. On top of this, annuity rates are not exactly mouthwatering.'

However, Ms Atanassova added: 'All that said, a pension plan should not be ignored completely. Subject to certain limits, tax relief is available on pension contributions at the investor's highest rates and, although the pension, when investors take it, is subject to income tax, the lump sum is tax-free.'

Tom McPhail, of IFAs Torquil Clark, said: 'Self-invested personal pensions (SIPPs) can be used to invest in commercial property, and are very useful for reducing tax liabilities – something Mike is keen to do – but non-pension investments such as individual savings accounts (ISAs) and residential property can form an effective retirement planning strategy as well.'

Mr Stonehouse's plan to use rental income from property to fund his retirement and provide a means to save now is a good one, the advisers said.

However, Wai Man Cheung, of IFAs WMC Investment Managers in Dorset, said: 'He should bear in mind that any gains on property disposals will incur capital gains tax (CGT) and, in respect of future inheritance tax (IHT), provide limited planning opportunities.'

Interest payments on buy-to-let mortgages can be offset against rental income for tax purposes, along with other expenses such as agent fees and maintenance costs. Ms Atanassova said: 'Before going

blindly into any buy-to-let deal, Mike needs to allow in his calculations for any likely period when the property is not let and, therefore, producing no income.'

On the investments front, the advisers agreed that Mike ought to
be using his ISA allowances to assist in tax planning. Mr McPhail
said: 'Using his £7,000 ISA allowance will give him tax-free growth
on his investments.' He recommended Invesco European Growth,
Framlington Health, ABN Amro UK Growth, Fidelity Managed
International and Artemis UK Smaller Companies unit trusts for
inclusion in an ISA.

LESSONS TO BE LEARNED

- They say you have to speculate to accumulate. However, while
  Mike has speculated he has not accumulated. The advantage of
  long-term investments is that money is locked up for your
  future.

- A pension plan may not be the best way to plan for the long-
  term future. A mix of property (in the form of buy-to-let) and
  shares (in individual and pooled investments) can provide
  greater returns. However, investors will have to forego the
  generous tax relief given by pensions.

- Managing your money yourself puts you in control. By self-
  investing his portfolio, Mike was able to go liquid (move into
  cash) as the stock-markets fell, protecting his capital. Investment
  managers, on the other hand, are under pressure to keep
  investing.

- If you like managing your money, why not manage your own
  pension – through a self-invest personal pension? It is similar to
  a personal pension except that you decide what to invest in and
  you get a wider choice – commercial property, shares, unit trusts
  and other collective investments, gilts and cash.

Case Study 36

PROBLEM: RESTRUCTURING INVESTMENTS TO PROVIDE INCOME IN RETIREMENT

Vital Statistics

Names: Martin and Kay Massey

Ages: Sixty-seven and sixty-three

Location: Mill Hill, North London

Occupations: Own engineering business

Combined income: £31,500 p.a. net

Savings: £56,050 in bank and building society accounts

Pensions: Scottish Amicable personal pension and two other paid-up pensions (Mr Massey); S&P personal pension (Mrs Massey)

Investments: £155,400 in pooled investments; £17,000 in with-profits bonds; £5,800 in high-yield bond; £35,000 directly invested in shares

Mortgage: None

Borrowings: None

Insurance: None

As retirement nears, Martin and Kay Massey aim to reallocate their investments from seeking growth into delivering an income.

Martin said: 'The aim is to achieve an income when we retire in 2003 of about £600 a week net. I am sure that is possible with my investments.'

Their London-based engineering business pays a salary of £20,000 after tax to Martin and £11,500 after tax to Kay, with the remainder of profits invested in the company.Although they need income, the couple's wide array of investments is mostly oriented towards growth. They have a further £12,000 in their current accounts waiting to be invested.

Martin has a total of £43,000 invested in personal equity plans

(PEPs) with Johnson Fry, Jupiter and Schroder and an individual savings account (ISA) with Schroder. He also has a £500 Prudential with-profits bond, £5,800 in a Newton High Yield Bond and £3,000 in a Warrant Portfolio Trust with Hargreaves Lansdown.

Kay has £10,000 invested in PEPs with AMR and Schroder. She contributes £100 a month to a Merchants Investment Assurance fund which invests in the Perpetual International Growth fund and pays £100 a month into a Sun Life deferred distribution bond that she took out this year.

Martin said: 'I have £80,000 tied up in unit trusts, of which £40,000 is in technology trusts, including Framlington Net Net and Aberdeen Technology.'

The rest of his unit trusts are spread across European, Japanese, Latin American, International and UK smaller companies funds with managers, including Newton, Invesco, M&G, Johnson Fry and Fidelity.

While her husband has gone largely for technology on the pooled funds side, Kay has concentrated on 'old economy' stocks for her shareholdings. She has £35,000 tied up directly in shares, including Cable & Wireless, Carlton Communications, Granada, 3i, Reuters, Pearson, Scottish & Newcastle, Sage, Whitbread and Unilever. Kay said: 'I have had my fingers burnt with recent trends so I am very cautious now. I have not bought shares for a while.'

To balance their stock-market investments, the Masseys have a total of £56,050 held on deposit, including TESSAs which are due to mature.

Both have made pension provisions for retirement. Martin's paid-up NPI personal pension has a projected value of £15,000 for 2003 and his paid-up Scottish Mutual personal pension has a projected value of £2,500 in 2003. More substantially, he contributes £600 a month gross to his main personal pension with Scottish Amicable which is projected to be worth £160,000 in 2003.

Kay puts £1,800 a year into a personal pension with Save & Prosper, which is projected to be worth £21,000 in 2002. They also have a number of endowment policies due to mature in 2003 with a total value of £98,000.

The couple's home in north London is worth £250,000 and they have no mortgage or other borrowings.

WHAT THE EXPERTS SAY

The Masseys should be able to achieve an income of £600 a week net – or £31,000 a year net – from their investments with a few careful changes, the advisers to Cash Clinic said.

Although this will involve switching to investments for income, the Masseys should not switch everything immediately, said Milena Atanassova, of independent financial advisers (IFAs) Rickman Tooze.

She said: 'Capital growth is important to ensure that their money grows sufficiently to keep pace with inflation. Therefore it is vital that part of their portfolio remains invested for growth, with the built-in flexibility to transfer to income-generating products at a later stage.'

David Baker, of (IFAs) Assured Benefit Consultants, said the Masseys should also maintain tax-free investments: 'At the end of the term, their TESSAs can be reinvested in TESSA-only ISAs.' This is in addition to their normal ISA allowance.

John Turton, of IFAs Best Investment in London, recommended that the couple consider reinvesting the proceeds of their TESSAs into income-bearing investments such as corporate bond fund ISAs.

Mr Baker added that the Masseys should also be switching to less risky investments in preparation for retirement: 'They should move generally towards cautious funds to protect fund values. Pension funds should be with-profits, managed or UK equity funds.'

He recommended, for example, switching the funds in their Schroder Pacific and US smaller companies ISA to a less risky fund within Schroders. He said: 'Staying with the same provider will minimize initial charges.'

The Masseys should aim to switch their unit trusts investing in Japan and Latin America to a more balanced fund such as M&G's Index Tracker fund or Barings UK Growth.

Mr Turton recommended that Martin switch from exposed single-company holdings to pooled funds over the three years to 2003, 'using up annual capital gains tax allowances to mitigate any tax on gains.' The couple should go for tracker funds to provide a balance against their more specialist funds.

Ms Atanassova said the Masseys need to go for investments that provide a rising income when they get to retirement: 'This is where distribution bonds can offer the best of both worlds, allowing you to take advantage of stock-market performance while enjoying a relatively cautious investment.'

She recommended that Kay top up her Sun Life distribution bond with the proceeds of one or two of the endowments due to mature in 2003. 'The real attraction of distribution bonds is their tax treatment. Mrs Massey is allowed to withdraw up to 5 per cent of her original investment each year free of income and capital gains tax at the time of the withdrawal, for up to twenty years.' The same applies to with-profits bonds.

LESSONS TO BE LEARNED

- Just because an investor wants income, this does not mean he or she should not invest for growth. As the Masseys have been advised, they need to have some growth investments to maintain their capital.

- Most retirees want rising – rather than flat-income when they retire. This is so that their spending power is maintained. Distributions allow this – and 5 per cent can be withdrawn each year free of income and capital gains tax.

- Those wanting income tend to be cautious investors as they are often retired and need to live off their capital for the rest of their lives. As you near retirement, switch out of specialist and high-risk funds investing in niche markets such as technology or Japan into a more general fund.

- Use up capital gains tax allowances by selling shares up to the allowance each year to avoid a hefty capital gains tax bill in later years. Invest the proceeds in an ISA to keep this cash tax-free.

Case Study 37

PROBLEM: GENERATING INCOME FOLLOWING RETIREMENT

Vital Statistics
Name: Judith Jones
Age: Sixty
Location: Clacton-on-Sea
Occupation: Supply teacher
Income: £15,248 a year pension income; £350 a month from supply teaching
Savings: £8,550 cash savings; £24,000 tax-free lump sum from pension
Pension: Mrs Jones is drawing her pension
Investment: Seventy-two CGNU shares; £4,500 in personal equity plan (PEP); home worth £120,000
Mortgage: None
Borrowings: £3,000 on credit cards
Insurance: Sun Life and Norwich Union life cover

After teaching five-to-seven-year-olds for more than twenty-eight years, Judith Jones has retired from full-time work but plans to continue as a supply teacher one day a week in two local schools until the middle of next year. She earns around £350 a month from this.

Now that she is starting to receive her state pension and £8,000 a year teachers' pension, she will lose her state widow's pension, which she has received since her husband, who was also a teacher, died at the age of fifty in 1989.

Judith, who has remained single since the death of her husband and has three children and three grandchildren all living in London, has lived in Clacton most of her life.

When she retired she received a tax-free lump sum of £24,000, which she would like to invest. On top of this, she receives £162 a month from the teachers' widows' pension fund as well as £102 a week from the state pension.

She said: 'I don't want to tie up my money too tightly but I would like to generate a little more income to add to what I have. I have a large dilapidated house which needs redecorating with a view to selling it in a couple of years' time and moving somewhere smaller.'

Judith keeps a surplus of between £200 and £300 in her Barclays current account, transferring £350 a month into a second Barclays account to pay direct debits and other bills. At the moment, there is £5,000 in her current account from the proceeds of a Prudential life insurance policy that has recently matured. This is earmarked for a new car. Judith also transfers £50 a month into a Barclays savings account, which holds £1,000 to pay for emergencies. In addition she has £200 in an Abbey National Instant Saver account and £150 in a Nationwide Anglia account. There is also a Barclays Savings Bond, which will mature at £2,200 at the end of October next year.

On the investments side, Judith holds seventy-two CGNU shares. She also has a Prudential UK Growth PEP, in which she invested £3,000 ten years ago. It grew to £10,000 but she released £6,000 to repay her mortgage when she retired. She also invested £3,000 in a Scottish Widows European Growth PEP in December 1998, which is worth about £4,500 now.

Judith does not have a mortgage on her £120,000 home and has no loans but finds she cannot repay her credit cards each month. There is now £3,000 outstanding on two cards – Capital One Visa and Barclaycard. She said: 'Part of that was for a new central-heating boiler recently. I pay off as much as I can afford each month.'

To save her family the costs of a funeral and legal expenses, Judith pays for two life insurance policies, which will pay out a total of approximately £4,000.

WHAT THE EXPERTS SAY

Once she has repaid her credit cards, Judith should turn her attention to investing the remaining £21,000 of her pension lump sum, the advisers to Cash Clinic said.

Tom McPhail, of independent financial advisers (IFAs) Torquil Clark, said: 'Judith should pay off her credit card debts first because the interest on them is money wasted each month and she has the capital to make a clean break.'

He said the bulk of her remaining capital should go into individual savings accounts (ISAs) – £7,000 for this tax year and £7,000 for the next – in funds such as Perpetual Monthly Income Plus, which invests mainly in bonds with some equities.

John Porteous, of IFAs IFP in London agreed that £14,000 of the remaining £21,000 should be devoted to ISAs. He recommended the M&G Corporate Bond fund and the Threadneedle Corporate Bond fund for income.

Darius McDermott, an IFA at the discount broker Chelsea Financial Services, said that Judith should not worry too much about generating a lot more income as she is better off now than she was before she retired. He said: 'It would be better to start her new investments for growth and adjust them later on for income.'

For the remaining £7,000, Mr McDermott recommended that Judith remain in a high-interest savings account such as Nationwide e-saver.

The advisers recommended that Judith consolidate all her cash savings into a higher-interest account in order to maximize the interest she can earn.

However, Mr Porteous said Judith should go for something more adventurous with the £7,000 remaining from her pension lump sum, recommending a fund of zero dividend preference shares. These have traditionally been less risky than ordinary shares because they are placed at the top of the queue for repayment of capital in the event of financial collapse of a company. However, some zero funds have recently run into difficulties.

He added: 'Judith should transfer her Scottish Widows PEP to a high-income fund – Aberdeen Fixed Interest. This will boost tax-free income.'

Mr McPhail agreed that she should switch away from the Scottish Widows fund but recommended moving to ABN Amro Equity Income.

The advisers suggested that Judith sell her CGNU shares to help with renovations on her home.

LESSONS TO BE LEARNED

- Before considering savings and investments, turn your attention to your debts – they cost you money and the interest you may incur can be more than the returns on your investments.

- Make the most of ISA allowances – ISAs do not have to cost any more than other investments but have the added advantage of being tax-free.

- Consolidate smaller amounts of savings into a larger lump sum – you will often get a higher rate of interest.

- Monitor performance of existing investments – in this case Judith's PEP – and if you are unhappy, switch to a better-performing or more suitable investment.

- Individual shares are riskier than pooled investments. So if you need the money – as Judith does for home renovations – sell them before selling unit trusts and ISAs.

Case Study 38

PROBLEM: PRODUCING ENOUGH INCOME IN RETIREMENT

Vital Statistics

Names: Geoffrey and Helen Shaw
Ages: Seventy-four and seventy-nine
Location: Croydon, south London
Occupations: Semi-retired musicians
Income: State pensions plus £13,000 annual investment income
Savings: £22,500 in Nationwide accounts
Pension: The couple are drawing their pensions
Investments: £35,600 in personal equity plans (PEPs) and
    individual savings accounts (ISAs); £40,000 in insurance bonds,
    £180,000 in property
Mortgage: None
Borrowings: None
Insurance: Long-term care fees insurance plan (Mrs Shaw)

Professional singers Geoffrey and Helen Shaw have managed to keep earning well into their seventies, doing a bit of teaching, singing and chorus direction work, but after three years of semi-retirement – earning about £1,000 a year – they have decided to retire full-time.

It means that the couple, who do not have children or any dependants, need to make their savings and investments generate enough income to see them through retirement.

Geoffrey said: 'We need to maximize income from what capital we have. If only we knew how long we have to live and could arrange to spend our last pound the day before! Preserving the capital is not important because there is no one we want to leave things to.'

At the moment, the couple both receive full state pensions plus about £13,000 a year from earnings and investments, including money from two £20,000 insurance bonds from which Geoffrey withdraws 5 per cent each year and the £8,000 gross he receives from his annuities.

The Shaws, who live in Croydon, south London, keep a £1,000 surplus in their Nationwide current account and have £2,000 savings in a Nationwide e-savings account in Helen's name. Also in this account is £19,500 from the proceeds of a matured TESSA and a matured National Savings bond. Geoffrey said: 'We want to invest this money to provide us with more income.'

In addition, Geoffrey has some stock-market investments wrapped in PEPs – £6,000 invested just before April 1995 in Perpetual's UK Growth trust which has grown to only £6,500, and £6,000 invested just after April 1995 in Schroder's UK Equity PEP, which is now worth around £10,800.

The following tax year, he invested his £6,000 PEP allowance in Morgan Grenfell's UK Equity fund and UK Equity index tracker. This is now worth about £9,500.

Helen invested £3,000 in a single-company PEP holding Marks & Spencer shares in April 1996. However, the value of this has fallen to £1,800.

In addition, Geoffrey has some ISA investments – he invested £7,000 in a Henderson European Bond ISA, which he took out in April 2000 and is worth roughly the same today.

Apart from their home, which is worth about £180,000, the couple have no other investments. They are happy to consider an equity release scheme, but would rather sell their property if they need to go into sheltered accommodation, and have arranged a long-term care insurance policy with PPP for Helen costing £20,000 which will provide £1,300 a month to pay for care fees.

WHAT THE EXPERTS SAY

The Shaws need to switch their PEP investments to higher-yielding funds in order to produce more income, the advisers to Cash Clinic said.

Mark Dampier, of independent financial advisers (IFAs) Hargreaves Lansdown, in Bristol, said: 'The most obvious area to increase their income is in their PEPs, which are all capital growth-oriented at the moment. They could, of course, keep them intact and withdraw capital as income, but the problem with this is that capital growth can be elusive and over periods when markets have fallen, it would generally be unwise to take money out.

'I would therefore suggest that the PEPs are transferred to high-yielding corporate bonds which will provide a tax-free income of between 7.5 per cent and 10 per cent a year.' He added: 'The existing Henderson European Bond ISA should be retained because of its yield.'

Of course, the Shaws ought to consider what level of risk to their capital they are willing to accept, as higher-yielding corporate bond funds tend to be riskier than lower-yielding ones. This is because they invest in companies, which are more likely to default on their debts and therefore offer higher rates of interest to encourage investors to buy their corporate bonds.

The Shaws have the option of using a fund supermarket such as Cofunds or Funds Network to complete their PEP transfers, the advisers said, but they should check the cost of doing this, depending on the funds they choose to switch to.

Darius McDermott, of advisory discount broker Chelsea Financial Services, said they should diversify, investing £4,200 into each of the following funds: ABN Amro Equity Income, Crédit Suisse Income, Perpetual High Income, Jupiter High Income, Norwich Union Higher Income Plus, Old Mutual Corporate Bond, Perpetual Monthly Income Plus and M&G Corporate Bond. He said: 'These funds offer a spread which generates a decent income with an underlying growth. This ensures that the value of the portfolio will not be eroded by inflation. As the value of the portfolio grows, so the level of income will increase.

'Helen should also adjust her single-company PEP, currently invested in Marks & Spencer. The rules have changed and it is now possible to spread the investment over a selection of holdings rather than in only one single share. This offers less volatile performance.'

An equity release scheme would provide a useful way to release capital from the couple's home, the advisers said. Milena Atanassova, of IFAs Rickman Tooze, said: 'The Shaws should not worry about having to go into sheltered accommodation later in their life if they are prepared to do equity release. There is a type of scheme called a 'reversion scheme' which involves the home owner selling part or all of the property to the reversion company in return for a lump sum or monthly income and lifetime tenancy.'

Finally, the couple need to invest the £19,500 they have from the proceeds of a matured TESSA and matured National Savings Bond. Ms Atanassova suggested they use £10,000 of this money to invest in an annuity. She said: 'For a purchase price of £10,000, Mrs Shaw could get an annuity of £1,022 a year from Standard Life, £685 of which represents the capital content so is tax-free. Although annuities have had some bad press, they can still be attractive at higher ages.'

Mr Dampier said the TESSA proceeds can be invested in a TESSA-only ISA within six months of maturity. This is on top of existing ISA allowances. He suggested the couple use £7,000 of the National Savings bond money to use up one of their ISA allowances for this tax year.

LESSONS TO BE LEARNED

- Diversification gives safety – the Shaws are relying on their capital to provide them with an income and have been advised to invest in a wide spread of funds, just in case some do not do as well as others.

- Investments need to be regularly reviewed – the Shaws have thousands of pounds in PEPs that are no longer suitable for their needs.

- Make the most of tax-free schemes. While the Shaws have PEPs, they have not maximized their ISA allowances, including the option to invest the capital from their maturing TESSA in a TESSA-only ISA.

Case Study 39

PROBLEM: HOW TO INVEST A £100,000 INHERITANCE

Vital Statistics

Name: Peter and Lynne Judge

Ages: Thirty-seven and thirty-nine

Location: Twickenham, Middlesex

Occupation: Information technology consultant and full-time mother

Income: £45,000 a year

Savings: Total of £115,000 in savings accounts; £680 in children's savings accounts

Pension: Company pension scheme (Mr Judge); frozen company pension schemes (both)

Investments: Shares in CGNU, Halifax and Abbey National; £30,000 Friends Provident endowment

Mortgage: £78,000 Halifax home loan, part repayment, part interest-only

Borrowings: £15,000 Tesco five-year car loan

Insurance: None

Peter and Lynne Judge have the kind of problem most people only dream about. They have inherited £100,000 and are not sure what to do with the money.

Lynne a full-time mother who used to work in marketing, inherited the money when her father died nine months ago and until now, the couple have kept it in a deposit account but would like to make it work harder.

Lynne said: 'We both have virtually no pension and we want to invest for the future.' The couple have been married since 1993 and have two children, Alexander, four, and Christopher, one. Lynne intends to return to at least part-time employment within three years.

Her husband earns £45,000 a year as an information technology (IT) consultant, with an additional car allowance.

To make investing a little more interesting, Lynne is keen to use around £5,000 of her money either to set up or join an investment club. One option for the inheritance money is to pay off the mortgage, a £78,000 home loan which they took from Halifax in 1987. Part of this – £48,000 – is on a repayment basis, while the rest – £30,000 – is supported by a Friends Provident endowment policy. The couple pay £615 a month to the Halifax and £44 a month into the endowment.

There is a redemption penalty in force on the loan until next month, at which time there will be around £68,000 outstanding to repay. Lynn said: 'I can't see any reason not to pay this off, but I do think we should keep the endowment going and use the proceeds in 2012 to pay for the children's higher-education costs or something.'

If the couple pay off their mortgage, they will be left with just over £30,000 to invest, along with the £9,000 they have saved.

Lynne said: 'I know we ought to be putting more into pensions, or perhaps investing in ISAs. If we pay off the mortgage, we will also be able to make regular savings of around £500 a month on top of our savings. I don't think we will need to be able to access the money we invest in anything under five years.'

The couple have two separate and one joint First Direct current account with around £1,000 in each. There is also a joint First Direct High Interest Savings account with £6,000 in it. The couple also have £340 saved for each of their children in National Savings accounts.

The £100,000 inheritance is currently in a Skipton Building Society thirty-day notice postal account. Although the couple both have pensions, neither has saved a large amount in them.

Although the couple have never invested in pooled funds, personal equity plans (PEPs) or individual savings accounts (ISAs), they do have a few shareholdings. They have fifty CGNU shares, 200 Halifax shares and 100 Abbey National shares.

WHAT THE EXPERTS SAY

The advisers to Cash Clinic suggested that the Judges be less hasty in any decision to repay the mortgage in full.

Maxine Harvey, of independent financial advisers (IFAs) Torquil Clark, said: 'Using £68,000 of the £100,000 available to repay the mortgage in full would limit the scope for investing to meet their other objectives. As an alternative, they could consider repaying the Halifax repayment portion and leave a reasonable lump sum to invest.

'The Friends Provident endowment should continue to run as a repayment vehicle for the interest-only portion because there is the possibility of a good return and it will continue to provide valuable life cover as Lynne has none.'

Adrian Shandley, of IFAs Balmoral Associates, said: 'The main point to get across is that even if they ultimately decide that they want to pay off the mortgage, they do not have to do it now. Whether the money is put into investments for the next five, eight or ten years, it could still pay off the mortgage at any point during its term. There is obviously the usual risk with regard to investments in that the value of the investment can fall as long as rise.'

However, against all that, paying off the mortgage involves no investment risk. If they are prepared to regard avoiding future interest bills as a form of 'return', then paying down mortgage debt provides a higher-rate taxpayer like Peter with the equivalent of a high rate of interest gross – risk-free. Even so, the advisers urged the Judges to go for pooled investments such as unit or investment trusts after noting that the couple hold shares only.

Ms Harvey said: 'For a sum of £50,000–£60,000, a discretionary portfolio fund such as the Edinburgh Managed Growth Portfolio would be a good idea. As a fund of funds, the portfolio is built of holdings from the wide range of unit trusts available on the market.

The decisions on when to buy and sell them would be made for them by experienced qualified fund managers.'

Janine Starks, of IFAs Chase de Vere, said the couple should make use of their annual ISA allowances as well. It is also possible to hold a wide variety of pooled funds in ISAs.

Ms Starks said: 'They both have ISA allowances of £7,000 this tax year that should be used. If they have a balanced level of risk, they could start to build up an investment portfolio by choosing two different ISAs with different sectors such as a UK fund, for example the Flemings Premier Equity Growth fund or a European fund such as the Gartmore European Selected Opportunities fund.'

If the couple want to start up an investment club they should contact Proshare (tel: 020 7220 1750), the advisers said.

There are some unit trusts designed for children's investments such as the Rupert Bear Growth fund from Invesco. Mr Shandley said: 'Though this is slightly higher on charges and has middle-of-the-road performance, it is an excellent vehicle with which to encourage children to save and to familiarize them with the principle of unit-linked savings.'

The advisers urged Peter Judge to make additional voluntary contributions (AVCs) to his pension.

LESSONS TO BE LEARNED

- Think twice before paying off your mortgage if you come into a lump sum – once it is repaid, you have fewer options. Investing the money – which should hopefully produce a higher return than the interest you are paying – gives the option to repay the mortgage at a later date or to use it for other needs such as children's education.

- Even if you do want to pay off your mortgage, keep any endowment policy going. Investors only get the maximum returns if they keep their policy for the full term and can often get back less than they have paid in if they cash it in during the early years.

Case Study 40

PROBLEM: MAKING A LARGE
INHERITANCE LAST

Vital Statistics
Name: Malcolm Ettridge
Age: Sixty
Location: Nottingham
Occupation: Retired bus driver
Income: £104 a week in state disability benefits
Savings: £900 in bank and building society accounts
Pension: None
Investments: None
Mortgage: None
Borrowings: None
Insurance: None

Malcolm Ettridge's father saved hard but failed to plan to avoid inheritance tax – and now the Inland Revenue is the biggest single beneficiary of his will, taking £200,000 in tax from his estate before the remainder is divided equally between Malcolm and his three siblings.

Malcolm, who now expects to receive about £133,000, said: 'I don't want to do what my father did – he stashed all his money away and never spent any of it on himself or my mother and now we have had to pay a huge amount of it to the Government in tax. I want to be able to enjoy the money I have now and not just leave it to rot away in the bank.'

Until now, Malcolm, a retired bus driver, has been living on disability benefits of £104 a week, plus housing benefit, because of an injury he sustained while working.

Malcolm, who lives alone in a rented flat in Nottingham, said: 'I used to drive double-decker buses but was retired on injury benefits two years ago.' He will now be able to afford to buy a home of his own. He said: 'I want to travel as much as I can, now that I can afford to. I really feel this money will give me the freedom to do all the things I have always wanted to do.'

However, he does not know what to do with the lump sum. 'The best thing I suppose is to invest it somewhere where it is tax-efficient,' he said. 'I have four children from my marriage, which broke up thirty years ago. I have been single since then, but my children are grown-up and quite well off, so I do not need to provide for them.'

Malcolm would like to spend around £50,000 or £60,000 on a house for himself and then invest the rest wisely to provide an income – particularly as he will not receive the state pension until he turns sixty-five and will lose benefits, including the £175 per month Nottingham Council currently pays for his rent, because he has inherited such a large lump sum.

Malcolm said: 'I am on unfamiliar territory here because I have never done any form of investment before.'

Malcolm has £900 in savings and no debts.

WHAT THE EXPERTS SAY

Malcolm should certainly spend part of his inheritance on a home for himself, the advisers to Cash Clinic said.

Kevin Minter, of the independent financial advisers (IFAs) David Aaron Partnership, said: 'The loss of £175 per month paid for by Nottingham Council is a major drop in his income. However, buying a property for up to £60,000 will reduce the effect of this loss, leaving £70,000 or more available to invest for his future.'

The advisers said Malcolm should keep some of his inheritance on deposit to meet emergency expenses. James Dalby, of IFAs Bates Investment Services, said: 'I would advise him to boost the surplus in his current account to £1,000 as this is a more reasonable level to have at his disposal.

'He should also have a decent amount in a no-notice deposit account – I would suggest about £25,000. This money will form the low-risk part of his investment strategy as well as being his easy-access fund to pay for travelling and other luxuries.' He could try a telephone or postal account to get the best rate.

John Dawson, of IFAs Momentum Financial Services in Hampshire, felt that Malcolm need only hold £10,000 on deposit. He said: 'This will not only act as a contingency fund for emergencies or unexpected expenditure for his new home but will also provide him with an additional income.'

The advisers said the bulk of his remaining inheritance should be invested for income. Mr Minter said: 'I would suggest a higher income level from his investments to start with, which will allow him to travel. Once the state pension becomes payable at sixty-five, the income level from his investments can be reduced to allow for more capital growth in his later years.'

Mr Minter recommended a corporate bond fund wrapped in an individual savings account (ISA), which will yield an income. He said: 'This is the most effective way of benefiting from the tax advantages of an ISA. The Aberdeen Corporate Bond ISA has an excellent record.' Malcolm can invest up to £7,000 in ISAs each tax year.

Mr Minter added: 'As Mr Ettridge is a non-taxpayer, an offshore corporate bond fund would also be suitable as it can pay him a gross return.'

He said the bulk of any remainder should go into a managed bond. He said: 'This would serve two purposes. First, it would allow Malcolm to select the income level he wants. Second, within the bond, he could set up a portfolio of medium-risk growth funds that, held within the bond, can produce income. For the bond, I recommend the Skandia High Investment Bond.'

Alternatively, Malcolm could invest part – £20,000 – of his inheritance in a with-profits bond. Mr Dalby said: 'The returns are paid out in the form of bonuses, with the aim being to smooth out the peaks and troughs over the life of the investment, and investors can take 5 per cent income from a with-profits bond for up to twenty years with the tax deferred until the bond is cashed in. This is because the 5 per cent is treated as a 'return of capital'.

Even after making these investments Malcolm will probably still be a non-taxpayer (the income from the corporate bond ISAs will be tax-free). As such, he should fill in form R85, available from the Inland Revenue, to receive the interest from his savings without paying tax.

LESSONS TO BE LEARNED

- What is the point of being frugal all your life if £200,000 of your hard-earned savings goes in inheritance tax? It is often the moderately-well off who end up paying inheritance tax because they do not realize their estate is worth more than the threshold (currently £250,000 for the 2002/2003 tax year).

- If you are a novice investor – like Malcolm – put your money into a wide spread of low-risk managed funds, with profits bonds and corporate bonds rather than investing in individual shares or in higher-risk equity funds.

- Make the most of ISAs for tax-free income – it does not have to be included on your tax return.

- If any other income (plus taxable state benefits and pensions) when totalled up is less than the personal tax allowance (£4,615 for the 2002/2003 tax year), do not forget to register to receive any savings interest gross (without tax deducted) by completing form R85, available from the Inland Revenue.

7 Insurance

It won't happen to me. That is what many people (rather hopefully) think. However, accidents, redundancy and long-term sickness are problems faced by millions each year.

What you should be thinking is, 'What would happen if . . . ?' Could you pay your mortgage if you could not work because of illness or following redundancy? How would you pay off your loans, overdraft and credit card balances if you suffered a dramatic fall in income? If you died, would your family be left financially secure?

These are difficult questions to address. Facing up to the possibility of years of unemployment, months of debilitating illness or death is not easy. However, dealing with the possibility of the events is far easier than dealing with the reality if you have made no financial provision to protect you – and your family – should the worst happen.

Fortunately there are several types of insurance designed to help keep individuals and their families afloat financially.

Most of us cannot afford every type of cover, but it is possible to find a policy or combination of policies that will suit your circumstances and your pocket.

LIFE INSURANCE

Anyone who has a family depending on them needs life cover. It is one of the cheapest types of insurance policy you can buy – and one of the most necessary.

Even those with no dependants may need cover. For example, if you have debts or business loans that would have to be paid off if you died, you need life cover.

There are several different types of life policy.

Death in service benefits

This is free life cover (usually for three or four times your annual salary) given to employees who are members of company pension schemes. However, remember that if you leave your job, the life insurance will cease. It is therefore advisable to have additional separate life cover.

Term assurance

This is the cheapest, most basic and most popular form of life cover. It pays out a tax-free lump sum if you die before the term of the policy is up. Survive for the full term, and you do not get a penny back. Term assurance can be:

- **Flat rate**: The same amount of cover for the term of the policy.

- **Increasing**: A rising amount of cover (and premiums) in line with inflation. These policies are for those wanting to protect their family's lifestyle.

- **Decreasing**: This is usually linked to a repayment mortgage – as the mortgage is repaid and the amount owed reduces, so does the amount of cover.

- **Family income benefit**: This gives dependants a yearly income rather than a lump sum, with the income paid only for the term of the policy.

Term assurance with critical illness cover

These policies pay out if you are diagnosed with a terminal illness before the end of the term and are expected to die within a short period. Alternatively they pay out on death. Again, if you survive for the full term, you do not get any money back.

Whole-of-life insurance

Just as the name implies, this covers you for the whole of your life – not just a limited term. So it will pay out – eventually (unlike term insurance, which will not if you survive to the end of the term). As such it is much more expensive. It is ideal for those wanting to provide a financial cushion for their family. There are two types:

- **Sum-assured policy**: Pays a set amount on death.

- **Investment policies**: The premiums are invested and the investment is paid to your family. However, in the early years this may be small although some do guarantee to pay out a minimum sum.

Endowment policies

Although these provide an element of life cover (usually enough to pay off an interest-only mortgage) they are really investments. The current consensus is that you are better off buying term assurance and buying a separate and more tax efficient and flexible investment such as an individual savings account (ISA).

Which is best?

If you simply want your debts to be repaid, term insurance is ideal. If, however, you want your debts repaid and to leave some money – or income – for your dependants, a mixture of term insurance and whole-of-life cover may be a better option. Term assurance should be taken out to end when your mortgage or other debts will be paid off or, if it is not to cover a specific debt, until your children reach eighteen or twenty-one when they will no longer be so financially dependent.

How much cover do I need?

You should have enough to pay off your debts (the mortgage, loans, etc.) and provide sufficient income or capital to provide for your family. Ideally, you should insure yourself for five to ten times your annual income.

If you cannot afford that amount of cover, any cover is better than none. You can always buy an additional amount of cover later on when you can afford to, but in the meantime at least you will have some protection for your family should the worst happen.

How can I cut the costs?

Premiums are based on risk, with older, less healthy individuals paying more than younger, non-smokers who are less likely to die and therefore make a claim.

- Buying a joint policy – which pays out when one of you dies – cuts the cost. However, the survivor is left with no cover.

- Buying through your pension plan means you can get tax relief on your premiums.

- Giving up smoking (premiums drop after twelve months) can cut the costs.

- Shop around – as with household or motor insurance, you can keep changing your policy provider to cut costs. However, the older you are the higher the premiums, so it is better to get a competitive quote from day one. You can even do this on-line (go to www.find.co.uk for useful websites).

What about tax?

The pay-outs from life insurance policies are tax-free. However, the value will be included in your estate when it comes to inheritance tax. Write policies in trust to benefit your dependants, and then the payout will not be subject to inheritance tax and can be used to pay any other inheritance tax liability.

CRITICAL ILLNESS COVER

You are more likely to suffer from a debilitating disease or life-threatening illness before you reach retirement than you are to die. Yet comparatively few insure against this eventuality.

This is partly because critical illness cover can be expensive. The main conditions it covers are:

- coronary artery by-pass surgery

- cancer

- heart attack

- kidney failure

- major organ transplant

- multiple sclerosis

- stroke

Those who are too ill or disabled to perform several 'activities of daily living' may also receive a pay-out. Watch out for exclusions for pre-existing conditions.

One in four men and one in five women will develop one of the conditions covered by critical illness policies before they reach age sixty-five, so this type of cover may be worth reconsidering.

These policies are particularly important for those who are single with no dependants, who may find critical illness cover more useful than life insurance as it pays out while they are ill rather than after they die. The money can be used to pay for nursing or home help for those who have no family to provide care or financial support.

How can I cut the costs?

- Buy less cover or only cover for a set term (until your financial commitment decreases, you retire, or your children leave home).

- Buy a combination of term assurance and critical illness cover – as only one part of the policy will pay out, it is cheaper.

- Buy joint cover. However, remember that it will only pay out for one of you.

INCOME PROTECTION INSURANCE

Eight in ten home buyers no longer receive any state benefits to help pay their monthly mortgage bills for the first nine months they are out of work. With consumer credit at record levels, these borrowers will also be struggling to meet their credit card and loan repayments and could find that their bank demands immediate repayment of any overdraft should they lose their jobs.

The solution, historically, has been to have enough saved to provide for a rainy day. The alternative is to buy insurance.

Mortgage payment protection

Rather than protecting or replacing your income, this pays some of your outgoings – in this case the interest (not any repayment element) on your mortgage usually for a limited period of time, twelve or twenty-four months. It pays out if you lose your income because of:

- A major illness

- An accident

- Termination of employment (but not if it was your own fault)

- The failure of your business (going bankrupt)

There is usually a thirty-, sixty- or ninety-days excess period before the policy starts to pay out and there are exclusions (you must have been in your job for at least six months, pre-existing medical conditions may not be covered, etc.), so read the small print.

Credit insurance

This is similar to mortgage cover. If you are made redundant or become too ill or disabled to earn an income, the policy pays your monthly instalments (if you have a loan) or a set amount of your credit card debt (say 5 per cent of the outstanding balance). You are usually offered it when you take out a loan or credit card. Once again, there are exclusions.

Accident, sickness and unemployment cover

Rather than paying the monthly repayments (as with the two previous types of insurance), this pays out a set amount of income – usually between £500 and £1,500 – if you lose your job or cannot work due to ill health or following an accident. As such, you can spend the money as you want. You can often buy the different elements separately, so if you do not want unemployment cover (for example, if you are your own boss) you can just buy accident and sickness insurance. Once again, the policies only pay out for a limited period, twelve months or until you return to work. A lump sum is usually paid in the event of death, loss of a limb or permanent total disablement.

Permanent health insurance

This is called permanent because – unlike the other income protection policies – it pays out a permanent income, well until you recover, resume work or retire. It provides a replacement income if you cannot work because of sickness or disability. The monthly payouts – which are tax-free – are usually for up to three-quarters of earnings, minus any state benefits. Policies differ on when they will pay out. Some will pay if you are unable to do your own job, while others only pay out if you are unable to do a similar job or any paid work.

The policies have a deferred period (a set amount of time before they start to pay out). Employees who would get full sick pay for six months can, for example choose a twenty-six-week deferred period and cut their premiums as a result. Limiting the amount of cover (say, to only half of earnings) or restricting the pay-out to five years, can also cut the costs.

Which type of policy is best?

The ultimate type of cover is permanent health insurance but it is expensive. For the self-employed who want something more affordable, accident and sickness cover should be an absolute minimum particularly if business is going well and you do not want unemployment cover.

Mortgage protection and credit insurance are optional. These policies do not pay out immediately, and only for a limited time, so if you have a spouse who is earning and some emergency savings you could find you can self-insure (protect yourself).

Saving twelve months of mortgage repayments has an added

advantage. If you do not lose your job, you keep your savings with interest added, whereas with a mortgage protection policy, your premiums are wasted.

Remember, these policies (apart from permanent health) only provide limited cover for a limited period. After twelve months or two years are up, the payouts stop. If your family relies on your income (particularly if you are self-employed and therefore will not qualify for some state benefits including sick pay), permanent health insurance along with term insurance will be the ideal. Critical illness cover can work out slightly cheaper (however, it does not provide an income and pays out in a much more limited range of circumstances).

PRIVATE MEDICAL INSURANCE

Private treatment is often seen as a luxury rather than a necessity. However, if you are self-employed or could not afford to be ill, it can be prudent financially. With one in six people spending some time in hospital each year, getting treatment quickly can mean the difference between being unable to work – or work at full capacity – for several months while on a hospital waiting list, or being back at work in a matter of days or weeks. So if your finances would suffer because of delays in getting treatment, consider private medical insurance.

As with all insurance, cover is limited and there are restrictions, and the more limitations and restrictions you are prepared to accept, the lower the premiums.

Six- and twelve-week wait plans, for example, dovetail with the NHS. You only get private treatment if you have to wait longer than the agreed number of weeks. As a result, the premiums are lower.

Other ways to cut costs include:

- **Cheaper accommodation**: You agree to be on a ward or in a shared room.

- **Restricted places where you can get treatment**: These are usually ranked by band, so you will probably end up somewhere less luxurious or in the private wing of an NHS hospital.

- **Higher excess**: The amount you pay towards each claim.

Case Study 41

PROBLEM: PROTECTING INVESTMENT IN BUSINESS AND INCOME

Vital Statistics
Name: Simon Beeby
Age: Forty-one
Location: Plymouth
Occupation: Director of yachting school
Income: £3,380 p.a. from his business; £15,000 p.a. rental income
Savings: £20,000 in NatWest Premium Reserve
Pension: Personal pension plan worth £10,000
Investments: £70,000 lent to his business
Mortgage: £30,000 NatWest mortgage
Borrowings: £22,000 secured loan
Insurance: Life assurance to cover his mortgage

Simon Beeby has been fighting the elements over the past few years to keep his yachting business, Liberty Yachts, afloat.

The company, which Simon bought from its previous owners four years ago, charters out yachts and runs a sailing school. However, the business is seasonal and it is still very much in its early days. As a result, Simon has been living frugally, drawing an annual salary of just £3,380 to allow the business to develop as quickly as possible.

Simon said: 'I am determined to stick it out until the business becomes profitable and I believe I am just about there. You need to persevere and build up a strong client base and now more than half my customers are repeat customers.'

He has also cut down the expenses of the business, reducing the number of staff from four to one and only hiring extra staff during the summer season when business picks up.

For the first time, Simon will be able to increase his salary to about £5,000 this year. He also has an annual income of around £15,000 from some industrial property in Leicester that he shares with his sisters.

His NatWest current account is always in credit, and he has around £20,000 in his NatWest Premium Reserve savings account. Simon is considering whether to invest his savings in the stockmarket – he is interested in taking out an individual savings account (ISA) – or to use the money to pay off his mortgage.

He has also made personal interest-free loans totalling around £70,000 to the company, which he can draw down whenever the company can afford it. The business also has a £22,000 loan secured on a yacht worth £50,000.

His pension is 'minuscule'. He was advised to transfer his old company pension scheme into a personal pension plan with Scottish Equitable in 1992, which he did. It is now worth around £10,000. 'I don't have any other pensions and this is something I want to address. I think it is much more important than trying to earn lots of money now,' Simon said.

On the borrowings side, Simon took out a £30,000 NatWest mortgage four years ago to buy his three-bedroom flat, which is now worth around £80,000. It is a repayment mortgage at the bank's variable rate for a twenty-five-year term. He said: 'I would like to get it paid off quicker than that if possible.'

Simon pays his credit cards off in full each month and holds a NatWest Gold Card with a £10,000 limit which he got when he was working in London. He said: 'I had to use it a year ago to help buy three boats. It comes in useful sometimes.' He has life assurance to cover the mortgage but he has no other policies.

WHAT THE EXPERTS SAY

Simon's top priority must be to take out critical illness cover to protect himself if he is prevented from working due to illness or disability, the advisers to Cash Clinic said.

Philippa Gee, of independent financial advisers (IFAs) Gee & Co., said: 'The problem is that Simon has invested a large sum of money as a loan to the company, for which he receives no interest, and he receives only a nominal salary.

'The amount of salary paid to him is actually less than the interest that would be paid if the £70,000 were simply held on deposit, therefore Simon is effectively working for nothing. While he feels that he could draw this sum out of the business if necessary, it is difficult to see where in the company Simon would actually obtain this money.'

She suggested that Simon concentrates on building up the business quickly as he needs to move into profits as soon as possible.

Harris Frazer, of IFAs Assured Benefit Consultants, said: 'As a single man with no dependants, Simon should consider making financial provision to secure his circumstances. He is at an age when the chances of being unable to work through a critical illness is five times greater than dying. The cost of £100,000 critical illness insurance until he is sixty would be £57 a month with Scottish Provident.'

Tracey Dell, of Vine House Financial Planning, said: 'As Simon receives income from the industrial property rental, he has no need for regular income replacement as this income would probably continue if he was ill. However, he should consider a critical illness policy in case he becomes seriously ill. For example, if he were to have an accident and suffer from paralysis, he might need cash urgently. Until he sells the yacht, he has an outstanding liability of £22,000 and he should also consider covering the debt within the critical illness policy.'

The advisers recommended that Simon should review his current mortgage arrangements as he is paying the standard variable rate when there are much better rates on offer. He should also start thinking seriously about his pension arrangements.

Finally, he was advised to steer clear of tying up his savings for a long period. Ms Gee said: 'Equity-based ISAs should be avoided for the time being as they would involve investing for at least five years, which would not be practical at the moment.'

Ms Gee recommended transferring the £20,000 on deposit with NatWest – which is earning an uncompetitive rate of interest – to Prudential's Egg account. Mr Frazer agreed: 'As Simon's income is seasonal, he should ensure that he has easy access to his cash while ensuring he maximizes the interest rates available.' He also suggested taking £3,000 from the total and investing it into a cash ISA as the rates are better than for many savings accounts and interest is earned free of tax.

LESSONS TO BE LEARNED

- Someone of Simon's age is five times more likely to suffer a critical illness than die. If Simon suffered a stroke or injured himself in an accident and could not work, his business would probably go bust, leaving him with no income – and possibly only a fraction of the £70,000 he invested in it. Everyone running their own business should therefore consider insuring their income (through critical illness or permanent health insurance).

- Simon is living frugally on a very low salary, but for far less effort than it takes him to earn his money he could boost his income by simply switching his mortgage and savings to a better rate.

Case Study 42

PROBLEM: NO INSURANCE TO PROTECT WIFE OR REPAY MORTGAGE

Vital Statistics
Name: Ian Leigh
Age: Thirty-one
Location: York
Occupation: Management consultant
Income: None while setting up business
Savings: £500 in Nationwide account
Investments: £4,000 in shares; £2,000 invested in a personal equity
    plan (PEP); £400 in investment trust
Mortgage: £60,000
Borrowings: None apart from mortgage
Insurance: None

Ian Leigh recently realized a dream by setting up his own management consultancy company, Bergander, which helps build employee commitment.

'I have found that a committed person can do 100 times what someone who is not committed can,' says Ian, who set up the limited company in York, sponsoring a roundabout in the city for £1,500 a year to help promote his new company.

Ian, who has a network of associates and visits companies to do his courses, charges around £700 a day for his services, with this amount varying according to the size of the company he is visiting and the length of the course.

In order to fund Bergander's start-up, Ian has paid himself nothing for the past two-and-a-half months. He and his wife of one-and-a-half years, Jo, are prepared to forego an income on his side for six months. The couple live just outside York and moved there when Jo landed a job as a clinical data systems manager. Ian said:

'Things will be OK for about four months, and very tight for another two.'

Ian gave up a £50,000-a-year job with pension scheme, car, bonus and private health insurance to start up his business.

Although he has his personal current account with Barclays, Ian decided to run his business account with NatWest. He said: 'Barclays did want to help, but they were hell-bent on discussing in detail my business rationale. NatWest didn't want to interfere too much and I felt more comfortable with that.'

He would like to investigate the possibility of setting up a savings account for the company in order to earn interest on any surplus cash it brings in.

Ian used £6,000-worth of shares and £6,000 held in a Sainsbury's Bank savings account to help him set up Bergander. He has just £500 left in savings in a Nationwide account.

Ian still holds shares worth £4,000. 'Unfortunately, I originally invested £6,000. I would like to wait for them to go back up, but I may need the money for the company. I tried to focus on small and medium-sized companies when I invested because I thought they might be takeover targets. A couple were taken over, but the rest flopped,' he said.

Ian has stopped using his current account as it has no money in it at the moment, and the business account is in credit.

Ian and Jo have been paying the mortgage out of the savings they have stockpiled to get them through the first few months of the company's life.

As far as pensions are concerned, Ian said, he has changed jobs a lot and cashed in the contributions he has made. He is still waiting for £1,500 to come through from his last pension scheme. He intends to put this money into the company.

Instead of a pension, Ian had been contributing £100 a month to a Virgin tracker PEP for twenty months until the end of 1998, and contributed £20 a month to the Templeton Emerging Markets Investment Trust savings scheme for the same period.

Ian and Jo have a twenty-year £60,000 repayment mortgage with the Yorkshire Building Society, which is still at a fixed rate with a £1,600 redemption penalty if they move it within the first five years.

The couple do not have any personal loans and make a point of paying off credit cards in full each month. The company, which also has no loans, can borrow money from NatWest if it needs to and owes Ian £10,000.

Ian has no life assurance, although Jo has life assurance linked to her company pension scheme.

He said: 'I don't have any income replacement or critical illness cover and I know this is a real issue. We haven't even got any cover for the mortgage, but my wife has been advised that if she is made redundant, she will be paid a sum that we could tread water on for a bit.'

WHAT THE EXPERTS SAY

The advisers to Cash Clinic immediately focused on Ian and Jo's lack of life assurance.

Vivienne Starkey, of independent financial advisers (IFAs) Haddock Porter Williams, said: 'I think the lack of mortgage protection is a real problem. Jo currently does have life cover as part of her company benefit package. However, if something were to happen to Ian, Jo would probably not be able to keep up the mortgage payments long term.'

Mrs Starkey suggested Ian consider paying £6 a month for an eighteen-year decreasing-term life policy from CGNU to cover the mortgage. The price rises to £13.50 a month if you add critical illness cover.

She said: 'If this is too much to pay at the moment, Ian could consider covering half the loan at a cost of £5 life-only cover with Zurich or £8 including critical illness cover with Legal & General. All of these premiums are guaranteed not to increase.'

Rebekah Kearey, of Roundhill Financial Management, suggested a mortgage protection policy from Scottish Provident for £11 a month, while David Gough, of Pen-Life Associates in York, recommended twenty-year level term assurance from Scottish Widows.

Ms Kearey said: 'Permanent health insurance pays an income in the event of long-term ill health or disability, and this should be considered for Ian. If such a calamity befell him in the early years of his new business, it would most likely destroy the business because in his line of work, business relationships and clients are established over months and years, but can be destroyed in minutes.'

Mr Gough also suggested that Jo organize unemployment cover as her contribution to the household is vital at the moment.

He said: 'This usually costs in the order of £3 per £100 and one or two insurance companies would be happy to accept the extra cover for household expenditure.'

On the investment side, Mrs Starkey said: 'As the major part of Ian's investments are in smaller companies and emerging markets, he would seem to have a fairly speculative attitude to risk. Once he starts to generate income again, I would recommend a rather more cautious approach to begin with.'

She suggested that Ian begin with a cash reserve and consider the £3,000 independent savings account (ISA) cash allowance for this year.

Mr Gough said: 'In most business ventures cash is really king. Ian seems to have a disproportionate amount of his capital invested in either a tracker PEP or straightforward shares.'

He suggested that Ian should think about selling his shares and the PEP and placing the cash on deposit. He said: 'Such long-term investments should only be entered into once the business future has been secured.'

Ms Kearey felt Ian was wise to try to obtain a return on surplus cash in the business while he is not using it. She said: 'There are a number of deposit accounts that are available for business. I suggest Ian considers Standard Life Bank.'

Mr Gough recommended business accounts with Scottish Widows and the Skipton Building Society.

Ms Kearey said: 'Pensions planning should form part of Ian's business plan. It is very easy to put off pension planning because there is always something that seems more pressing to pay for.'

As far as Ian and Jo's mortgage is concerned, the advisers said it might be better to switch to a new loan within the Yorkshire Building Society. Mrs Starkey said: 'They can then calculate how long it would take to recoup the £1,600 penalty.'

Ms Kearey said: 'One way to reduce the mortgage costs is to extend the term. I recommend this mortgage is extended to run until Ian is sixty.'

By remortgaging to a better rate they could save £3,900 over two years, added Ms Kearey, 'reducing monthly personal expenditure at a time when Ian and Jo most need to.'

LESSONS TO BE LEARNED

- It is vital to think about what would happen if you suffered a serious illness or died. How would your spouse pay the mortgage? What would you live off if you could not work? Ian is not alone in failing to address these issues.

- Like Simon in the previous Cash Clinic case study, Ian is struggling to earn an income while getting his business off the ground. That is why he needs to make every penny work from him including cash in the business, money tied up in shares and savings and his mortgage.

Case Study 43

PROBLEM: NO CONTINGENCY IF UNABLE TO EARN A LIVING

Vital Statistics

Name: Rupert and Margaret Bateson-Hill
Ages: Forty-one and thirty-nine
Location: London
Occupation: Postgraduate medical student and children's writer
Combined income: £500–£600 a month (Mrs Bateson-Hill); student
    loan (Mr Bateson-Hill)
Savings: An emergency fund
Pensions: None (Mrs Bateson-Hill); Scottish Widows personal
    pension plan and previous company scheme (Mr Bateson-Hill)
Investments: Unit trust for the children; 250 shares
Mortgage: £15,000 variable endowment mortgage with Abbey
    National
Borrowings: Student loan
Insurance: None

Margaret Bateson-Hill became a children's writer after the sharp
rise in value in her house – upon which she and her husband Rupert
pay just £90 a month each in mortgage payments – afforded her
enough financial security to start writing for a living. She has
written two children's books, one being *Lao Lao of Dragon Mountain*,
which is based on the unusual subject of the Chinese art of paper-
cutting, and in addition she runs drama clubs twice a week at the
local primary school and museums.

Margaret, who has three children, Charlotte, thirteen, Michael,
eleven and Joanna, six, earns between £500 and £600 a month
although she said: 'In an amazingly good month, I might make
£1,000.'

She shares a Midland Bank current account with her husband

from which they pay all the bills and the mortgage. Rupert is a postgraduate student in occupational therapy at Barts Hospital and receives a student grant.

The couple have a £15,000 variable-rate endowment mortgage with Abbey National and some savings held in an Abbey National account into which they pay all their income before transferring what is needed for bills into the Midland account. They also have a postal account with Abbey National which has a more substantial amount of savings kept for emergencies.

'We just chose the bank or building society that was local and my husband had been with the Midland for some time,' Margaret said. The children have Abbey National savings accounts and the couple have set up a Friends Provident ethical unit trust fund for the children. 'The money is for them to go to university or college,' Margaret said. 'When the stock-market rose and fell recently, I did phone Friends Provident about it and they put me in touch with a financial adviser who said it would be better to leave the fund alone.'

Margaret also holds 250 shares in a publishing company.

Rupert has a personal pension plan with Scottish Widows and a company scheme from when he worked for Mencap. Margaret said: 'I know that I should have one and I have reached a stage where I think I could afford to start putting money away each month.'

WHAT THE EXPERTS SAY

The advisers to Cash Clinic were concerned that the Bateson-Hills do not have insurance cover or adequate pension provision.

Bryn Walker, a partner at independent financial advisers (IFAs) Regency Financial Management in Walsall, said: 'Margaret is the major breadwinner at present. If she were unable to work due to incapacity or disability, the family finances would be stretched to breaking point.' He advised her to take out a permanent health insurance (PHI) policy.

Andrew Cowan, of IFAs Aitchison & Colegrave in Glasgow,

agreed: 'This is the most vulnerable area. As an example of costs, a plan which provided private income of £5,000 a year to age sixty for Margaret would cost £15.56 a month with Norwich Union.'

The couple should also consider term assurance, Mr Walker advised. 'Assuming they do not smoke, a joint-life term assurance policy which would pay out £100,000 on either person's death costs around £30 each month.'

Turning to pensions, Bhavesh Amlani, of IFAs Rickman Tooze, said: 'Margaret is understandably concerned about her lack of pension provision. The premium does not have to be high – some plans start at £30 a month – but I would suggest that the couple make use of some of the surplus funds held with Abbey National to make a one-off payment into a pension as the tax breaks on pension contributions are very attractive.'

Mr Cowan said: 'Due to her irregular earnings, however, it may be wiser for Margaret to start contributions at a lower level – say £50 a month – and make single contributions at the end of each tax year as top-ups once she knows what her overall earnings position is.'

The consultants felt the couple had so far been prudent to keep some money on standby for emergencies but both Margaret and Rupert should invest their maximum allowances (£3,000 a year each) into an individual savings account (ISA) where interest is tax-free.

The couple were praised for opening savings accounts for the children. Mr Walker suggested they consider putting the children's money into a pooled investment fund, such as a unit trust, if they do not mind tying it up for five years.

Mr Cowan added that the couple should look at their Friends Provident unit trust: 'As it has been held for over ten years, there may be a large potential capital gains tax liability. But with careful planning, some of the profits could be reinvested without any tax to pay.'

Although Margaret and Rupert's mortgage is small, Mr Walker said they should reconsider moving lender. 'Abbey National's variable rate is not competitive. However, they should only remortgage with a lender who will pay their valuation and legal fees.'

LESSONS TO BE LEARNED

- Even if your income and outgoings are very low – as is the case for Margaret and Rupert – you still need money to live off – particularly if you have three young children. Yet the couple has no contingency plans should Margaret – the main breadwinner – be unable to earn an income.

- It is not just high earners who need to worry about tax. Margaret might face a large capital gains tax bill on her unit trust investments, has not made use of tax relief on pension contributions and is not saving tax-free using an ISA.

Case Study 44

PROBLEM: SHOULD CRITICAL ILLNESS OR INCOME PROTECTION COVER BE TAKEN OUT?

Vital Statistics
Name: Alison Smyth
Age: Thirty-four
Location: North Walsham, Norfolk
Occupation: Charity manager
Income: £20,000 p.a.
Savings: £600 in bank account
Pension: Two personal pension plans
Investment: £50 Premium Bonds
Mortgage: £60,325 Nationwide repayment mortgage
Borrowings: £500 overdraft
Insurance: None

Alison Smyth, who recently returned to her childhood home in Norfolk and bought her first property, is manager of an educational charity, Elm Farm Research Centre, which aims to promote organic farming to farmers and the general public.

Alison, who had been working in the Home Counties for sixteen years, said: 'I was born here and eventually moved back last September after managing to persuade my employer to let me work over here.'

With her first-ever mortgage arranged, Alison, who is single and has no dependants, has left it late to get on to the property ladder.

She said: 'I am a bit of a late starter and realize that my first goal now should be to build up some short-term spending money. I had hoped to build an extension on the back of my house, so I wanted to save around £7,000 for that. I also realize that I need some longer-term savings as well.'

Alison, who earns £20,000 a year, has very little in the way of cash savings at the moment. Although she has around £600 saved in an Abbey National current account, and pays £100 a month into this, these savings are offset by a £500 overdraft on her NatWest Advantage Gold current account, which she expects to run to a £1,000 overdraft.

She said: 'I want to fit out an office at the end of my garden and my savings are earmarked for that. I have opened a Nationwide Flex Account to pay my mortgage and bills and I pay £700 a month into that.'

Her £60,000 twenty-five-year repayment mortgage from the Nationwide is currently on a one-year special fixed rate of interest, so her payments may rise at the end of this year.

As for longer-term investments, Alison has two personal pension plans. One is for her SERPs (state earnings-related pension scheme) rebates and is set up with Allied Dunbar. The other was set up with a previous employer through Albany Life, but Alison has taken it with her. She said: 'I currently put £140 a month into this after tax. My employer does not contribute, but I am unsure if it would be better to switch over to their stakeholder pension.'

Alison has been considering insurance. She said: 'I couldn't care less about life insurance: I do not have any dependants and my house can be sold if I die. However, I am worried about critical illness or income protection cover. I am not sure which of these would suit me best and I feel I ought to have some protection.'

WHAT THE EXPERTS SAY

Income protection cover should be Alison's priority, the advisers to Cash Clinic said.

Milena Atanassova, of the independent financial advisers (IFAs) Rickman Tooze, said: 'Alison should not have a problem getting a competitive quote for income protection insurance.'

James Little, of IFAs WMC Investment Managers, added: 'She needs to protect her income against being unable to work. Generally, the maximum benefit through an income protection scheme is about two-thirds of original income, and will be paid tax-free. She should also opt to have payments indexed to keep pace with inflation.' The minimum waiting period for a claim to be paid is usually four weeks. Leading providers include Canada Life and Friends Provident.

Ms Atanassova recommended that Alison consider permanent health insurance, which would pay out if she had an accident or if illness forced her to stop working as well.

She said: 'To provide £1,500 a month of cover, the cost would be £51.31 a month through Royal & Sun Alliance. The cover would kick in after thirteen weeks and the plan runs to age sixty.'

John Owen, of IFAs Willis Owen in Nottingham, also said felt that income protection should be a priority. He said: 'If necessary, she should reduce her pension contributions to finance this priority. The recommended contract is from Scottish Provident and the premium is £46.65 a month.'

The alternative is critical illness cover, which pays out a lump sum instead of a monthly income. Ms Atanassova recommended

Scottish Mutual Assurance Pegasus cover which provides just under £150,000 of cover for £30 a month.

In the meantime, Alison needs to generate savings and pay off her overdraft. One way to reduce the cost of her debts would be to use a flexible 'current account' mortgage. She is tied into her present mortgage until the end of the year, but will be free to switch once her early redemption penalty period is finished.

Ms Atanassova said: 'By offsetting savings against borrowings, credit balances earn the equivalent of the mortgage rate, which is generally up to one percentage point higher than the best savings rates. As interest is not actually earned – it is saved – no tax is paid on the interest.'

Alison could also use a flexible mortgage to finance the extension on her house and the new office space. Mr Owen suggested she take out a loan to cover these expenses now, rather than pay high overdraft charges, and switch it over to a flexible mortgage along with her home loan at the end of the year. Mr Owen recommended flexible mortgages from Virgin or Intelligent Finance, the Internet arm of the Halifax, while Mr Little and Miss Atanassova recommended the Woolwich Open Plan mortgage.

Ms Atanassova said: 'The main advantage is the ease with which Alison can draw down the equity in her home to pay for her extension at a future date.'

In the meantime, Alison should stop paying unnecessary overdraft charges by repaying her overdraft with her savings. Mr Little said: 'She should use the funds in her Abbey National account to clear the overdraft on her NatWest account. She should then only go overdrawn when she is actually forced to. I would also question whether her NatWest account is the best for her. Her Abbey National account would be cheaper to be overdrawn on and has no monthly fee.'

For regular short-term savings, Alison should consider a mini cash individual savings account (ISA), the advisers said. She can save £3,000 each tax year into one of these. Mr Little recommended the cash ISA from Smile. Although Alison should increase her pension contributions as and when she can afford to do so, the

advisers agreed that she should avoid stock-market-related investments for the time being.

LESSONS TO BE LEARNED

- At Alison's age – and taking into account the risks of losing her
  job as well as suffering from ill health – income protection
  insurance and/or permanent health insurance are the most
  suitable policies as she needs to keep paying her mortgage.

- Single, childless people do not have to go to the expense of
  buying life cover to ensure their dependants are protected (as
  they have none), but they are vulnerable in other ways. They do
  not have a partner to rely on should they suffer a drop in income
  or be unable to work due to ill health. So they need to buy
  insurance to protect themselves.

8 Coping with Change

The earlier chapters in this book have looked at ways of preparing your finances for the future. However, the reality is that most of us do not make major financial decisions because we should or we want to – we make them because circumstances force us to.

It is only when a major upheaval occurs – marriage, divorce, children, redundancy, a new job, early retirement or deciding to go it alone and start a business – that we are forced reassess our finances. Waiting for events to rule your decisions means that it is often too late to prepare. There is no point in taking out redundancy insurance after you have lost your job, saving to start a family when the baby has already been born, or buying critical illness cover when you are terminally ill.

So what can you do if your finances are not prepared?

The most important thing is to make sure that you adapt to your changing circumstances. In Cash Clinic Case Study 52 in this chapter Mary Gelder, who has been made redundant, has been advised to look at her spending and outgoings now she is living on a much-reduced income. In Case Study 46, would-be first-time buyer Donella Gayle was advised to remain living with her mother if she wanted to be in a position to afford to buy in London. And in Case Study 48, Mike and Paula Redmond, who have just had triplets, need to look at life insurance, income protection and critical illness cover now they have such a growing family.

They are all cutting their coats according to their cloth.

LEAVING HOME

The average age of first-time buyers is now over thirty-four as a result of soaring house prices in recent years. It means that more

and more young people are having to remain in rented accommodation – or at home – for longer. In fact, if they are ever to afford to
save up a deposit to buy a property many – like Donella Gayle in
Cash Clinic Case Study 46 in this chapter – are advised to stay at
home where overheads are low, so that they can start to save.

The Cash Clinic advisers warn Donella that it is not just mortgage
repayments – or rent – that she needs to factor into her budget. For
anyone leaving home the advice is:

• Work out what your total outgoings will be, including council
  tax, rent/mortgage, insurance, gas, electricity, telephone bills,
  food and laundry as well as travel and entertainment.

• Set aside this much cash each month before leaving home so that
  you get used to paying out such a large chunk of your income
  for bills.

• If you find you cannot afford this much, reassess your plans –
  move to a cheaper property or wait until you have more savings
  before leaving home.

As renting is now the first step for most of those leaving home,
they need to be aware of the financial pitfalls of renting a property
or sharing a flat.

Make sure you have a tenancy agreement – a legally binding
document with the landlord which you should both sign. That way
there should be fewer disagreements. It should set out:

• The amount of rent and to whom it is payable

• The length/term of tenancy

• When rent is payable

• What the rent includes/excludes

• The tenant's rights and responsibilities (for example, no pets
  allowed)

• The amount of the deposit

- Notice periods to terminate the agreement

- Bills for which the tenant is responsible

Deposits are one of the largest areas of dispute. Many landlords keep the deposit at the end of the tenancy to cover repairs and cleaning even though any deterioration is due to normal wear and tear. Make sure an inventory is taken before the tenancy begins and also at the end, to avoid disputes.

Another problem area is flat-sharing. When one sharer leaves, it is up to the others to find another tenant and in the meantime cover the extra rent. There can also be numerous disputes about who owes what proportion of the bills (the telephone, for example). To protect your pocket, make sure these day-to-day issues are covered in a written agreement.

STUDENT LIFE

The image of students spending their grants in the union bar while missing lectures has now been replaced with one of poverty, student debts and a gruelling schedule of studying part-time while keeping down a job to finance their way through university.

The introduction of tuition fees and the lack of grants mean that many students leave with debts in excess of £10,000. Borrowing is a fact of student life. The National Union of Students has calculated that in London the average student has a £4,928 shortfall in income even after taking out a student loan. However, there are ways to spread the costs and make money go further:

Student loans
Borrow as much as you can using student loans as the rate of interest is very low (just 2.3 per cent until September 2002) and payments can be spread over a number of years. The amount that can be borrowed depends on where you study, whether you live at home or not and, depending on how old you are, your parents', spouse's or co-habiting partner's income. Those living away from

home and studying in London can in the 2002/2003 academic year, borrow up to £4,815 for a full year and £4,175 in the final year. Outside London, these amounts drop to £3,905 and £3,390. Those living at home can borrow up to £3,090 and £2,700 in the 2002/2003 academic year. A quarter of the loan is means-tested and the full amount borrowed is repayable. However, it is only repayable when you earn more than £10,000 a year and then it is repayable at 9 per cent on earnings above this threshold.

Student bank accounts
Banks offer preferential rates – fee- and interest-free overdrafts and loans at preferential rates – which can continue for up to two years after leaving university if you switch from a student to a graduate account. So borrow as much as you can at these preferential rates. Do not be seduced by free gifts. Check the interest rates, charges, unauthorized overdraft penalties (these are best avoided) and availability of branches.

GIVING UP WORK TO RAISE CHILDREN

Starting a family or expanding your existing one is probably the biggest investment you will ever make – it now costs over £110,000 to raise a child to the age of eighteen, according to a recent survey by Legal & General. No wonder the survey found that one-third of people felt unprepared for parenthood. However, it is not just the huge life-style change you need to prepare for but the financial commitment that the patter of tiny feet brings. This is partly why more of us are leaving starting a family until later in life when we are more financially secure.

If you possibly can, save as much as you can afford before you start your family.

- Choose tax-free savings schemes such as independent savings accounts (ISAs) to save before the birth and afterwards. Many parents invest child benefit (£15.75 for the eldest child and £10.55

for each subsequent child in the 2002/2003 tax year) in savings schemes such as friendly society children's bonds for their children's future.

- Your biggest monthly expense is probably the mortgage, so it is worth looking at: remortgaging to a cheaper rate; switching to a flexible loan that allows you to take repayment holidays (for example, during maternity leave) provided you do not exceed an agreed borrowing limit; or extending the term of the mortgage to cut the monthly bills.

- Life insurance is vital when you have dependants and not just for the father. While a quarter of men have life cover through work, only 4 per cent of women do. Yet it can cost over £378 a week to replace a mother with home helps and nannies. Shop around for the best rates for term assurance (which can be taken out until the children reach eighteen).

- Make a will, particularly if you are not married.

- Invest as much as you can in your pension while you are still working, to make up for losses during maternity/paternity leave. A break in a woman's career can cost her up to £52,000 in her pension. Experts urge women with personal pensions to restart their payments as soon as possible, even if they invest a much smaller amount than before.

SELF-EMPLOYMENT

Many of us dream of going it alone, being our own boss, working hours that suit us, not having to take orders and yet earning a decent wage. The reality, however, is usually long hours, more responsibility, stress and worry and often struggling to earn a living.

Self-employment also involves more paperwork (tax and VAT as well as PAYE if you employ staff) and uncertainty.

To cope with this change, particularly if you have previously been in secure employment:

- Prepare a proper business plan. Nearly half of all businesses fail to reach their second birthday mainly because there was no plan or the business plan was not realistic or well thought through.

- Make sure you have enough to keep you afloat. There are often delays in getting paid and you will have to spend money to start up and keep you going until you start to earn an income.

- Remember that your income will fluctuate. Can your finances cope? Consider flexible mortgages that enable you to vary your monthly payments or setting up a savings account with enough to pay your bills for the first few months.

- Cut back on your outgoings so your finances will not be stretched when you start self-employment. Pay off debts and remortgage to keep your monthly outgoings down.

- When you are self-employed, you can no longer rely on an employer to provide you with a pension and life insurance, so you will have to arrange this for yourself – do not be tempted to assume that your business is your pension.

- Self-employment also means you are responsible for your own taxes (there is no longer a payroll department sorting out your PAYE). Many self-employed people fall into the trap of living hand to mouth and leaving nothing aside to pay their tax bill.

- You do not pay tax on everything you earn – only your profits, which is your income minus any allowable expenses such as premises (including part of the cost of running your home if you work from home), telephones, staff, transport, etc. Work out roughly what profit you earn (for, example 60 per cent of income) and then set aside roughly a quarter, if you are likely to be a basic rate taxpayer to cover tax and national insurance.

- The self-employed pay two types of national insurance, one flat rate – Class 2 which for the 2002/2003 tax year was £2 a week for those earning more than £4,025 a year – and Class 4-based, which is 7 per cent of profits between £4,615 and £30,420.

• It is important that you inform the Inland Revenue that you have become self-employed.

• Think about how you would cope if you became too ill to work. You will no longer have an employer to pay you sick pay. Consider taking out accident and sickness insurance or income protection insurance to ensure that you – and your business – could keep afloat.

• If your turnover (that is sales, not profit) exceeds – or is likely to exceed – the VAT threshold of £54,000 for the 2001/2002 tax year, you must register for VAT and charge it on all goods and services provided (unless they are exempt).

• Make sure you are genuinely self-employed. If you work for one main company and work from their premises, using their equipment and are paid by the hour, day or week instead of per job, you may have to be taxed as an employee even if you are not one. Those in the building trade have special rules under the Construction Industry Scheme to prove they are not employees, and for those using service companies or partnerships there are guidelines under IR35 (the Inland Revenue helpline for IR35 matters is 0845 303 3535).

• Have a fallback position – another means of earning a living or a safety-net of savings – just in case your business fails.

REDUNDANCY

Most of those opting to take redundancy – rather than being forced to – manage to leave with a reasonable pay-off. However large it may seem at the time, remember you may have to make it last a long time, so it needs to be managed carefully.

Tax

The first £30,000 of any redundancy pay-off is tax-free. However, sums over that amount are taxable – so factor this into any calculations.

Pensions

When you leave employment, you will also cease to have contributions paid into any company pension scheme. However, you may be able to pay in a lump sum out of your redundancy money to boost your pension and cut any tax liability. This should only be considered if you could live without this money until you retire.

Mortgages

Tell your lender as soon as you lose your job – that way you may be able to agree to restructure your repayments (but check if there are any financial penalties). Even if you have mortgage payment protection insurance to cover monthly home-loan bills in the event of sickness or redundancy, this will only be a short-term solution – the payouts often only last for twelve months.

Current account

If you have an overdraft, this can be withdrawn at any time. If your bank notices that no money is coming in, it could withdraw the facility. Talk to your bank in advance to agree payment terms. It may be tempting to dip into an unauthorized overdraft but remember that the penalties are steep and will plunge you further into debt.

Benefits

Most home buyers no longer qualify for help from the state in making their monthly mortgage repayments for the first nine months after losing their jobs. In addition, any redundancy money you have received will be assessed in calculating any means-tested benefits – so you could have little to live off.

Budgeting

Cut your coat according to your cloth – do not blow the redundancy cheque in the hope that you will get another job tomorrow. Assume the worst.

EARLY RETIREMENT

An estimated 13 million of the 39 million adults of working age are facing poverty in retirement according to recent research, so if your vision of retirement is a life of luxury, lazy days spent in the sun in your second home in Spain, you may have to think again. Three in every four people who retire early are forced by financial pressure to seek a job again, according to a survey by Mintel.

Increasing numbers of older workers never get to the stage where they can fund their pension to the maximum before retiring as they are forced out of the workforce well before then. Of the 9.3 million people aged between fifty and sixty-four in the UK today, some 3.7 million are not in work and this is set to rise to nearer 4 million over the next decade, It means that the numbers of inactive people aged between fifty and sixty-four are double the unemployment numbers for the entire country.

The financial implications of being put on the scrap-heap at fifty are vast, covering everything from the ability to borrow to mortgages and pensions.

Mortgages and debts

While employers may feel that the over-fifties have fewer financial commitments as their children have grown up and they are expected to have repaid their mortgage, this is not so true today.

The average age of first-time buyers has risen to thirty-one in the past few years, so today's home buyers will not repay their mortgages until they are in their mid to late fifties and one in seven home buyers is over age fifty, according to the Halifax. So the first priority should be to repay your mortgage if you can afford to (unless you have an endowment maturing shortly to cover the mortgage). Other debts should also be repaid as they are a drain on your income and usually cost far more than you could earn by keeping the same amount in a savings account.

Pensions

Only a third of those being asked to take early retirement receive their full accrued pension from their employer's pension scheme according to the National Association of Pension funds. In addition, as many employer pensions are based on the number of years of service, those taking early retirement suffer again as they have fewer contributions or years of service to count towards their final pension. While there is less time to build up a pension, it has to last even longer. A male retiring at fifty will live for over thirty years on average life expectancy and a female just under thirty-five years. They also need to protect their pension against inflation. Over twenty years with an average 2.5 per cent inflation rate, the buying power of £1,000 would reduce to £610. With 5 per cent inflation, that buying power drops to £377.

Those forced into early retirement have three main options:

- To take their pension from age fifty onwards – this will result in a lower pension because it will have to be paid for a longer period.

- To defer their pension until the state retirement age. The only drawback is what to live off in the meantime.

- To opt for income drawdown if they have a personal pension, instead of buying an annuity. The pension is then invested and they can take an income (which they can vary) before buying an annuity at age seventy-five.

Case Study 45

PROBLEM: SAVING UP TO BUY A FIRST HOME

Vital Statistics

Name: James Hodgson
Age: Twenty-four
Location: Torquay
Occupation: Sainsbury's branch assistant manager
Income: £17,600 p.a.
Savings: £300 in bank account
Pension: Company pension scheme
Mortgage: None
Investments: £5,800 in stock-market investments; £50 a month to
    Sainsbury's Save As You Earn scheme
Borrowings: £1,000 student account overdraft; £6,500 interest-free
    Citroën car loan
Insurance: None

James Hodgson has the usual student debts to overcome, but he has already made a head-start on investing for the future. For the past six months he has been working as an assistant personnel manager at Sainsbury's in Torquay, where he moved from Yorkshire with his parents in 1983. He earns £17,600 a year.

James said: 'Before that I did a trainee management scheme for about a year after I graduated in three-dimensional design from Plymouth University in Exeter.'

He now lives with his girlfriend, Shelley, twenty-three, in a flat they rent for £240 a month in Torquay. His parents still live nearby.

He is still £1,000 overdrawn on his Lloyds TSB graduate account, which used to be a student account. He said: 'There is no interest charged on that, so it is not worth repaying it until December when they start charging interest. I will either start paying interest then or take out a low-interest graduate loan to repay it when the time comes.'

He also has a £6,500 interest-free car loan from Citroën, which costs £185 a month for three years. It has two years more to run. On top of this there is £3,200 of student loans which he has not yet started repaying.

James said: 'So far, I have missed the earnings threshold each year when the chance to defer comes up in March. I do not know yet if I can defer this year, but I do know it will cost about £50 a month when I have to start paying it back. I would rather put it off for another year and start putting £50 a month somewhere else before having to pay back the loan. If this is the case, I would want to invest £50 a month either in an individual savings account (ISA) or by topping up my pension contributions.'

On the borrowings front, James does not have any credit cards and pays for everything with his Switch card or cash. However, he only has £300 in his Alliance & Leicester savings account.

His investments are more substantial, with more than £5,800 in stock-market investments, including 250 Alliance & Leicester shares and 400 Sainsbury's shares, and over £3,000 in a Virgin Tracker Growth personal equity plan (PEP). He also contributes £50 every four weeks to the Sainsbury's Save As You Earn scheme, giving him the option to buy shares in three years' time at a discounted price: 'If you stay in the scheme for three years, they pay a bonus as well.'

James has been contributing to the Sainsbury's company pension scheme for almost two years. He contributes 4.25 per cent of his earnings and Sainsbury's pays in another 3.25 per cent.

James and Shelley, who earns £15,000 a year, are thinking of buying a house or flat together as an investment. James does not have any life assurance or critical illness cover.

WHAT THE EXPERTS SAY

James has made a good start with his investments but needs to focus more on building up his cash savings, the advisers to Cash Clinic said.

Milena Atanassova, of independent financial advisers (IFAs) Rickman Tooze, said: 'As a starting-point, James should transfer his £300 savings from the Alliance & Leicester account to one with a better rate of interest.'

Cash savings are the most appropriate way to build up a deposit for a property, she said: 'Generally he will be best advised to avoid stock-market investments for this purpose. The underlying volatility, or the risk that prices may fall, means that, if he can only invest over just a few years, he may end up with less than the amount invested.'

Harris Frazer, of IFAs Assured Benefit Consultants, said: 'While Mr Hodgson's immediate objective is to go for a higher-risk investment, he should remember that this should be considered as a medium- to long-term investment over a minimum of three to five years. Is this the right strategy if he is looking to purchase a property, repay his graduate overdraft in six months and begin repayments on his student loan?'

Ms Atanassova advised that James should initially pay £50 a month into a savings account and then use the money to repay his overdraft. He should aim to repay his debts as quickly as possible before attempting to get a mortgage.

She said: 'When calculating the maximum amount of mortgage that he can afford, the unpaid loans currently in place will be taken into account.'

However, Tom McPhail, of IFAs Torquil Clark, said: 'James is not liable to pay interest on his borrowings for now, so it makes sense to save any surplus income. If there is spare cash above the £50 a month he wants to save in the stock-market, he should save it until it is needed, either to repay debts or to use as a deposit for the property purchase.'

Looking at James's investments, Ms Atanassova urged him to move away from direct investment as this is too risky. Instead, he could go for a pooled fund such as a unit or investment trust which will give him access to a wider range of companies for his money and wrap this in an ISA to shield his investments from tax.

Mr McPhail encouraged James in his appetite for risk, but within a pooled fund so that risks can be diminished by diversification. He said: 'Given that he is relatively young, this is a good idea, provided he is happy to accept that high risk can mean big losses as well as big gains.'

LESSONS TO BE LEARNED

- Get your priorities right. James wants to buy a property and that means saving up a deposit. He can afford to forget long-term and stock-market-based investments until he achieves that goal.

- Everyone should make the most of tax-free schemes such as ISAs. Why pay tax when you don't need to?

- James may be happy taking an element of risk with his investments. However, investing in individual shares is not ideal if your main priorities are safe cash savings.

Case Study 46

PROBLEM: NOT EARNING ENOUGH TO LEAVE HOME AND BUY A FIRST HOME

Vital Statistics
Name: Donella Gayle
Age: Nineteen
Location: London

Occupation: Public relations assistant
Savings: £1,400 in bank accounts
Pension: None
Investments: None
Mortgage: None
Borrowings: £400 on HSBC credit card
Insurance: None

Donella Gayle landed her first proper job, as an assistant in a public relations consultancy, after finishing her A levels, and now wants to leave home.

She said: 'I am living at home with my mum and my two foster-brothers in New Barnet, north London, at the moment. I want to move into a place of my own, but I know I can only afford to rent a place for the time being. I am looking but haven't found anywhere to live yet. I want to stay in the same area and I want to live on my own.'

Although the idea of buying her own home has crossed Donella's mind, she does not think she is old enough yet to be able to get a mortgage. She said: 'I want to get a good mortgage, so I still need to save up for a sizeable deposit. Before I can do that, though, I want to buy a new car, so I am also car-hunting at the moment.'

She wants to trade in her old car for a newer one. She said: 'I have got some savings and I want to see if I can get a loan to help with the rest.'

Although Donella has the potential to earn a high salary in her chosen career, she is on a low income at present. She said: 'I have been told there is the chance to earn a lot more, but I have no idea when that might be.'

She keeps her HSBC current account in credit, although there is not much surplus at the end of the month. She has £300 saved in her Abbey National Instant Access savings account and there is another £100 in a NatWest savings account.

Donella said: 'I don't really have enough to save each month, but I do save if I can.' The bulk of her savings – £1,000 – is kept in a savings account controlled by her mother. 'That will not be enough to buy a new car, so I am looking to borrow around £2,000 to help.'

Like most people aged nineteen, she has yet to start a pension or make any investments and does not have life assurance.

She said: 'My priority at the moment is to buy a new car and amass as much cash as possible to put down a deposit on a flat.'

Her only debt is a balance of £400 on her HSBC MasterCard. She said: 'I pay off £70 a month but I do keep using my card regularly.'

WHAT THE EXPERTS SAY

Donella should consider staying at home for a while longer before taking on the rent of a flat on her own, the advisers to Cash Clinic said.

Wai Man Cheung, of independent financial advisers (IFAs) WMC Investment Managers in Dorset, said: 'One of her priorities is to build up her cash position and head towards a decent deposit to buy a flat.

'Even in cheaper parts of London, a decent flat won't leave any change from £100,000 and most lenders want a 5 per cent deposit. So that's £5,000 needed before legal and other bills raise their head. If she really wants to rent, she should be renting for at least two months before embarking on savings. Even renting can throw surprises at you.'

Colin Jackson, of IFAs Baronworth, said: 'Donella is probably being a little over-ambitious in wanting to move into a rented flat, borrow money to buy a new car and save for a deposit for a new home – all on a fairly low income and about £1,400 in savings.

'I suggest she continues to live at home and each month pay into a savings account an amount equivalent to her future mortgage repayment and other outgoings once she owns her own property – council tax, gas, electricity and insurance, for example. This will give her some idea as to whether she can afford to buy a property. Second, it will help her build up some savings. Even if she applies for a 100 per cent mortgage, she will still need some money behind her to cover legal fees and unforeseen expenses.'

Donella will also have to pay stamp duty when she buys a property – starting at 1 per cent on a property valued £60,000 and above.

Most lenders will be happy to lend to her, but not much more than three to three-and-a-half times her salary.

On obtaining a loan to buy a new car, Mr Jackson said Donella should ask the car dealer first if it can arrange an interest-free or low-interest loan. If not, she needs to delve through the mass of products on the market. Mr Cheung said: 'The best place to look for a loan is not at your local bank branch. The Internet will save time and money. Moneyfacts.co.uk will point her to the best loans with the lowest interest rates. The Internet Banks, such as Cahoot, Egg or Smile, offer good deals. She should decide how quickly she can pay the loan off. The sooner, the less interest in total she will pay.'

The advisers said Donella should consider repaying her credit card with some of her savings now. Kerry Nelson, of IFAs Deep Blue Financial, said: 'The interest she is paying is far higher than the interest she receives on her savings accounts.'

When she is able to afford to save on a regular basis, Donella should look for a savings account with a good interest rate as well, the advisers said.

Ms Nelson added: 'She already has two savings accounts with a total of £400. Both accounts are paying very little interest, however. I would therefore advise her to open a mini cash individual savings account (ISA) to make the most of higher rates. Even though Donella is a basic-rate taxpayer, she will benefit from receiving the interest paid gross – tax will not be deducted – and she can invest up to £3,000 each tax year.'

The advisers agreed you can never be too young to start a pension. However, Mr Jackson urged Donella to wait until she can really afford it.

LESSONS TO BE LEARNED

- You can't always have it all. Donella wants to rent a flat, save up to buy her first home and buy a new car – all with few savings and on a low salary. Like many of those leaving home, she will have to make a sacrifice, which could mean staying at home for longer in order to build up a deposit to buy a flat.

- Buying a home is expensive – not just in terms of mortgage bills. Donella has wisely been advised to pay the equivalent of the costs of running a home – including bills and council tax – into an account each month to see if she could really afford to buy.

Case Study 47

PROBLEM: DEALING WITH STUDENT DEBTS

Vital Statistics
Name: Helen Feane
Age: Twenty-two
Location: Manchester
Occupation: Student
Income: £60 a week allowance in term-time
Savings: None
Pension: None
Investments: None
Mortgage: None
Borrowings: £1,500 overdraft; around £6,000 in student loans
Insurance: None

Helen Feane, a student in Manchester about to start her final year reading Neuroscience with French, is luckier than most in that her parents can afford to offer her some financial assistance at university.

'I've been well off compared with other people: lots of my friends spend forty hours a week working while studying for their degree because they can't manage otherwise,' she said. 'I started my degree before students became liable for tuition fees and my parents have helped me a lot.'

Helen's parents pay her rent and give her living expenses of £60 a week during term-time. However, she will pay £60 a week in rent including bills in a shared flat – higher than for many students because she had to leave finding somewhere to the last minute as she spent the last academic year abroad, in France.

So even with the help from her parents, Helen has not found being a student easy. She has spent up to her overdraft limit and has gone over it on several occasions.

She admitted: 'I find budgeting difficult. My parents give me the money at the beginning of the term, so I have got plenty, and then I don't budget and find I have very little towards the end of the term. This year, my parents have made out a monthly standing order to my account, and I hope that will help me manage better.'

Helen is considering going into research when she finishes her degree at the end of next year and has been to an adviser at the Careers Research and Advisory Centre in Manchester, which also provides students with financial advice. She said: 'You can get grants to do a PhD but I wouldn't do one if I didn't get a grant.'

She has a student e-bank account with Lloyds TSB that allows her a fees-free £1,500 overdraft. Helen does not have any other bank or building society accounts.

She said: 'I use a Visa Delta debit card. I used to have a Switch card with a Halifax account but I switched because Lloyds TSB offered a higher overdraft and I thought the Visa Delta card would be easier to use abroad. I don't want to get into debt on a credit card.'

She has taken three student loans and plans to take a fourth in her final year. These were for around £1,500 in her first and second years, £1,800 in her third, and will be for another £1,300 or so in her final year.

Helen does not know how she will go about paying off her student debts after she graduates next year, although she expects to be at least £8,000 in debt by the time she finishes. She said: 'I have no plan of action on how to tackle that.'

WHAT THE EXPERTS SAY

Although Helen's debts are something she will have to think about carefully when she graduates, the advisers to Cash Clinic told her not to worry.

Milena Atanassova, of independent financial advisers (IFAs) Rickman Tooze, said: 'According to the National Union of Students, because of the erosion of grants and the introduction of tuition fees, students are expected to have debts to the tune of £10,000 or more by the time they finish their degree courses.'

She added: '£8,000 is a big financial millstone with which to start a career, though, and psychologically it may seem better to get rid of it as soon as possible. However, before a final decision is made, both sides of the coin need to be examined carefully – does it really make financial sense to pay off the loans as a priority?'

Richard Ogdon, a financial adviser from the Cambridge branch of the Careers Research and Advisory Centre, pointed out that the interest rate on student loans remains low as it is linked to inflation as measured by the Retail Prices Index (RPI). He said: 'Helen should take out the maximum amount of student loan for next year since student loans are the most advantageous form of debt available to her: the interest rate is low and you only have to make payments when you are earning in a regular job, and then only in stages over quite a long period of time.'

This means that if Helen does choose to go into research and complete a PhD after she graduates, she will not even have to think about her student loans.

Ms Atanassova said: 'Helen is best advised to start building up an emergency savings account first before she pays off her student loan so that she will have something to fall back on if she finds herself out of work or in need of emergency cash.'

It would make sense to set up a savings account now and have her parents pay her allowance into this. She could then transfer it into her current account on a weekly or fortnightly basis to help herself budget better.

Ms Atanassova added that a competitive savings account would pay a far higher rate of interest than the interest charged on her student loan.

As far as her student overdraft is concerned, Helen will be able to convert it into a graduate overdraft at the end of next year. Janine Starks, of IFAs Chase de Vere, said: 'The Lloyds TSB e-bank current account overdraft remains interest-free until the end of her degree and then Lloyds TSB offers an interest-free overdraft of £2,000 for up to two years after she has completed her degree.'

Ms Starks also pointed out that if Helen decides to get a job after graduation, she can take advantage of a graduate loan at favourable rates of interest if she is in need of money after graduation.

Mr Ogdon suggested Helen consider replacing her overdraft with an unsecured personal loan after graduation. He said: 'Many banks are willing to extend such loans to people in regular employment. The advantage of it compared to an overdraft is that it can be repaid over a longer period of time – overdrafts are basically short-term loans that the bank can recall at a moment's notice – and the rate should be no more expensive.'

Mr Ogdon said that in order to manage her finances better now, Helen must try hard not to go over her overdraft limit again, 'Otherwise the bank will start charging her penalties for sending letters and also higher interest rates.'

Ms Starks praised Helen for avoiding credit cards. She suggested she also save money by paying utility bills by direct debit, taking full advantage of all student discounts available and using supermarket loyalty cards.

LESSONS TO BE LEARNED

- The less money you have, the harder you have to work at making it go further. Helen has been advised to keep money in a savings account before switching it to her current account when she needs it and to make the most of discounts available as a student and for paying bills by direct debit. Although each measure may save only a few pounds, the savings mount up quickly.

- Always compare the interest charged on debts with the interest you are earning on savings. In most cases it pays to use savings to repay debts as savings rates are usually far lower. For students such as Helen, however, special loan deals mean that it pays to borrow as much as possible.

Case Study 48

PROBLEM: COPING WITH THE FINANCIAL COST OF HAVING TRIPLETS

Vital Statistics

Names: Mike and Paula Redmond

Age: Thirty-seven and thirty-eight

Location: Liverpool

Occupation: Both are general practitioners

Combined income: £74,000 net p.a. (however, Paula will earn less in future)

Savings: £10,300 plus a TESSA

Pension: Both members of NHS scheme; Paula pays into an AVC while Mike pays into a personal pension

Investments: Several life insurance company investment plans; a PEP each; £5,000 in unit trusts; a children's bond for their eldest daughter; endowment for £50,000

Mortgage: £92,000 repayment mortgage
Borrowings: None
Insurance: Joint life policy plus life insurance tied into Mike's
    personal pension

Mike and Paula Redmond's lives have been turned upside down
after the birth of triplets: two girls, Elise and Francesca, and a boy,
Nicholas.

They have also just moved house and have drained most of their
savings. Paula is on maternity leave on full pay but this is due to
run out soon and she has not yet decided if she will go back to
work.

'I want to do much less than I was doing before,' she said and
estimates she will need to find £1,200 a month to pay for childcare
if she does go back to work. She is paying a live-in maternity nurse
£450 a week to help with the babies.

Before Paula had the babies, the couple, who also have a seven-
year-old daughter, Claire, had about £50,000 in a deposit account
and £7,800 in a tax-exempt special savings account (TESSA) with
the Hinckley & Rugby, which matured right on time for the birth in
December.

After moving house in Liverpool, where both are general practitioners with local medical practices, there is now about £10,000 left
in a Midland Bank savings account, £200 in the expenses account
they set up with the Midland for the move, and £100 invested in
Paula's roll-over TESSA.

Mike, who earns about £42,000 a year after tax, holds a TESSA
with the Lambeth Building Society which is due to mature next
year, but he has not invested the full amount allowed.

Paula, who was earning about £32,000 a year after tax, said: 'We
have tried to take advantage of tax-free savings; because we are
both 40 per cent taxpayers, it makes sense.'

Both took out a personal equity plan (PEP) a few years ago and
also invested £5,000 in a Schroder's emerging markets unit trust in
1995. 'Unfortunately that hasn't done very well and I think it is
worth about £4,800 now,' said Paula.

When Claire was one year old, her parents started a Child Bond for her with Tunbridge Wells; they put in £225 a year.

Both Mike and Paula pay 7 per cent of their earnings into the National Health Service pension scheme, which they joined when they qualified as doctors in 1984.

Paula also pays £75 a month into a free-standing additional voluntary contributions (AVC) plan. Mike pays the full 20 per cent of his salary that he is allowed into a personal pension plan with Allied Dunbar which he has held for three years, which means he loses the tax benefit on his NHS pension scheme.

Mike is able to pay into both his NHS scheme and a personal pension because of a special provision for doctors and dentists made by the Inland Revenue which takes account of the fact that they often have a combination of private and NHS income every year.

Paula said: 'The reason he started the personal pension was because we were hoping to retire at the age of fifty-five. But now that the triplets are here, everything is different. They'll probably still be at school when we are fifty-five.'

The couple also have a number of savings accounts allied to life assurance policies. 'They leap on you when you're just out of medical school,' Paula said. One of these, for example, is a family assurance plan, which costs £27 a month.

On the borrowing side, their major debt is their £92,000 repayment mortgage with the Portman Building Society, which has twenty-two years to run. About £16,000 of this is at a fixed rate and the balance at the building society's variable rate.

Two previous mortgages, one for £30,000 and one for £50,000, were backed by endowments from Standard Life and Scottish Amicable, which the couple have held on to. Mike also has life assurance attached to his Allied Dunbar pension that accounts for £22 a month of the premiums. He pays a further £32 a month for a joint life policy, also with Allied Dunbar.

Paula said: 'I think I should have more life assurance in case something happens to me and Mike is left with four children.'

The couple's two credit cards, Midland MasterCard and a Barclaycard, are repaid every month.

WHAT THE EXPERTS SAY

Reducing the couple's monthly outgoings now that Paula is likely either to give up or take on a reduced role at her surgery was the first target for the advisers to Cash Clinic.

Vivienne Starkey, of independent financial advisers (IFAs) Haddock Porter Williams, managed to negotiate a better mortgage offer from the Portman, which would immediately reduce outgoings by £140 a month.

Mrs Starkey said: 'The Portman is willing to consolidate the two mortgage accounts and waive the three months' interest penalty on the £76,000. For a fee of £50, they would offer Paula and Mike a one percentage point discount to the standard variable rate for two years.'

Andy Harris, of IFAs Maddison Monetary Management, also suggested switching to an interest-only mortgage which could reduce monthly outgoings by £100 a month. He said: 'The couple have endowments in place to repay £50,000 of the mortgage a lot sooner than they are currently due to do. The remainder could be cleared from the tax-free lump sum from Mike's pension.'

On the pensions front, IFA Philip Harper urged Mike to spread his pension payments around other providers. 'I might suggest that contributing 20 per cent of salary is rather too high to one company. Allied Dunbar has certainly experienced periods of poor investment performance and also, to be fair, other periods of above-average results.'

He suggested Mike direct future additional payments to products by CGNU Life, Scottish Equitable or Standard Life. 'These all have well-designed products which offer excellent scope for flexibility of premium payments, are competitively charged and are all able to demonstrate a fine investment track record.'

On the savings side, both Mrs Starkey and Mr Harris suggested Paula and Mike switch their savings account to one with a higher rate of interest, such as a postal account.

Mr Harper suggested Mike consider a corporate bond individual savings account (ISA) when his TESSA matures: 'Bond funds are lower in risks than equity versions and access to ISA funds will be available at any time. Investment groups with high-performing corporate bonds are Aberdeen Prolific, Hendersons, Perpetual, CGNU and Prolific.'

All the advisers felt that the Redmonds needed urgently to review their life cover position now that the family has doubled in size. Mr Harris said: 'They are both under-insured, particularly Paula. Should the worst happen and Paula were to die prematurely, Mike would need to employ a full-time nanny to take care of the children.'

Mr Harris advised both Paula and Mike to consider income-replacement cover, which would pay out over a period of time in the event of illness. 'The maximum cover available is only 60 per cent of your income. If Paula does not return to work, she would need what is known as "housewife benefit".'

He said it would cost £59.10 a month to provide cover with benefits up to an annual income of £36,000 with Norwich Union, the best deal he could find on the market.

Mr Harper urged the couple to buy at least £250,000-worth of life insurance for Paula.

Mrs Starkey said: 'As doctors, they will appreciate the value of critical illness cover. Paula estimates the cost of childcare to be around £14,000 a year and this would increase each year.'

LESSONS TO BE LEARNED

- New responsibilities such as new children – three in this case – mean you should re-evaluate all your finances, particularly life insurance, income protection insurance and critical illness cover.

- With so many people depending on him, Mike needs to be adequately insured. However, many couples fail to realize that if the mother died or became ill, there would still be a large financial burden on the family and as such mothers need adequate insurance too.

Case Study 49

PROBLEM: HOW TO SAVE WITH A GROWING FAMILY

Vital Statistics

Names: Andy and Maria Spooner

Ages: Thirty-six and thirty-five

Occupation: Manufacturing consultant and occupational health
   adviser (on parental leave)

Location: Somerset

Combined income: £50,000–£65,000 p.a.

Savings: £13,000 cash

Pensions: Two frozen schemes with previous employers with
   additional voluntary contributions (AVCs); £300 a month into
   Equitable Life personal pension (Mr Spooner); Scottish &
   Newcastle company scheme (Mrs Spooner)

Investments: Virgin personal equity plan (PEP) each and single
   company PEP investing in Scottish & Newcastle; Baillie Gifford
   unit trust; shares in Caradon, Halifax, Marks & Spencer, Scottish
   & Newcastle and 3i; £60,000 Standard Life endowment
   supporting mortgage

Mortgage: £100,000 sixteen-year Standard Life mortgage; part
   repayment, part interest-only, supported by endowment

Borrowings: None apart from mortgage

Insurance: Axa Sun Life joint life insurance including critical illness

Maria Spooner is undecided about whether to return to work after
taking parental leave to look after her two children, Jake, four and
Barney, two. She has already been away from work at Scottish &
Newcastle for three years but is entitled to take up to five years off.
She works ten days a year while on parental leave, and earns £750.

Her husband Andy works for a small manufacturing consultancy, Suiko – Japanese for 'performance' – based in Bristol, which

helps manufacturing companies improve efficiency by working out improvement plans which involve the entire workforce.

Last tax year, he earned £30,000 basic, plus a further £20,000 through fee income and a share of company turnover. This year he expects to earn around £65,000 as company turnover is rising.

'Maria is undecided about when she wants to return to work,' said Andy. 'When we had the children, we were living in Nottingham and now we are in Somerset, so it is unclear whether there would be a position for her down here anyway. Any job she returns to would need to be quite flexible.'

Andy would like to be able to retire at fifty if he decides he wants to and to pay for private education for their children. The Spooners would also like to pay down the repayment part of their mortgage early, ideally within ten years. The couple have already paid down £8,000 of the sixteen-year £100,000 Standard Life Freestyle mortgage they took out in April last year. It is part repayment and part interest-only supported by a £60,000 endowment which costs them £120 a month and matures in sixteen years' time.

The couple have a joint First Direct current account. All their cash savings are in Maria's name as she is a non-taxpayer. They have £3,000 in a First Direct High Interest savings account and £3,000 in a First Direct mini cash individual savings account (ISA), which they took out last tax year. There is £1,500 in a Nationwide tax-exempt special savings account (TESSA) which is due to mature.

They also have £2,000 in a Cheltenham & Gloucester savings account, £2,500 in a West Bromwich account and £1,000 in a Bradford & Bingley one-year bond that they have renewed each year for the past three years. The couple have started some savings for their children in the Invesco Rupert Bear fund and Smart 2 Save at Nationwide.

Andy has frozen pensions with two previous employers and now has an Equitable Life personal pension with part of the lump sum he earned at the end of last year. He pays £300 net a month into this. Equitable has since run into problems as it could not afford to meet the guarantees it gave to some pension investors.

Maria contributed to the Scottish & Newcastle company pension scheme. Andy said: 'Provided she goes back to work, she will get a percentage of her pension contributions for the five years she has taken for parental leave.'

The Spooners each have a Virgin FTSE 100 Tracker Growth PEP and Maria also has a Scottish & Newcastle single-company PEP. Andy also invested in the Baillie Gifford UK Smaller Companies Growth fund fifteen years ago when it was first launched.

The couple hold 225 shares in Caradon, 200 shares in Halifax, 450 shares in Marks & Spencer, 3,500 in Scottish & Newcastle and 600 shares in 3i. Andy said: 'We have held all those for quite a while.'

They have joint life insurance with Axa Sun Life, including critical illness cover, which costs £120 a month.

WHAT THE EXPERTS SAY

The first thing the Spooners must do is set about paying down their mortgage early if they want to be in a position to consider retiring early, the advisers to Cash Clinic said.

Maxine Harvey, of independent financial advisers (IFAs) Torquil Clark, said: 'The major expense currently is the mortgage. If the Spooners want to retire in fourteen years' time, they need to have the mortgage reduced to a manageable level. There are two ways they can do this. Either they can save up to pay the loan down early in one fell swoop or make regular overpayments, starting straight away.'

Milena Atanassova, of IFAs Rickman Tooze, said: 'Monthly payments should be increased by around £220 a month in order for the repayment part of the loan to be repaid within nine years. Part of this could be funded out of monthly income, with the rest at the end of the year when Andy receives his share of the company's turnover.'

Bryn Walker, of IFAs, Regency Financial Management, suggested the couple consider putting the £6,000 savings with First Direct and the £2,000 from Cheltenham & Gloucester straight into the mortgage as they can draw back money they have paid to their mortgage later on if they need it. Mr Walker said: 'This will give a better return.'

Ms Harvey suggested they start saving up the capital needed to pay down the mortgage early via ISAs. She said: 'If they do not in the end use them for mortgage clearance, they will have achieved good growth in a tax-efficient environment.'

Long-term investments are essential for the Spooners – whether or not they are used to pay down the mortgage.

Ms Harvey said: 'They need to maximize their ISA allowances for this year. They should start taking a more balanced approach with their investments as they are currently invested cautiously. The Fidelity Managed International ISA will give them more exposure to equities in a managed environment.'

Both Ms Atanassova and Ms Harvey urged the Spooners to switch from their Virgin PEPs to managed funds. Ms Harvey said: 'Their Virgin PEPs have performed better than sector average, but it may be time to transfer to something more dynamic like the Gartmore European Select Opportunities fund, although this will be higher-risk.' Similarly, Mr Spooner should move out of the Baillie Gifford fund as soon as possible, Ms Harvey said. Mr Walker added: 'Spending it would be a better alternative to keeping it where it is.'

He said the couple should think carefully about retiring early. He said: 'In fourteen years' time, the children will be sixteen and eighteen and possibly needing funding for college and university.

'At thirty-six years old, with £65,000-a-year earnings, Andy can contribute up to £13,000 a year into a personal pension plan. He is actually contributing £4,608, meaning he should pay an additional single premium of £6,500 net into his pension when he receives his annual bonus.'

As Equitable Life has since run into difficulties, the consensus is that investors should take out a new pension – preferably a stakeholder – with a different company. They should also consider switching their Equitable pension to a new provider, although they will incur a hefty penalty if they are invested in the with-profits fund, so should take advice.

Saving for their children is important to the Spooners and they should look to stock-market investments for this, the advisers said.

LESSONS TO BE LEARNED

- It is one thing having a dream, another turning it into reality. Retiring at fifty will remain a dream for the Spooners unless Andy starts investing the maximum allowed into his pension.

- Paying off your mortgage quickly may make more financial sense than investing any spare cash as the cost of the mortgage may exceed the returns on any investments. Also, once the mortgage is repaid outgoings are lower, so there will be more spare cash to save and invest.

Case Study 50

PROBLEM: KEEPING AFLOAT AFTER GOING SELF-EMPLOYED

Vital Statistics
Name: Paul Bew
Age: Thirty-one
Location: North London
Occupation: Sailing instructor
Turnover: Just under £15,000 p.a.
Savings: £9,000 in TESSA 2; £7,000 in savings account; £100 in
     Premium Bonds
Pension: None
Investments: None
Mortgage: £60,000 Northern Rock endowment, fixed for five years
Borrowings: None apart from mortgage
Insurance: None

After being at sea for twelve years, Paul Bew decided to return to land last year to settle down with his girlfriend in Stoke Newington,

London. However, he has not left the water behind completely and has set up a sailing school based in London called Capital Sailing, which teaches practical sailing in the Solent, off Portsmouth, and also offers corporate entertainment. He also teaches people to use radios and radar and provides Royal Yachting Association (RYA) training and examinations.

He said: 'We are the only school to offer these courses over two evenings in central London. Normally people have to travel out to the country and give up much more time to do the courses.'

Paul has not had to borrow money to set up the business and managed to keep overheads to a minimum by offering his services over the Internet. He invested £3,000 which 'went into printing, hardware, the website, paying for classrooms and buying a domain name.'

When the business was making a loss at the very beginning, Paul supplemented his income by doing as much examining for the RYA as possible. He can still do this if necessary to bring in cash.

Although Paul does most of the teaching himself, he sometimes needs to hire extra instructors, which is an additional expense.

His business account is with HSBC and he is about £500 in credit at the moment. He has a company cheque book.

Paul said: 'I have been promised a Visa facility as well so that people can pay me by card and it doesn't have to be a cheque all the time, but HSBC is being a bit slow providing it. However, the rates for accepting Visa are very high. They really skin you alive.'

So far Paul has turned over just under £15,000, which keeps his tax return simple for the time being. He has not set up as a limited company and instead is registered as self-employed. He has downloaded what he can from this after expenses, but hopes he will start to make more when things get busier.

Paul's personal bank account, with the Halifax, is kept in credit. He also has a Halifax TESSA 2, into which he rolled the full £9,000 from his first tax-exempt special savings account, which is due to mature in about four years' time.

Paul also has £7,000 saved in a Halifax savings account and a

£100 Premium Bond given to him by his grandfather twenty years ago. He has won £50 once.

Paul's £40,000 mortgage is a twenty-five-year endowment loan from Northern Rock which he took out with his girlfriend to pay for their home in Stoke Newington last year. Although Paul put down the £20,000 deposit, the mortgage is in her name only as Paul could not provide proof of income so lenders 'would not touch me'.

The couple pay £80 a month into the endowment, which is with Friends Provident, and £190 in interest to Northern Rock.

There is no pension, and Paul has never contributed to one, and he does not have life or critical illness cover apart from his Friends Provident endowment.

WHAT THE EXPERTS SAY

Paul should concentrate on more immediate concerns rather than worry about long-term investments for the time being, the Cash Clinic advisers said.

David Holland, of independent financial advisers (IFAs) PIFC Benefit Consultants in London, said: 'Having only just started his business, Paul would be unwise at this stage to consider any long-term savings commitment. As expected with any new business, things are slow to start, but future prospects look good.'

Similarly, Angus Millen, of IFAs Millen Financial Management, said that Paul could afford to hold off putting money into a pension for the time being.

He said: 'Although Paul has already missed five of the most important years in terms of saving for his retirement, he should not be persuaded or panicked into establishing a pension plan straight away.'

Mr Millen said that as Paul's business is in its first year, he will not know what sort of profit he is likely to make until at least the end of the year, so committing himself to unrealistic pensions contributions would be unwise.

In the meantime, Paul needs to stockpile an emergency cash

supply. Mr Millen said: 'I would recommend that he opens up an easy access deposit account with Egg to earn a higher rate of interest and transfer from his existing Halifax savings account an amount he feels comfortable with keeping readily accessible.'

He also suggested that Paul transfer the balance from his Halifax account to an individual savings account (ISA). Each year Paul can invest £3,000 free of tax in a cash savings ISA. However, he should consider a stocks-and-shares ISA when he comes to a point where he can afford to make a long-term commitment to investing.

Mr Miller said: 'Paul should only tie up money in an ISA if he can afford to leave the money to grow for a minimum of five years.'

Mr Holland pointed out that it is important for Paul and his girlfriend to make wills, as they have bought a property together and the mortgage is in her name only. He said: 'If they have not already done this, there is a risk that if she dies, the property could revert to her parents.'

LESSONS TO BE LEARNED

- It may be prudent in terms of financial planning to start a pension as young as possible and to invest for your long-term future, but if you are starting a business that should be your priority. Cash is king when you are self-employed, so do not tie up money in long-term investments.

- When you are starting in business and money is tight, it is wise to have a means of supplementing your meagre – or non-existent – income like Paul, who does examining work.

Case Study 51

PROBLEM: PROVIDING FOR FUTURE AFTER BUILDING UP TWO SUCCESSFUL BUSINESSES

Vital Statistics

Name: Rob Mamuda

Age: Thirty-three

Occupation: Restaurateur

Income: £25,000 p.a.

Savings: £200 a month invested in two savings accounts

Pension: ICI company pension (deferred with ceased contributions) and single-premium personal pension plan with Legal & General

Investments: None

Mortgage: £64,000 repayment mortgage with Halifax

Borrowings: None, although the business has a £5,000 loan

Insurance: £90,000 life and critical illness cover from Friends Provident; £50,000 life and permanent disability cover from Skandia Life

After running a buildings maintenance company for five years, Rob Mamuda decided to set up a bar-restaurant, Mad Monki, in Bristol's Redlands.

Rob, whose first business, Guild, provides maintenance services for high-street stores, pubs and restaurants, had been planning to open a restaurant for a while.

He said: 'We set targets for the restaurant and so far we are approaching our wildest dreams. As this was my first bar I have learned lots. Now I want to open another one – probably in Clifton.'

Guild has twenty-four staff and a turnover of £2 million a year. Profits come in at around £130,000 a year. The restaurant turns over £8,000–£9,000 a week and is expected to pick up even more.

Rob, who trained as an electrical engineer, is not yet drawing an income from the restaurant. He said: 'I won't for the first six to eight months and then I will look at how much the restaurant can afford at the time.'

From Guild, he pays himself a salary of £25,000 a year – £18,000 through PAYE (Pay As You Earn) and the rest through dividend income. He also takes bonuses from time to time. He said: 'If we have had a very good quarter, I can take an extra £2,000 or £3,000 and I don't pay for my car and some other expenses.'

Rob's current account is at NatWest and he does not run into overdraft. Both business accounts are also with NatWest. He has two personal savings accounts with Bristol & West and Lloyds into each of which he puts £100 a month and has been saving for a while.

Rob said: 'I have had a pension since I was sixteen because my mother made me join the ICI company scheme when I started training there. I was advised to leave my pension there as it is a very good one. After I left I received letters saying that it would provide me with £7 a week in retirement; now the letters are saying £70 a week.'

Rob also started a single-premium personal pension plan with Legal & General when he was twenty-three but he has not contributed for a couple of years. At retirement at age sixty, this fund is projected at the lower rate of assumed growth to produce £90,600 and, at the higher rate, £424,000. While these figures do not strip out the potentially illusory effect of inflation, they do illustrate the value of making contributions early and allowing as long as possible for investment returns to accumulate.

Rob is setting up a pension scheme for his restaurant staff (under the new stakeholder rules any employer with five or more employees must offer their staff a stakeholder pension, although the employer does not have to contribute to this). Rob said: 'This is a competitive market and it is hard enough to find good staff, so I want to give them something to make them feel they belong.'

Rob lives with his girlfriend, Rekha near Mad Monki. He bought the house eleven years ago for £64,000 on a straight twenty-five-year repayment mortgage from the Halifax on the lender's variable rate.

He said: 'I think I have got it down to about £50,000 now. I know it is an expensive mortgage but I am thinking of moving now, so I am keen to see what is available at the moment.'

Rob has no personal loans but the restaurant has a £5,000 business loan from NatWest. He said: 'It was to buy kitchen equipment and to act as a cushion when I started the business. I could pay it off straight away, although there is a small penalty.'

He has two life assurance policies. His Friends Provident policy covers him to £50,000 and incorporates permanent disability insurance. It costs £25 a month. The other, from Skandia Life for £90,000, includes critical illness cover and costs £32 a month.

WHAT THE EXPERTS SAY

Graham Duckett, of independent financial advisers (IFAs) Millfield Partnership, said that it is admirable to be concerned about staff pensions but Rob must also pay closer attention to his own situation.

He said: 'As the owner of two businesses, he is in an ideal position to funnel profits into a tax-efficient area and he could do this by using an executive pension plan. This could also be used later for loanback purposes to the company, or even to purchase commercial premises via a small self-administered scheme (SSAS). He could make a pension contribution as an alternative to paying himself a bonus or dividend.'

Vivienne Starkey, of IFAs Equal Partners, said that as far as staff benefits are concerned, pensions are the obvious place to start.

Mr Duckett agreed, saying: 'Rob could start by offering to fund a percentage of each employee's salary, say, a maximum of 5 per cent salary.'

Although employers do not have to contribute to stakeholder pensions, this would provide a valuable employee perk.

On the savings front, Ms Starkey advised Rob to consider saving into a stocks-and-shares individual savings account (ISA). She said:

'He regularly saves £200 a month into Lloyds and Bristol & West. If he was happy to tie this up for at least five years, he could invest in an ISA. As he is not risk-averse, he may wish to consider using a combination of both UK and international funds.'

Ms Starkey liked the Fidelity ISA, which invests in a combination of funds such as the American fund, European fund and UK Special Situations fund. She also recommended Perpetual and Crédit Suisse.

If Rob prefers to keep his savings liquid, Mr Duckett said, he could consider a mini-cash ISA instead, which will still shelter his money from tax. 'He could move £3,000 into a mini-cash ISA. For the rest of his savings, he could achieve a higher rate of return by opening an Internet account with Egg.'

For the mortgage, Mr Duckett said Rob could benefit from switching to a better rate. He liked Standard Life's Freestyle mortgage, which has a variable rate.

LESSONS TO BE LEARNED

- When you run a business, that business relies on you and you on it. So it is wise – as Rob has done – to buy permanent disability insurance and critical illness cover which pays out if you can no longer work.

- Protecting your assets and income involves more than just buying insurance. Rob relies on attracting good staff to run his bar-restaurant – without the right staff his business would suffer. Providing staff with a valuable perk such as a pension is one way to keep your best personnel.

- Many self-employed people and those running their own companies believe that their business is their pension. However, there are no guarantees that the business will survive that long or that they will be able to sell it upon retirement at the right price. That is why a pension is always advisable.

Case Study 52

PROBLEM: MAKING A REDUNDANCY CHEQUE LAST

Vital Statistics

Name: Mary Gelder
Age: Thirty-seven
Location: South London
Occupation: Made redundant
Income: None
Savings: £9,000 in bank accounts
Pension: Occupational scheme, AVCs and personal pension plan
Investments: £7,600 worth of American Express shares
Mortgage: £74,000, fixed for two years
Borrowings: None apart from mortgage
Insurance: None

Mary Gelder thirty-seven was made redundant from her post as head of marketing for American Express's corporate card division just before Christmas.

She had been with American Express for ten years and decided to accept redundancy when it was offered because it looked like a good opportunity to have a break and assess her options.

Mary, who lives in Wandsworth, London, took a degree in economics before working for an insurance company. She spent 1993 and 1994 working in New York for American Express. She lives alone and bought her flat a year ago.

She is now living off the £25,000 redundancy payment – seven months' salary – she received from American Express. She started her search for a new marketing job in the financial services industry immediately and hopes to go on holiday to India once she has found one. She said: 'I feel quite positive about leaving my job.'

When she received her redundancy payment, Mary immediately

put £9,000 into an Egg account, which she opened especially for this purpose, and £5,000 into her NatWest Premium Reserve account.

There is about £2,000 in her NatWest current account but Mary does not have any tax-free savings.

She used £2,500 to pay off her credit card bills and £5,000 to buy her company car. 'The rest has gone towards paying off bills,' Mary said. She added: 'I haven't been very organized but I don't want to tie up my money too much as I do not yet know when I will be working again.'

After initial confusion because of a computer fault at the Department of Social Security, Mary has successfully claimed the Job Seeker's Allowance of just over £50 a week. After six months, this will be reassessed according to her income.

At American Express, Mary was able to participate in the company's non-contributory occupational pension scheme where the company paid in the equivalent of 5 per cent of her salary. She joined the scheme seven years ago, as the entry age is thirty. 'I have also been contributing £40 a month in additional voluntary contributions for the last two years.'

Before joining the American Express scheme, Mary contributed for three years to a personal pension plan she took out with Equitable Life, which is now worth a little more than £10,000.

On the investments side, Mary does not hold any personal equity plans (PEPs). She has participated in the American Express share save scheme about four times. She said: 'I liked doing that because they take the contributions from your salary at source, so I couldn't get my mitts on it.'

Under a share-save scheme, American Express employees can save over a three-, five-, or seven-year term and at the end use the savings to buy shares in their company at the price that was quoted at the beginning of the term. At the moment, Mary has a total of around 331 American Express shares. She can exercise her option to cash 100 of them in now because she has been made redundant and that scheme had been running for more than three years. The rest will have to wait for at least one year.

The first time she participated, between 1992 and 1997, Mary saved £2,500 and was able to buy shares worth £10,000 at the end of the term. 'I used it for the deposit on my flat,' Mary said.

She bought her flat in December 1997 for £84,000 and it is now worth about £120,000. Mary is considering the possibility of renting it out.

Her mortgage is fixed for two years, with no early redemption penalties. 'I have thought of changing it to get a better rate, but I don't think anyone will lend to me while I'm not working,' Mary said.

She holds an American Express charge card and an RBS Advanta Platinum Mastercard. Mary did hold a Save & Prosper Visa card but she cut it up before Christmas.

She does not hold any critical illness or life cover, and she has not made a will.

WHAT THE EXPERTS SAY

The advisers to Cash Clinic pointed out that unemployment makes this a particularly difficult time for Mary to plan her finances.

Kim North, of independent financial advisers (IFAs) Pretty Financial Partnership, said: 'Mary is in a difficult situation for financial planning purposes as she is in between jobs and does not know when she will gain employment.'

Rebekah Kearey, of IFAs Roundhill Financial Management, said: 'Mary needs to calculate how much she needs as a minimum monthly sum to maintain her life-style at its most basic and then calculate whether or not she has a shortfall. I suspect that the shortfall may be larger than she thinks – if only while she adjusts from a well-paid post with all the trimmings to an income of £50 a week. Her mortgage commitment alone is nearly three times the Job Seeker's Allowance she is receiving.'

Ms North pointed out that Cheltenham & Gloucester will allow Mary to take a payment holiday. 'C&G can defer capital and interest payments for up to three months.'

She added: 'Once employment is secured, Mary could consider

remortgaging to reduce her monthly payment and to release some of the equity to repay any debts she has built up during her unemployment.'

Andrew Baggott, of IFAs Excalibur in London, suggested that Mary consider renting out a room in her flat to increase her income. He said: 'She can rent one out under Government rulings but she should be very careful about renting the whole flat out as some building societies can be awkward about this and she may find her interest rate being switched to a commercial rate.'

Ms Kearey said that another way for Mary to reduce her outgoings could be to stretch the term of her mortgage to be paid off at age sixty-five.

The next step for Mary is to decide whether or not she has put her redundancy payment to the best use she can. Ms Kearey noted: 'If Mary continues to spend at the level her old salary afforded, she will have spent the whole of the remaining redundancy money in five months.'

Ms North suggested she try to make the money in her bank accounts work a bit harder. She said: 'Mary's current account should only hold a sufficient amount which she is happy about: for example, to pay her bills and to run her car.'

As for Mary's savings, the advisers urged her to switch all of these to Egg as NatWest is giving her such a low amount of interest.

Although she is concerned to keep her money accessible, she should tie some of it up for the future, Ms Kearey said: 'You tend to try harder to find work if your sources of financial security are drying up and the temptation is to spend until it is all gone.'

The American Express shares to which Mary is entitled by virtue of the savings scheme turn out to be worth £25,200; a handsome gain on the £10,000 which Mary has invested. She does not own all of them yet, but will be able to download them from the Amex share save scheme at later dates. At the moment she only owns £7,600 worth of shares.

Ms Kearey said: 'The yield on this portion is only £53 a year and consequently worthless as a source of extra income. Mary should therefore consider reinvesting these shares into an investment which could generate income if she believes she will not return to work for some time, for example, a maxi ISA investing in corporate bonds.'

Mr Baggott suggested that Mary switch some of her American Express shares into an ISA once the share-save schemes mature at a later date, to 'throw a tax-efficient envelope around them.'

As far as pensions go, Mr Baggott said Mary should not worry about this until she is back in work and can put her existing provisions in the context of her new employer. However, following the problems at Equitable Life she should take advice about switching her pension to a different provider.

All three advisers strongly urged Mary to avoid further debt as much as she can. Ms Kearey added: 'As a single person, however, she should consider income replacement in the event of long-term ill health, and also critical illness cover. However, these decisions can be put on hold until she finds new employment or has settled into a new life-style.'

LESSONS TO BE LEARNED

- Losing a job leaves you in limbo while you look for another. But that does not mean you can leave your financing in limbo too. Mary needs to make every penny work for her so should invest in ISAs, earn the best rates on her savings and cut her outgoings by looking at restructuring her mortgage.

- When you lose a job with a large employer, you lose more than your salary. A pension scheme, life insurance and sick pay are all things you can no longer take for granted. It is important that you replace these with private provision as soon as you can afford to.

Case Study 53

PROBLEM: AFFORDING TO TAKE EARLY RETIREMENT

Vital Statistics

Names: Phil and Sue Jones

Ages: Fifty-three and fifty

Occupations: Scientist and administration clerk

Location: Luton

Combined income: £39,500 p.a.

Savings: £2,550 in bank and building society accounts

Pension: Final salary company scheme plus Scottish Widows AVC scheme (Mr Jones)

Investments: Three endowment funds totalling £49,000 from Friends Provident, Scottish Provident and Abbey Life; £100 in Premium Bonds

Mortgage: £59,000 part repayment, part interest-only, supported by endowments, loan from Coventry Building Society

Borrowings: £1,200 interest-free loan; £3,000 personal loan from Frizzell Bank

Insurance: None

Phil Jones, a scientist at a large agricultural research institute in Hertfordshire, had been planning to retire at age sixty, but is now considering stopping work sooner. 'I may get the opportunity to retire at fifty-five, because in two years' time, they are going to be looking for 150 voluntary redundancies,' he said. 'It is quite tempting.'

Retiring at fifty-five would enable Phil and his wife Sue to return to their roots in Shropshire, where most of their family is still based. It would also allow them to focus on their main interest – their classic car, a Triumph TR6, which they enter in rallies all over the country.

The couple currently live in Luton, in Bedfordshire. They have two sons, Gareth, aged twenty-five, a musician who is getting married this summer, and Richard, aged thirty, a hairdresser who is married with one child.

Phil said: 'We had always planned to retire at sixty, but now this opportunity has presented itself, we need to start making retirement plans now.'

The couple have not decided if Sue, a part-time administration clerk, would stop work completely as well if her husband decides to take voluntary redundancy in two years' time.

They currently earn just under £40,000 a year between them, with Phil's income representing the majority of this – £32,000.

Under the terms of the redundancy package, the institute would top up his pension scheme to make up for early retirement. He has been paying £250 a month net into an additional voluntary contribution (AVC) scheme with Scottish Widows since 1995. Sue has never contributed to a pension.

The Joneses have £200 in an Abbey National joint current account, £500 in an Alliance & Leicester account earmarked for the house, and £1,750 in a cash ISA in Phil's name, which is earmarked for their son's wedding. There is also £100 in a Post Office account in his name.

The couple have £100 in Premium Bonds but no direct stock-market investments.

They do have three endowment funds, although these are currently supporting their mortgage and are due to mature in 2011. Phil said: 'One option may be to pay down the mortgage more quickly and then be able to use the endowments as investments instead.'

The mortgage, from Coventry Building Society, is part repayment and part interest-only.

The couple have other debts as well. There is a one-year £1,200 interest-free loan from Sue's place of work which must be repaid by November this year.

The Joneses also have a £3,000 personal loan from Frizzell Bank, which they are repaying over three years from January 2000 with 12.7 per cent interest.

They have no separate life or critical illness cover.

WHAT THE EXPERTS SAY

The advisers to Cash Clinic felt that for the time being, the priority for the couple is to pay off their debts before they can start planning for retirement.

Darius McDermott, of independent financial advisers (IFAs) Chelsea Financial Services, said: 'It would make sense to repay the Frizzell Bank loan.' He also suggested that the couple start building up some more substantial cash savings in a mini cash ISA, switching money from savings accounts where interest is taxed to top up Phil's ISA savings to the £3,000 maximum.

Warren Perry, of IFAs Whitechurch Securities, said: 'Contingency funds are running at a relatively low level. I would look to top up the savings accounts to cover emergencies. The accounts should be reviewed to ensure that the interest rates are competitive and perhaps be placed in Sue's name to ensure tax efficiency.'

The advisers to Cash Clinic also noted that the Joneses should make a profit on their move to Shropshire. Mr Perry said: 'A similar home in Shropshire is likely to cost less than in Luton and therefore some equity may well be released from the sale of the existing home.'

He suggested that they invest any profit from the move in with-profit bonds, corporate bonds or equity funds, depending on their risk requirements at the time.

As Phil already has a mini cash ISA this year, he cannot take out a maxi ISA for investment purposes until next tax year. However, Sue has her own ISA allowance and could take one out instead to start saving for retirement, particularly as she has no pension provisions of her own.

Mr McDermott said: 'Sue should consider making provision for income in retirement. Currently she would be provided for as a widow, but that is far from ideal. Perhaps an appropriate way to invest would be to build up a portfolio of ISAs, contributing monthly.'

Janine Starks, of independent financial advisers (IFAs) Chase de

Vere, said: 'A point to bear in mind is that, should Phil die at an early age, the widow's benefit is usually only 50 per cent of the pension income.'

Mr Perry estimated that Phil's pension should pay out a lump sum of £40,400 and an income for life of around £13,500, based on his twenty-seven years' service and contribution to the civil service pension. He should aim to reinvest part of the lump sum and use part to pay down a bit of the mortgage if he retires early.

If they want to choose just one of these options, rather than trying to spread the lump sum too thinly, Ms Starks preferred the option of investing the money. She said: 'Stock-market returns over the medium to long term should outweigh the costs of paying the interest on the mortgage. The investments can be set up to achieve a realistic level of income to add to their pension as well as capital growth.'

Mr Perry liked corporate bond funds for ISA investments. He recommended funds from Scottish Widows and Schroder.

He also urged Sue to look at lower-risk investments. He said: 'If they choose to invest the money, they should look at with-profit bonds from Prudential and MGM Assurance and distribution bonds from Sun Life and Royal Sun Alliance.'

As far as their endowments are concerned, Ms Starks said: 'The endowments should be kept running regardless of the decision to pay off the mortgage. The charges on endowments are incurred in the early years and as investments, the biggest benefits will not be seen until the end when terminal bonuses are paid.'

The advisers also urged the Joneses to change their Alliance & Leicester current account to one paying a higher rate.

LESSONS TO BE LEARNED

- If you want to retire early, clear your debts – including your mortgage – as quickly as you can. The rate of interest charged is always higher than the rate of interest you can earn – so it makes financial sense.

- Don't cash in an endowment to pay a mortgage off early. The penalties mean you will lose out. If possible, look at alternatives and keep the endowments running until maturity.

- Wives should not rely on their husband's pension alone. In the event of Phil's death Sue will only receive half his pension. If she had savings and investments of her own, it would be less of a financial shock.

Useful Addresses

FINANCIAL ADVISERS

Aitchison & Colegrave: 10/11 Park Circus, Glasgow G3 6AX.
Tel: 0141 332 5961

Alexander Forbes Financial Services: Lennig House,
Masons Avenue, Croydon, Surrey CR0 9XS. Tel: 020 8686 0660

Argent Consulting: 69 Eccleston Square, London SW1V 1PJ.
Tel: 020 7411 4700

Ashton House: 87 High Street South, Dunstable,
Bedfordshire LU6 3SF. Tel: 01582 478 877

Askfigaro: www.askfigaro.com, Tel: 01923 683 300

Assured Benefit Consultants: 239 Bury New Road, Whitefield,
Manchester M45 8QP. Tel: 0161 7664321

Balmoral Associates: 139/141 Cambridge Road, Churchtown,
Southport, Merseyside PR9 7LN. Tel: 01704 507 111

Baronworth: 370 Cranbrook Road, Gants Hill, Ilford,
Essex, IG2 6HY. Tel: 020 8518 1218

Bates Investment Services: Upper Bank House, Stoneythorpe,
Horsforth, Leeds LS18 4BN. Tel: 0113 295 5955

Best Investment: 20 Masons Yard, Duke Street, St James's,
London SW1Y 6BU. Tel: 020 7321 0100

Calkin Pattinson: 40 Piccadilly, London, W1J OHR.
Tel: 020 7734 2176

Careers Research and Advisory Centre: Sheraton House, Castle
Park, Cambridge CB3 0AX. Tel: 01223 460277. www.crac.org.uk

Chamberlain de Broe: 5 Cromwell Place, London sw7 2JE.
Tel: 020 7584 3300

Charles Dickson Financial Planning: Brackenwood, Grove Road,
Hindhead, Surrey GU26 6PH. Tel: 01428 608803

Chartwell Investment Management: Queen Square House,
Queen Square Place, Bath BA1 2LL. Tel: 01225 321 700

Chase de Vere: 2 Queen Square, Bath BA1 2HD. Tel: 01225 469 371

Chelsea Financial Services: St James' Hall, Moore Park Road,
London sw6 2JS. Tel: 020 7384 7300

City Independent Intermediaries: 40a, Dover Street,
London w1s 4NW. Tel: 020 7535 6700

David Aaron Partnership: Shelton House, High Street,
Woburn Sands, Milton Keynes MK17 8SD. Tel: 01908 281 544

David Allsup Investment and Insurance Services:
19 Denbigh Street, Llanrwst, Conwy LL26 OLL. Tel: 01492 641 333

Deep Blue Financial: 3 Quayside Commerce Centre, Lower Quay,
Fareham, Hants PO16 0XR. Tel: 01329 233364

Dennehy, Weller & Co.: 75 High Street, Chislehurst, Kent BR7 5AG.
Tel: 020 8467 1666

Dover Financial Services: 6 Park Place, Ladywell, Dover,
Kent CT16 1DF. Tel: 01304 214 500

Equal Partners: 6 St Mary At Hill, London EC3R 8EE.
Tel: 020 7867 0038

Excalibur: Glenhouse, 200–208 Tottenham Court Road,
London w1P 9LA. Tel: 020 7636 0888

Gee & Co.: Foresters Hall, 1a Wyle Cop, Shrewsbury,
Shropshire SY1 1UT. Tel: 01743 236982

Haddock Porter Williams: Closed

Hargreaves Lansdown: Kendal House, 4 Brighton Mews, Clifton, Bristol BS9 2NX. Tel: 0117 988 9880

IFP: Lion House, Red Lion Street, London WC1R 4FB. Tel: 020 7400 1860

Johnstone Douglas (now Alexander Forbes): Lennig House, Masons Avenue, Croydon, Surrey CR0 9XS. Tel: 020 8686 0660

London and Country Mortgages: Beazer House, Lower Bristol Road, Bath BA2 3BA. Tel: 01225 408000

Maddison Monetary Management (now part of Lamensdorf): Regency House, 1–4 Warwick Street, London W1B 5LT. Tel: 020 7287 3663

Millen Financial Management: Bankfield House, 9 Hill Street, Southport PR9 0NW. Tel: 01704 501166

Millfield Partnership (head office for Nationwide Network of IFAs): Knollys House, 17 Addiscombe Road, Croydon CR0 6SR. Tel: 020 8680 5200

Momentum Financial Services: 1st Floor, Pyramid House, Solartron Road, Farnborough, Hampshire GU14 7QL. Tel: 01252 557 300

Options for Women, Rockwell House, Two Rivers, Station Lane, Witney, Oxon OX28 41B. Tel: 01993 773889 [also offices in Kent and Berkshire]

Pen-Life Associates in York: 63–65 Heworth Road, York, North Yorkshire YO31 0AA. Tel: 01904 430 961

Philip Harper Financial Management: The Old Post Office, Wycombe Road, Studley Green, Buckinghamshire HP14 3XA. Tel: 01494 485 820

PIFC Benefit Consultants: Dresden House, 72 King William Street, London EC4N 7HR. Tel: 020 7283 3232

Pretty Technical Partnership: 40 Picadilly, London W1V 0HR. Tel: 020 7734 9899

Regency Financial Management: 39 Anchor Road, Aldridge, Walsall, West Midlands ws9 8pt. Tel: 01922 745540

Rickman Tooze: 2 Silver Street, Cirencester, Gloucestershire GL7 2BL. Tel: 01285 650 331

Roundhill Financial Management: 145 Islingword Road, Brighton, Sussex BN2 9SH. Tel: 01273 674 614

Thomson's Wealth Management: Diamond House, 36–38 Hatton Garden, London, EC1N 8EB. Tel: 020 7421 4300

Torquil Clark: St Mark's Church, Chapel Ash, Wolverhampton wv3 7br. Tel: 01902 570 570

Towry Law: Towry Law House, Western Road, Bracknell, Berkshire RG12 1TL. Tel: 01344 828 000

Vine House Financial Planning: Deepwell House, East Park Parade, Northampton, Northamptonshire NN1 4LA. Tel: 01604 622 117

Whitechurch Securities: Kings Weston House, Kings Weston Lane, Bristol, Avon BS11 0UR. Tel: 0117 373 0400

Willis Owen: 98–100 Mansfield Road, Nottingham, NG1 3HD. Tel: 0115 947 2595

WMC Investment Managers: 9 Tabernacle Walk, East Street, Blandford Forum, Dorset DT11 7DL. Tel: 01258 456 399

OTHER USEFUL CONTACTS

Financial planning

For details of independent financial advisers in your area: IFA Promotion: tel. 0117 971 1177. Website: www.unbiased.co.uk

To check if an adviser is authorized, and for general information about financial planning: Financial Services Authority, 25 The North Colonnade, Canary Wharf, London E14 5HS. Tel: 0845 606 1234. Website: www.fas.gov.uk

The registry of fee-based advisers: tel. 0870 0131 925

To find a solicitor to help you make a will:
The Law Society of England and Wales: tel. 020 7242 1222
Law Society of Scotland: tel. 0131 226 7411
Or www.make-a-will.org.uk

For useful information and leaflets about tax:
www.inlandrevenue.gov.uk or tel: 0845 9000 404

Savings
National Savings and Investments: tel. 0645 645 000
(8.30 a.m.–8 p.m. Mon–Fri and 9 a.m.–1 p.m. Saturday).
Website: www.nationalsavings.co.uk

To claim back tax deducted from savings:
Inland Revenue Taxback Helpline: tel. 0845 077 6543

For best-buy savings rates:
MoneyFacts, www.moneyfacts.co.uk

Credit cards and loans
To request a copy of a credit reference:
Equifax, Dept 1E, PO Box 3001, Glasgow G81 2DT
Experian Ltd, Consumer Help Service, PO Box 8000,
Nottingham NG1 5GX

For help and advice on coping with debt:
National Association of Citizens Advice Bureaux,
115–123 Pentonville Road, London N1 9LZ.
Tel: 020 7833 2181.
National Debtline: tel. 080 8808 4000

Property
To find out how much you can borrow and what it could cost:
John Charcol, www.charcolonline.co.uk

Buy-to-let information: The Association of Residential Letting Agents: tel. 01494 431 680

For information on equity release: Safe Home Income Plans: PO Box 516, Preston Central PR2 2XQ.
Tel. 0870 241 6060

The Age Concern Guide to Raising Capital From Your Home, Age Concern, Astral House, 1268 London Road, London, SW16 4ER. Tel: 020 8765 7200. www.ace.org.uk

For information on selling an endowment: the Association of Policy Market Makers: tel: 020 7739 3939.

Pensions
For help in tracing an occupational pension:
The Pensions Tracing Service: tel. 0191 225 6316

For information on occupational schemes:
The Occupational Pensions Advisory Service: tel. 020 7233 8080

Stakeholder pensions – a decision tree:
The Financial Services Authority: tel. 0845 6061234.
Website: www.fsa.gov.uk

Investments
Investment trust information: The Association of Investment Trust Companies (AITC), Durrant House, 8–13 Chiswell Street, London EC1 4YY. Tel: 020 7282 5555. www.itsonline.co.uk

For details on share ownership and investment clubs: ProShare: tel. 0207 220 1730. www.proshare.org.uk

Unit trusts and open-ended investment companies: Association of Unit Trust and Investment Funds (Autif), 65 Kingsway, London WC1B 6TD. Tel 020 8207 1361 (9 a.m.–9 p.m., seven days a week). www.investmentfunds.org.uk

For performance comparisons of funds:
Standards & Poor: www.funds-sp.com

Insurance

For information about insurance: Association of British Insurers,
51 Gresham Street, London EC2V 7HQ. Tel: 020 7600 3333.
www.abi.org.uk

Coping with change
Student life

National Union of Students: www.nusonline.co.uk

Self-employment

Inland Revenue/National insurance help for self-employed:
Tel. 0845 91 54655

Shopping around

To find a financial firm's website go to www.find.co.uk.
To compare best buys go to www.moneysupermarket.co.uk,
www.moneyextra.co.uk or www.moneynet.co.uk

Index